Main

# FELTING

The Complete Photo Guide to

**Creative Publishing international**

Copyright © 2012 Creative Publishing international, Inc.
First published in the United States of America by
Creative Publishing international, Inc., a member of
Quarto Publishing Group USA Inc.
400 First Avenue North
Suite 400
Minneapolis, MN 55401
1-800-328-3895
www.creativepub.com

ISBN: 978-1-58923-698-1

Library of Congress Cataloging-in-Publication Data

Lane, Ruth, 1961-
The complete photo guide to felting / Ruth Lane.      p. cm.
Summary: "This richly illustrated how-to book is a comprehen-
sive reference for various felting techniques, including needle
felting, wet felting, and nuno felting. With these easy-to-follow,
step-by-step directions and hundreds of full-color photos,
you'll be able to explore these easy projects that provide fun
opportunities for you to try the techniques. Galleries of unique
felted designs and creations by renowned fabric artists act
as beautiful examples and inspiration to pursue the hobby
yourself"– Provided by publisher.

ISBN 978-1-58923-698-1 (pbk.)
1. Feltwork. 2. Felting. I. Title.

TT849.5.L36 2012
677'.63–dc23

2012010630

Copy Editor: Ellen Goldstein
Proofreader: Peggy Wright
Book and Cover Design: Kim Winscher
Page Layout: Kim Winscher
Photography: Creative Publishing international; Ruth Lane;
Boltin Picture Library/The Bridgeman Art Library (pg. 9);
Courtesy of USDA (pg. 11, top); Shutterstock.com, pg. 171:
young woman: Ariwasabi; young man: Yuri Arcurs; old man:
Voronin76; baby: Victor Shova;
Photography Coordinator: Joanne Wawra

Printed in USA

# The Complete Photo Guide to
# FELTING

Creative Publishing
international

# CONTENTS

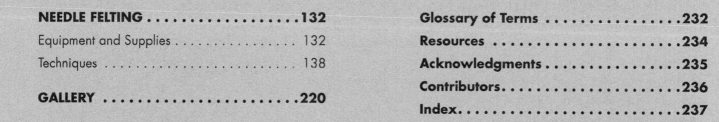

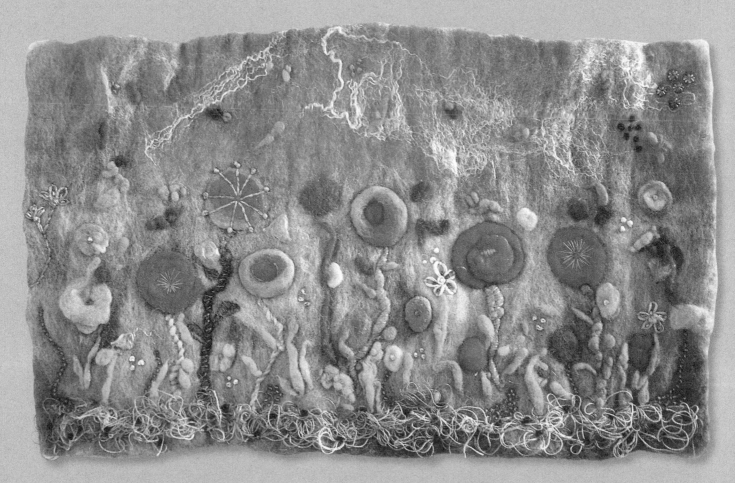

Mixed media wall hanging by Karen Erickson

# Introduction

Felting is an ancient technique, but it is quite versatile and is flourishing in the twenty-first century.

The technique of wet felting hasn't changed much over 2,000 years, and although the tools and supplies might have a changed a bit (there certainly wasn't any bubble wrap in fourth century BCE), the basic fundamentals of felting are the same. It is wonderful to think about people making felt over 2,000 years ago and how contemporary felt makers are still following the same basic directions of using moisture, heat, and agitation to tangle wool fibers together into an unwoven fabric.

Nuno and needle felting are more recently developed. Needle felting has become extremely popular in the last several years; the number of needle felters has increased exponentially. One reason for this increase is the Internet, which allows felt makers from all over the world to interact and share ideas and knowledge about their craft. Through forums, lists, and video sites, felt makers share their expertise with anyone who has access to the Internet.

When I first began felting, I started with needle felting. I soon began searching online for more information about my new craft. I found numerous sites with information about felting and tutorials that encouraged me to begin

An early needle-felted dog, core wool, brown Romney locks, and Merino

experimenting with wet felting and nuno felting. The first time I made a piece of wet felt, I was completely amazed by the process. By starting with a pile of wool and adding soap, water, and a little elbow grease, it turned into a piece of fabric which I had made myself. I was hooked. This book includes as much information about felting and wool properties as possible. The range of knowledge of felting from experience, research, and practice included here makes this book a resource to return to for information and inspiration. But don't feel as if you have to read it cover to cover. Read the sections that interest you the most. Check the end of the book for the glossary or list of resources. Perhaps your main interest is to make a wet-felted project. If you read the basics in wet felting, you will be able to make a project easily. Then you might want to come back and read more about different kinds of wool and fiber or perhaps skip to needle felting. Take what you learn from these pages and keep experimenting. Try different techniques, use different breeds of wool, and add something new. Develop a distinct style through your own creative innovations.

(continued)

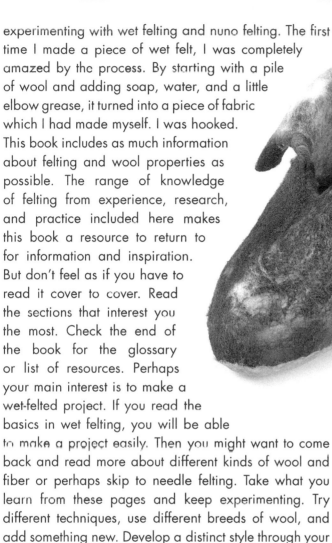

Slippers, wet felted, Merino, silk top accents, and dyed

Jack, a needle-felted doll made from core wool, Corriedale, and Merino

Felt is also quite forgiving; most "mistakes" can be either corrected or made into part of the design. Even a total mess of fibers can be reused in another piece of felt—just cut them up and work them into a different project. So enjoy yourself, take your time, and don't rush the outcome. Many felt makers say that the wool has a mind of its own and they follow the direction that the wool leads them. As you learn how various wools and fibers interact, you will gain a better understanding of the possibilities that felting has to offer.

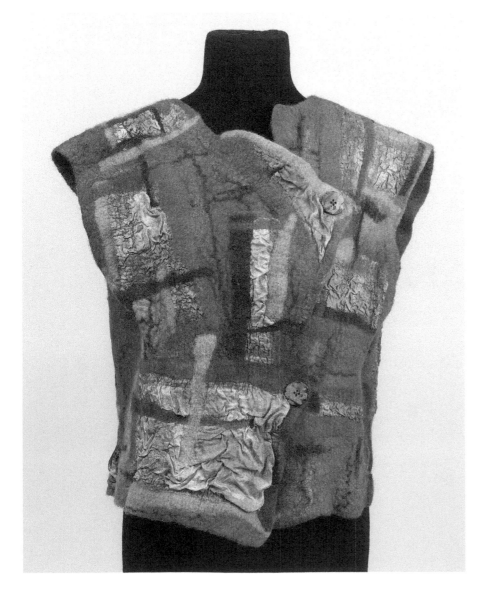

This vest includes 8-mm silk scarf pieces, Falkland wool, silk top, prefelt, and alpaca yarn made with wet-felting, nuno-felting, and machine-needle-felting techniques. At first the silk scarf pieces did not adhere well because there wasn't enough wool around the edges to hold them in place. Pieces of prefelt were used to machine needle felt around the silk and then it was felted again to "fix the mistake." What could have been a disaster was actually improved by the addition of the prefelt pieces.

# A Brief History of Felting

There are many myths about the origin of felt. One story is that someone put wool in his or her shoes, walked a long distance, and then discovered that the wool had felted due to the perspiration and agitation of the feet caused by walking. The truth is that the original felt maker is unknown. What is known is that cloth made from felt has been found from cultures 2,500 to 3,000 years ago and is the oldest acknowledged textile fabric.

Since the fourth century BCE, felt was used in Central Asia for items such as hats, horse blankets, carpets, yurts or gers, door flaps, boots, socks, and cloaks. Felt allowed nomadic tribes to survive in harsh climates and to travel more simply. Tents made from felt were lightweight and portable, allowing the nomads to pack and transport their shelters easily. As these tribes traveled and traded, sheep herding and the practice of felt making spread.

During the height of the Roman empire, Roman soldiers used felt pads as armor and wore felt tunics, boots and socks. Felt making was widely known in Western Europe by the first century CE with established felt-making guilds. In the 1500s, the Ottoman empire also had felt-making guilds that made intricately patterned robes, carpets, and felt hats.

Archeologists have unearthed many felt items and one of the more exciting finds was in the Pazyryk tombs dated to the fourth and fifth century BCE. The tombs are located in the Altai region of southern Siberia and because of the subzero conditions, felt items that under normal circumstances would have deteriorated were perfectly preserved. Thirty different felt objects were contained in the Pazyryk tombs and are now housed at the State Hermitage Museum in St. Petersburg, Russia. Many of these items display highly technical felt-making ability including felt inlays and even three-dimensional felt objects.

The felt swan pictured here was one of four found in the Pazyryk tombs. It is made from felt and deer hair and is 1 ft. (30.5 cm) in length. The swan is composed of six different colors of felt and its feet are stretched over wooden stakes that most likely were used to attach it to a tent. This swan symbolized the creation of the universe in Altaic beliefs and the three spheres of life, air, earth, and water.

# ALL ABOUT WOOL.

**W**ool is a very versatile fiber. It is flexible and elastic, which allows it to be stretched approximately 30% when dry and 70% when wet. The elasticity allows it to return to its original shape after it is stretched.

Wool insulates against heat and cold. Because it absorbs moisture and has scales on the fiber, wool clothing leaves a dry layer of air against the skin, which insulates against both warm and cold conditions. Wool is naturally antibacterial and has a tendency for odor absorbency, making it useful for underlayer garments. It is also naturally fire resistant. It will not support a flame and doesn't melt, so it won't stick to the skin and cause burns. Wool is often used for firemen's uniforms, and wool blankets are recommended for use in putting out fires.

The wool fiber consists mainly of the insoluble protein keratin. The surface of the fiber has microscopic scales, arranged like the scales on a pine cone. These scales open with moisture and heat and are one of the causes of the felting process. As moisture is added, the scales open slightly. Adding heat causes the scales to open wider. Once the scales are open they only allow movement in one direction. Once the scales are locked, they cannot move back in the opposite direction. The fibers enmesh, shrinking the wool, and felting occurs.

The other properties that affect the felting process include creep, elasticity, crimp or twist of the fiber, and the difference between the outer and inner layer of the fiber when wet. Creep means that the fiber tends to migrate toward its root end and pull adjacent fibers with it.

Shrinkage therefore takes place along the length of the fiber. The elasticity of the fiber in a low alkaline situation (i.e., when it mixes with soap) increases, causing the fiber to stretch and recover repeatedly, which makes the mass of fibers become tighter and tighter. The crimp is the natural twist and waviness of the fiber. When wet, the fiber twists more and turns rapidly. When dried, the fiber will try to return to its original shape causing further enmeshment of the fibers. Last, the outer layer of the fiber called the cuticle and the inner layer called the cortex, act differently when wet. The cortex tends to contract more than the cuticle when wet and causes the fiber to curl, opening the scales more. When dried, the cortex regains its former shape. All of these properties contribute to how well a fiber felts, and the felting process doesn't rely on just one factor.

So why don't sheep shrink in the rain? The fibers on a sheep lie mainly in the same direction and therefore the scales don't rub against each other in a way that would cause them to lock. The natural lanolin that is produced in the sebaceous glands of the sheep coats the fibers and deters felting as well.

(continued)

Wensleydale sheep at Carlson Farm, Loma Rica, California

Wool is graded by three different methods. The oldest, the blood system, is based on the bloodline of the breed as related to the Merino breed. The blood system is unable to take into account newer breeds and is not used on a regular basis.

The second grading system is the Bradford Count. It is based on the number of hanks (560 yd. [512 m] long) of yarn that can be spun from 1 lb. (0.5 kg) of wool top. The finer the wool, the higher the Bradford Count because the yarn is longer and finer. The count system ranges from 36, which is very coarse, up to 80, which is very fine.

The third method of grading wool, which is also the most accurate method, is the Micron System. One micron equals 0.0001 mm. The fiber's diameter is measured with a micrometer, and the average fiber diameter places the breed into one of sixteen grades. The finer the fiber, the smaller or lower the micron reading. The range of the Micron System is from 40.2, which is very coarse, to 17.7 or less, which is very fine.

Other factors that affect fibers when felting include staple length, crimp, and whether or not the wool comes from a meat or down breed of sheep. Staple length is the natural length of a lock of fiber and can range from 1½ inches (3.8 cm) up to 15 inches (38.1 cm). Crimp refers to the twist or waviness of the fiber. Finer fibers have a tendency for greater crimp than coarser fibers. Fibers with greater crimp tend to felt more easily. Meat or down breeds are raised for mutton. The fleece from a meat or down breed does not felt tightly, and the results can often be spongy and not densely felted. The most common of these breeds in the United States are Suffolk, Dorset, and Hampshire.

The differences in crimp can be seen in these various breeds of wool. Finn (1), Gotland (2), Icelandic (3), Pelsull (or Pelssau) (4), Wensleydale (5)

So why should you care about the kind of wool you use? Certain fibers are more suited to certain types of felting, and if you have knowledge of the breed and fiber qualities, you will have more successful results. All types of wool can be used for one or more projects, but none can be used for all purposes. There are many types of wool available, and there is no need to be limited to using just one fiber. For example, Merino top, which is widely available, is a fine fiber with a longer staple length. It wet felts easily and is perfect for making accessories that will be worn next to the skin. However, when a longer-staple Merino is used for needle felting, it is more difficult to needle, and it takes much longer to get a solid figure. Many first-time needle felters become discouraged when attempting to use Merino or other fine, longer-staple fibers. A fiber with a shorter staple length and a lower micron count is better suited for needle felting.

Eighteen-micron Merino wool is more difficult to needle felt than 32-micron Norwegian C1. Shown: Merino (1), Norwegian C1 (2)

## SHEEP AND WOOL VARIETIES

There are more than 200 different breeds of sheep worldwide and thus many wool varieties from which to choose. Every felt maker has his or her own favorite wool to use when felting, but often people limit themselves to just a few different types of wool. Knowledge about the characteristics of different breeds allows more diverse results. The following chart lists many preferred breeds of wool and their uses, grades, and staple lengths. Merino is probably the best known and most frequently used wool for wet felting. As Merino is widely available, many times it is the only wool that a felt maker will try. But if you branch out and try other breeds of wool, you may find that other types of wool are better suited to certain projects.

Black Leicester Longwool Sheep at 38th Annual Maryland Sheep and Wool Festival (photo by Patti McAleenan)

| Wool Breed | Count | Microns | Staple Length | Felt Characteristics and Possible Uses |
|---|---|---|---|---|
| Blue-Faced Leicester | 56 to 60 | 28 to 24 | 3½ to 6" (8.9 - 15.2 cm) | Easy and quick to felt; smooth finish; good for hats and bags |
| Corriedale | 46 to 62 | 34 to 23 | 3 to 3½" (7.6 - 8.9 cm) | Felts easily; less likely to pill; more durable felt; good for bags, slippers, outerwear; good for needle felting |
| Falkland | 52 to 56 | 30 to 28 | 3 to 5" (7.6 - 12.7 cm) | Felts easily; smooth finish; good for clothing, hats, and bags |
| Finn | 50 to 60 | 31 to 23½ | 3 to 6" (7.6 - 15.2 cm) | Fast to felt; strong and smooth felt; good for vessels, hats, and bags; Finn wool from Finland is difficult to obtain in the United States; American Finn wool is more easily obtained |
| Gotland | 48 to 50 | 34 to 29 | 5 to 7" (12.7 - 17.8 cm) | Quick to felt; smooth finish; holds shape well for vessels or other 3D pieces; good for slippers and bags |
| Icelandic (outer wool) | 56 to 60 | 30 to 27 | 8 to 12" (20.3 - 30.5 cm) | Slow to felt; felts better mixed with other wools; may be hairy; fairly water resistant; good for slippers, bags, and vessels |
| Icelandic (under wool) | 64 to 70 | 22 to 19 | | Easier to felt than outer wool with a softer hand; good for scarves and hats; many times the outer/under wool are sold unseparated |
| Merino | 60 to 80 | 22 to 18 | 2½ to 4" (6.4 - 10.2 cm) | Easy and quick to felt; soft and light handle; good for accessories or clothing worn next to the skin; good for nuno felting |

| | | | | |
|---|---|---|---|---|
| Norwegian C1 | 34 to 50 | 36 to 29 | 2 to 3"<br>(5.1 - 7.6 cm) | Longer to wet felt but sturdy and durable; good for bags, slippers, outerwear and upholstery; excellent for needle felting in batt form |
| Pelsull or Pelssau | 48 to 52 | 32 to 28 | 8 to 12"<br>(20.3 - 30.5 cm) | Fast to felt; gives heathered look due to mottled gray to black coloring; good for hats, bags, and upholstery |
| Polwarth | 58 to 64 | 26 to 22 | 4 to 6"<br>(10.2 - 15.2 cm) | Felts quickly and has similar feel to Merino but is more lustrous; good for accessories, clothing, and nuno felting |
| Romney | 40 to 48 | 38 to 31 | 3 to 5"<br>(7.6 - 12.7cm) | Lustrous fleece that hangs in separate locks; felts to a more durable fabric; good for bags, slippers and vests |
| Wensleydale | 44 to 48 | 36 to 31 | 8 to 12"<br>(20.3 - 30.5 cm) | Longer to wet felt; curly fleece/locks that are good for embellishment, cobweb felt curtains, and for use as hair in needle felting |

To give a better idea of each of the wool's characteristics, a sample was wet felted and is shown with an explanation. The samples were made with two layers of wool and all were felted under the same conditions. Times noted were from beginning rubbing to complete fulling. Making your own samples is still suggested as the conditions may vary and cause different results.

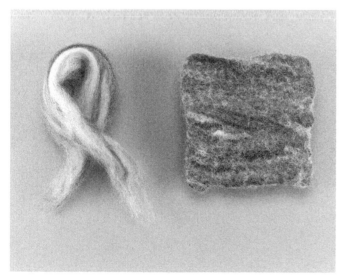

Blue-Faced Leicester is medium to fine grade wool. It forms a soft felt quickly but takes a little longer to full for a total of 10 minutes to form a firm felt. The shrinkage rate was 27% with a resultant firm felt that is fairly smooth. The mix of grays, whites, and taupe in the wool make a beautiful combination when felted.

Corriedale is medium-grade wool. It felts fairly quickly and took 10 minutes to completion. The shrinkage rate was 20% and the resultant felt was sturdy but slightly hairy.

(continued)

Falkland is medium-grade wool. It felts fairly quickly and took 8 minutes to felt completely. The shrinkage was 25%, and the finish was soft and fairly smooth.

Finn is medium- to medium-fine-grade wool. It has a fairly short staple length. Finn felts fairly quickly and took 9 minutes to felt completely. Shrinkage rate was 25%. The sample used had darker guard hairs and was durable but hairy. If dehaired, the felt would have been smooth and strong.

Gotland is coarse- to medium-grade wool. It felts quickly and forms a firm, durable felt in 6 minutes. The shrinkage rate was 21%. The felt was somewhat hairy but sturdy.

Icelandic under wool is fine-grade wool that forms a soft felt quickly but is slow to full, taking 12 minutes for a completely firm felt. The shrinkage rate was 29%, and the resultant felt was sturdy and smooth.

Merino is fine-grade wool with a medium staple length. The sample shown here is completed with, short-fiber Merino batt. The batt is the short fibers that are left over after combing; they are chopped for a consistent ½" (3.8 cm) length. Short fiber Merino felts very quickly, and the sample took 6 minutes to form a very solid, smooth felt. Shrinkage rate was 29%. This fiber will easily dry-felt by being rubbed in your hands, and when wet, begins the soft-felt stage almost immediately. It is perfect for making beads and cords.

Norwegian C1 is a crossbreed that is coarse to medium grade. It is sheared in autumn and has a short fiber length because of the timing of shearing. It felts to a soft felt fairly quickly but takes 11 minutes for full felting. Shrinkage rate was 17%, and the final felt was sturdy but hairy.

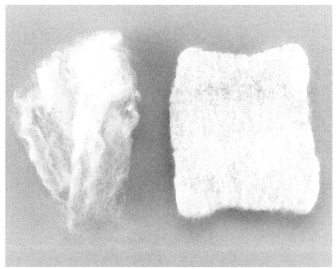

Pelsull (or Pelssau) is medium-grade wool with a medium-to-long staple length. It felts fairly quickly and was felted in 8 minutes. The shrinkage rate was 25%. The resulting felt is durable and sturdy and has a heathery appearance.

Polwarth is medium-fine to fine wool. It felts quickly; forms a soft, smooth finish; and took 9 minutes to completely felt. The shrinkage was 25%, and it is similar to Merino in feel.

(continued)

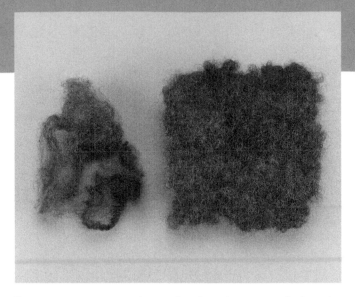

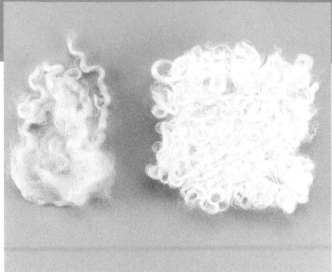

Romney is coarse-grade wool with a shorter staple length. It is slow to felt and took 16 minutes to completely felt. The resultant felt is very sturdy but hairy. The shrinkage rate was 33%.

Wensleydale is coarse-grade wool with a long, curly staple length. It is slow to accept water and slow to felt. This sample took 18 minutes. The shrinkage was 33%, and it was difficult to maintain smooth edges. The resultant felt has a beautiful sheen and texture.

Try a few of the breeds mentioned above and see if you can find other types of wool and fiber with which to experiment. So much can be learned about felting by taking a chance on a new type of fiber. However, if you see anything labeled "Superwash," avoid it. This fiber has undergone a chemical treatment to prevent felting of wool so that a wool garment can be machine washed and dried. The process coats the wool fiber with a microscopic layer of resin, which reduces friction and fiber entanglement. It is an irreversible treatment, and the resultant wool will not felt.

## OTHER FIBERS THAT FELT

Most animal fibers matt or felt in some form, but wool fiber is the easiest to felt by far. Alpaca, angora, llama, and cashmere all wet felt well and are readily available, although often more expensive than wool. These fibers can also be used in needle felting, but the silkier, longer staple fibers will take longer to needle felt than wool. Bison, yak, and camel felt but not easily, and the result is a soft felt that doesn't firm up. These would be best used as an embellishment or blended with wool if used for wet felting.

The following samples show the processed fiber and also a wet-felted sample. An explanation is included about the characteristics of the fiber and how the fibers felted.

Alpaca fiber is fine with a soft handle. It comes in natural hues from white to black. It felts fairly easily and took 18 minutes to felt completely. It forms a soft felt, and the shrinkage rate was 31%.

Angora goat fiber or Mohair is a very fine fiber and is the whitest of the natural animal fibers. It forms a very soft felt and took 10 minutes for complete felting. The fiber is somewhat resistant to water, and it is difficult to remove all the air from the fiber when wetting down. The soft, silky fiber shifts easily, and it's difficult to control the edges. The shrinkage rate is 17%, although this might be a factor of the fiber spreading and shifting when wet.

Angora rabbit is another very fine fiber, and is very white. It forms a soft felt quickly but takes longer to full. The sample took 12 minutes for complete felting. The fiber contains guard hairs that will not felt, and therefore, the felt is very hairy but soft and luxurious. The shrinkage rate was 26%.

Bison is a downy fiber in a natural brown. When wet down, the fibers tend to float apart, and initial felting is slow and difficult. Holes tend to develop easily, and the felt formed is very soft and would not be functional. Minimal shrinkage was obtained, and after 13 minutes, no further shrinkage occurred.

(continued)

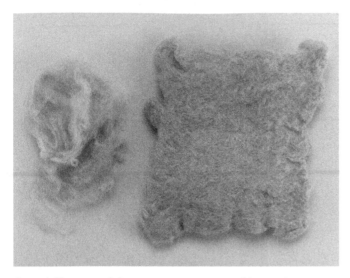

Camel fiber is soft but may contain guard hairs. It is a natural reddish brown and is another fiber that doesn't wet felt very well. When wet down, the fibers float apart, holes form, and the fibers don't hold together well. After 9–10 minutes, a soft felt forms but fulling does not cause any further shrinkage. Minimal shrinkage occurred with this sample.

Cashmere is the fiber from a Kashmir goat and is soft and luxurious. It comes in a variety of natural colors including white, gray, and brown. It felts fairly quickly to the soft stage but takes longer to full. The felt formed is soft and does not become firm or durable. Cashmere took 12 minutes to felt and had a shrinkage rate of 25%.

Llamas have a soft undercoat with coarse guard hair over top. There are a variety of natural colors including black, white, gray, and brown. Dehairing is recommended as the guard hair will not felt. Llama fiber felts quickly and forms a sturdy felt, which is somewhat hairy. It took only 7 minutes to felt and had a shrinkage rate of 25%.

Yak down is a luxurious fiber with a natural brown color and is often substituted for cashmere in spinning. The fiber is very soft and looks like it would felt easily but actually took more than 40 minutes to felt. The fiber shifts and moves when wet down, so use a minimal amount of water. The edges were very difficult to control, and there was no shrinkage obtained due to the shifting and moving of the fibers away from the center when wet down. The felt formed is fairly sturdy, but the length of time taken to felt is hardly worth the effort. Blend this luxury fiber in with other wools for a softer finish, but avoid felting it on its own.

## LOCAL FIBER MILLS AND FIBER FESTIVALS

Many felt makers find their supplies online, but depending on where you live, there may be sources much closer to home. Small fiber mills are located throughout the United States and are a great resource for fiber and information about wool. Many of these mills specialize in a specific fiber type or a particular process in fiber preparation.

Fiber mills process wool and other animal fibers usually in preparation for spinning, but the same methods are used to make wool ready for felting. The steps for processing in these small mills include tumbling to remove as much dirt and vegetable matter as possible, followed by washing and then drying. The fiber is then sent through a picking machine that opens up any matted fibers caused by the washing. If the fiber has guard hair (e.g., llama or alpaca), it will be put through a dehairing machine. The final step is to run the fiber through a large carding machine that realigns the fibers and forms them into roving or batt form. At this stage, the fiber is ready for felting.

To find a fiber mill near you, search online or attend a fiber fair or festival. Many times, local fiber-mill owners are involved in setting up and running fiber festivals. Numerous fiber fairs are held throughout the United States each year. Most are held in the spring after shearing, and fleece from a variety of breeds will be available for sale. A fleece requires washing and preparation but will be much less expensive per ounce than already processed roving or batt.

Sheep shearing at 38th Annual Maryland Sheep and Wool Festival (photo by Patti McAleenan)

Fiber festivals are great resources for learning more about wool, fiber, and felting. Most festivals have vendors with a vast array of fiber and supplies. The vendors also have a lot of information to share. Many times, felting classes are available at fiber festivals as well.

Another good source of information is the local spinning and weaving guild. Spinners use the same types of fibers as felt makers and will know of sources for wool. Felting classes may also be taught at the guilds. Guilds may have a loaner drum carder or hand cards that you could borrow and experienced people to help you with fiber preparation.

Carding machine, Going to the Sun Fiber Mill, Kalispell, Montana

## EMBELLISHMENT FIBERS

There are amazing arrays of fiber, yarns, wool locks, and surface design techniques that can be applied to felt whether you are wet felting, nuno felting, or needle felting. Numerous specialty fibers exist, such as various plant-based products, manmade fibers, silk, and even luxury fibers from other animals. The word luxury when applied to fiber does not always mean expensive; instead it expresses the feel, or hand, of the fiber. Specialty fibers can be carded and blended with wool and will felt in easily as they are then well mixed with the wool fibers.

The samples here show what some of the individual specialty fibers look like so that you can get an idea of what you are ordering and how they will work in a project.

Silk top (1) is combed silk fiber with two varieties normally available, Bombyx and Tussah. The Bombyx silk comes from the silk-producing caterpillar that feeds on mulberry leaves and is reared throughout Asia. Bombyx is the finest and whitest of the silk fibers. Tussah comes from

Avalanche Creek, wet-felted, needle-felted, Pelsull, Merino, mixed-breed wool, Jacob wool, banana fiber, flax, Tencel, SeaCell, pelsull locks, Angora goat fiber, silk top, fake cashmere, silk noil, and wool slubs.

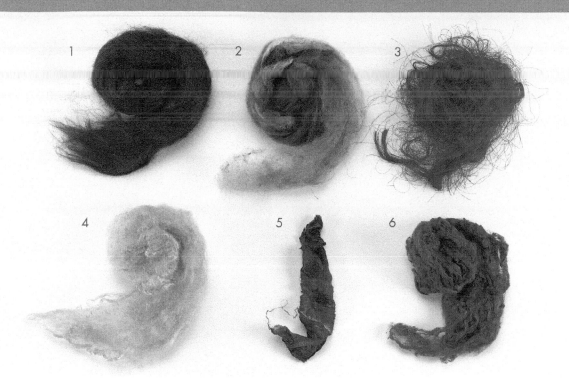

a wild caterpillar that feeds on arjun, asan, or oak leaves. This caterpillar is raised in the forested regions of China, Korea, and India. The resultant silk is a beige/golden color. Silk top can be used in wet felting, nuno felting, and needle felting. Its sheen contrasts nicely with the more matte appearance of wool.

Silk caps (2) are formed after a silk cocoon has been degummed. Degumming removes the sericin or natural gum from the silk by boiling in a solution with soap. Once the cocoon is partially degummed, the fibers of the cocoon are stretched and expanded over an arch-shaped piece of bamboo. Caps are multilayered and can be pulled apart to form very thin layers. Care must be taken to not catch the silk on any rough skin when caps are being pulled apart as they are quite fine.

Silk throwsters waste (3) is a byproduct of silk-reeling production. As the silk is spun from the cocoon, the fibers may tangle and catch in the gears of the reels and become waste of the silk-making process. The resultant silk is usually curly or kinked and is usually stiffer than silk top.

Silk hankies (4) are similar to caps in their production. They are partially degummed and stretched over a wire frame about the size of a handkerchief. Hankies also have multiple layers and can be pulled apart easily. Hankies can be used in all forms of felting.

Silk carrier rods (5) are a byproduct of reeling silk from the cocoon. They look like a slit tube and often the tubes are split into two or more sections. During the production of silk, the filaments are unraveled from the cocoon on to a reel, but some of the silk filament wraps around the machinery. This excess silk is then cut off and removed. The rods have not been degummed and are stiff. They can add an interesting textural component. The easiest way to use them is to let them soak in water and then thinner layers can be pulled apart and used on the surface of wet felt. As carrier rods are usually thick and stiff, it is difficult to needle felt them although if cautious you can use them with a needle-felting machine once separated into thinner pieces.

Silk noil (6) is the short, snarled fiber left over after combing silk into top. The fiber length of silk noil is uneven and quite short. There are different grades of silk noil with "A" being the highest quality. As in most forms of silk, it can be used in all aspects of felting.

(continued)

Nylon top (1) is a manmade fiber with a shiny, sparkly appearance. It accepts acid dyes, which result in vivid colors. If blended with wool, it will add strength and resilience, increasing durability.

Angelina fiber (2) is an iridescent synthetic fiber that comes in multiple colors. It can be blended with wool to give shine and sparkle. There are two types of Angelina, one of which is heat bondable. Either will work for applying to felt or blending with wool, but the heat-bondable feature is not needed with wet felting. Heat-bondable Angelina makes beautiful, thin wings to be added to figures in needle felting.

Fake cashmere (3) is a manmade fiber that is combed into top. It is very soft and is made to feel like cashmere. It accepts acid dyes readily.

Tencel (4) is a specific brand of viscose fiber. Viscose is a manmade fiber made from wood pulp and short cotton fibers that are unusable for spinning. Tencel has a lustrous appearance like silk, but as it is a plant-based product, it doesn't accept acid dye well.

Banana fiber (5) is a relatively new plant-based fiber that is white and soft. Banana also is a good substitute for silk, but it doesn't accept acid dyes well.

Flax or linen top (6) is one of the oldest plant-based fibers in the western world. Flax has low elasticity and feels much stiffer than wool and other luxury fibers. Its natural color is a golden tan. It doesn't accept acid dye as it is a plant-based fiber.

SeaCell fiber (7) is a luxurious fiber made from seaweed with silklike properties. It does not accept acid dye well.

Wool nepps (1) are little felted wool balls. They can be dyed with acid dyes because they are wool. Nepps can be used to form a bumpy texture on the wool when wet felting but will not work well with needle felting, as they are quite hard and would most likely break the needles.

Wool slubs (2) are a combination of felted strings and balls very similar to nepps. They accept acid dyes readily since they are wool and should be treated the same as nepps.

Wool locks (3) of curly, longhaired breeds can be wet felted completely to the surface of felt or just the ends can be felted down. Locks can add texture in needle felting for a 2D piece or for hair on figures. Many colors are available already dyed or in natural colors.

Pre-yarn (4), also known as hahtuvalanka or plotulopi, is yarn that hasn't been put through the spinning machine yet. It is harder to find in North America but is available in Europe. It works well for adding thin lines to a design in wet felting or needle felting.

Cotton fiber (5) is a widely used fiber for textiles. It is white and nonlustrous with a short and uniform length. As it is a plant-based fiber, it should be dyed with fiber-reactive dyes instead of acid dye.

Soybean fiber (6) is a good substitute for silk as it is strong and lustrous. When blended with other fibers, it improves the draping qualities of the blend. It is a plant-based fiber and should be dyed with fiber-reactive dye (see page 38).

Specialty yarns (7) are readily available in a wide range of styles and colors. Any type of yarn can be used but remember that yarn that isn't fuzzy will not wet felt in easily. Specialty yarns can be used in needle felting, and as long as they have some loose fibers, will adhere fairly well, especially if using a needle-felting machine.

# PREPARING TO FELT

There are a few things that need to be done before you begin to felt. The wool needs to be cleaned and carded, color needs to be applied, and the design of the project needs to be determined. All these steps aren't necessary, as wool can be used in its natural state. But it is possible and rewarding to process the fiber yourself if you have the time. Even if all the supplies are purchased already processed, a few minutes should be spent planning the felting project, deciding on a color scheme, and determining the appropriate wool, fibers, and embellishments to use.

## FIBER PREPARATION

Although wool can be felted from a raw fleece (unwashed wool sheared from the sheep), most people process the wool first or buy it already processed. All of the steps for preparing the wool can be done at home, which makes the wool more economical. Preparing or processing fiber at home takes time but is straightforward. Raw fleece will need to be washed and carded into a roving or a batt. A roving is a long, ropelike piece of fiber with the fibers running lengthwise. A batt is a flat sheet of fiber with fibers running in different directions.

Many people are apprehensive about dyeing, but when done in small batches, it is quite simple. Common food dyes can be used. Wool can be dyed before or after wet felting, and the satisfaction of creating your own color scheme is considerable.

Design is another topic that some people feel unsure about. Design should just be thought of as advance planning. Before beginning to plan, find a source of inspiration. Inspiration can be found anywhere; it is really a matter of looking more closely and taking the time to see the beauty in ordinary things that surround you. Once a source of inspiration has been found, it can lead to a color scheme, a focal point, or even the function of the planned project.

### Washing Wool and Fiber

Once a fleece is obtained, it needs to be examined, and any dirty, stained, or matted parts need to be removed. This is called skirting and is usually performed before the fleece is sold. Washing will be easier if the fleece is well skirted. Unless you have a top-loading washing machine that is dedicated to washing wool, it is easiest to wash the fiber in small batches by hand. The temperature of the wash water depends on the breed of the fleece. Fine wools have grease that is more tenacious and waxy and require 160°F (71°C) temperature water to loosen and remove the waxy grease. Coarser or long-staple wools only require a temperature of 140°F (60°C) as they are only moderately greasy. Care needs to be taken with both fine and coarser wools to prevent excess agitation, which could result in felted or matted fleece, although coarser wools are less apt to felt than the fine wool varieties.

### YOU WILL NEED

- large sink, tub, or tank
- water
- raw fleece
- large mesh bag
- thermometer
- liquid dish detergent, 1 cup (250 mL) of detergent for every 4 lb. (1.81 kg)
- heavy rubber gloves

**1** Separate the fleece into small batches so that the mesh bag is filled with wool but not overfull. Water and detergent must be able to seep into the wool easily, and if too much wool is forced into the bag, the wool in the center will not come clean.

**2** Fill a sink, tub, or tank with hot water, 160°F (71°C) for fine breeds and 140°F (60°C) for coarser wools. If the water out of the tap is not hot enough, boiling water may need to be added. Be careful when using hot water to avoid being scalded. Use heavy rubber gloves throughout the washing process.

**3** Add plenty of detergent to the water after filling the tank. It's better to add more detergent than not enough. Any kind of detergent can be used, but liquid dish detergents that are made to cut grease work especially well. Avoid using detergents that include bleach.

**4** Put the wool-filled mesh bag on top of the water. Gently press the bag down until it is completely submerged. Don't forget the heavy rubber gloves to avoid scalding your hands. The bag should immerse fairly easily. Let the bag soak in the hot water for 15 to 30 minutes. Coarser wool usually takes less time than finer wool. Do not leave the wool in the water long enough for it to cool or the wool may attract the grease again. Fine wools with tenacious grease may need to be put into wash water twice, especially if the wool has been sitting for a long period before washing and the grease has hardened. Other wool may also need more than one wash. This can be judged by how dirty the water is after the first wash. If the water is really dirty, do a second or even third wash.

**5** Carefully remove the mesh bag full of wool from the wash water. Hold each end of the bag and avoid agitating the wool. Let the water drain out of the bag without squeezing the wool. It helps to let the wool drain as much as possible before rinsing to get rid of as much dirty water as possible.

**6** Prepare a rinse bath of clear water with a temperature of 120°F (49°C). Put the bag of wool in the water and gently submerge it. Let the bag soak for 15 minutes.

**7** Repeat the rinse bath two more times using cooler water with each rinse.

**8** To remove excess water from the wool, place the mesh bag in the washing machine on the spin cycle and spin out the water. Don't leave the wet wool in a mesh bag for more than four to five hours to prevent mildew.

## Technique

For a small amount of wool, use a salad spinner dedicated to wool to remove excess water. If you are washing several batches of wool, you can wait and spin all the water out at once.

**9** Spread the wool out to dry. Drying wool outside on a screen or netting will speed the process. Spread the fiber thinly and turn it over once or twice until completely dry. After drying, if the wool feels tacky or sticky, it will need to be rewashed.

**10** To store wool, avoid using plastic bags. If the wool is stored in plastic where the temperature will change, condensation will form on the bag and may stain or damage the wool. Wool should be stored in large paper bags, cardboard boxes, cloth bags, or an old pillowcase. Tie the bag closed tightly.

**11** To protect the wool from moths while being stored, use mothballs or naphthalene flakes. Lavender is another good deterrent and can be added in a sachet to the bag of wool. Moths are less attracted to clean wool, so store the wool clean if possible.

## Technique

Smaller amounts of fiber can be washed in a smaller mesh bag. To wash locks and keep the structure of the lock, place one layer of locks in a mesh bag without overlapping or roll the locks into netting. Wash and rinse as shown in the steps above, being careful to not move the locks excessively in the bag. Unwashed locks can also be used as embellishments for felting as they will be cleaned during the felting process and will hold their structure better if not washed beforehand.

### Carding and Combing

Wool can be used for felting without further preparation, but most felting projects will benefit from starting with evenly carded wool. Beginning with a nice soft batt or roving will result in more even placement of wool when either wet or needle felting. Spending the time to prepare the fiber well will produce a better quality and more even felt.

To open up the fibers in preparation for carding, the fiber needs to be picked or teased. This can easily be done by hand by gently pulling apart the individual locks and spreading the fibers out to open and separate them. The end result should be a handful of fluffy fibers that are loose and not clumped together.

(continued)

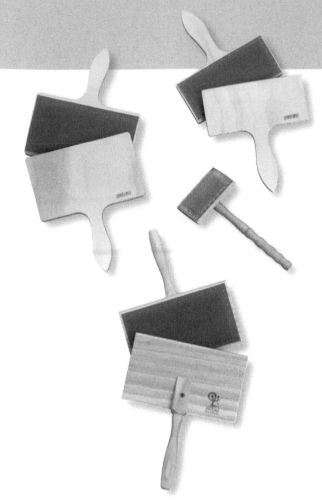

A mechanical picker is a machine that has a swinging cradle with large teeth or nails protruding from the base of the cradle. Wool is fed in from the front as the cradle is swung back and forth, picking and separating the fibers with each swing. Proper precautions should be taken when using a picker. This includes the use of heavy leather gloves, apron, and safety glasses; not reaching under the cradle; and securing the picker to prevent accidents when not in use. Mechanical pickers also come in a box form and are less dangerous than the swinging pickers.

Carding can be performed with hand carders or a drum carder. The drum carder is more efficient and can handle more fiber, but it is an expensive investment. Hand carders work well for small batches of fiber. Many people substitute slicker wire dog brushes when starting to hand card as they are less expensive than hand carders.

Hand carders are used in pairs except for the special flick carder. A flick carder is used to open up individual locks of wool without removing any of the shorter fibers. It is a similar process to picking or teasing. To use a flick carder, hold the lock of wool in one hand and pull the flick carder through the opposite end of the strands of wool with a flicking motion, pulling up and away.

When using two hand carders, sit with the left carder resting in your lap. The right carder can be held in your lap if you are left handed. Use an old sheet to cover your lap to catch any loose fibers or vegetable matter that falls from the carded wool. The carders should be held with your palm and the teeth or face of the carder facing upward and your palm facing downward if the teeth are downward.

Hand carders are convex handled paddles lined with short needlelike teeth. The teeth are anchored to the carder through the carding cloth, which is usually rubberized canvas or leather. Carders with teeth that are more closely spaced and have finer wire are used for finer fibers such as cotton or silk. Coarser carders are used for wool. The heel of the carder refers to the long side that attaches to the handle, and the toe is the opposite long edge (photo courtesy of Ashford Handcrafts, Ltd. NZ, manufacturers of textile equipment).

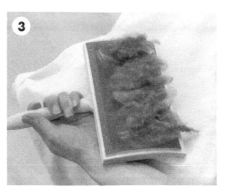

**1** Load or charge the left carder with wool. To load, lay locks of wool onto the carder and lightly attach the wool to the teeth. Start by laying a lock of wool with the cut or butt end about ½" (1 cm) from the edge of the heel of the left carder.

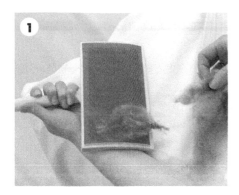

**2** Continue applying locks of wool until the teeth are covered.

**3** Once the left carder is loaded, hold the handle in your left hand with the teeth facing upward and resting against your lap.

## Technique

It is better to have less fiber than to overload the carder. If you have problems, try removing some fiber.

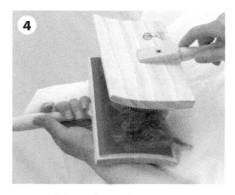

**4** Hold the right carder in your right hand with the teeth facing downward.

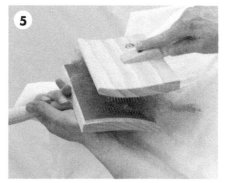

**5** Gently stroke the right carder over the wool held in the left carder. Do not push down with force or grind the two carders together.

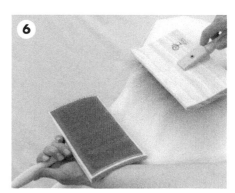

**6** Pull the right carder completely away from the left carder with each stroke. The wool on the two carders should be completely separated.

(continued)

**7** Keep gently stroking the right carder over the left one, keeping the carders parallel. Two-thirds of the right carder should come in contact with the wool. Complete at least 5 to 6 strokes of the right carder over the wool.

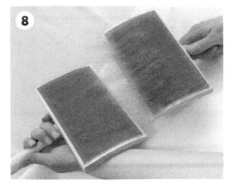

**8** To transfer the remaining wool on the left carder over to the right carder, turn the right carder teeth upward.

## Caution

If the wool is still connected between the two carders, the fibers can fold back upon themselves and become tangled.

**9** With the left carder teeth upward, place the toe of the left carder against the heel of the right carder gently joining the two at the first couple of rows of teeth.

**10** Turn the left carder to about a 60° angle to the right carder so the teeth of both carders face each other.

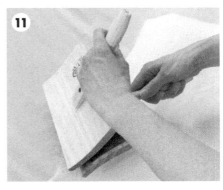

**11** Pull the right carder back toward you and push the left carder forward and away from you, keeping the teeth in contact and maintaining the 60° open angle. This movement will pull the remaining fiber off the left carder and move it onto the right carder.

## Technique

The wool that needs the most work should be on the topmost carder.

**12** Hold the left carder face up in your lap and gently stroke the right carder over the left.

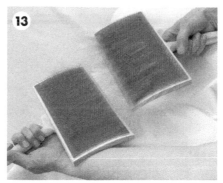

**13** Keep carding and transferring the fiber back and forth between the two carders until the fiber is straight and aligned with no clumps.

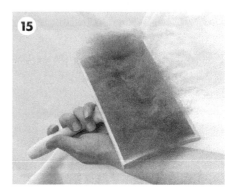

**14** Keep carding with as many passes as necessary to straighten the fiber.

**15** Remove the fiber from the carders by transferring it by using the method of toe to heel twice. The fiber should now lie lightly on the carder.

**16** Put the fiber in your lap and gently roll the fiber lengthwise so it forms a long tube of fiber. This is called a rolag.

Hand combing is usually performed with two combs and rids the wool of the shorter fibers, leaving the long fiber smooth and parallel. It is performed by loading a stationary comb with wool and combing through the fiber with a second comb. The wool is gradually transferred to the moving comb leaving any short fibers behind. Combing creates what is called wool top and is more important for spinning than felting as it removes the shorter fibers from the wool. Combing adds an extra step to fiber preparation, but it is one that can often be skipped if the wool will be used for felting.

(continued)

## Technique

Steam will increase the crimp in combed or carded wool, returning it to its more natural form. If more crimp or curl is needed, hang the wool in a steamy place, such as in the bathroom while taking a shower.

Drum carding allows a greater quantity of fiber to be processed at one time and produces a batt that works well for both needle and wet felting. Hand-cranked and electrical drum carders, are available. The drum carder is more efficient than hand carders but it is also considerably more expensive. If you will be carding a large volume of wool, then a drum carder is a good investment. If you only plan to card small batches or blend small amounts of fiber, hand carders would be a better choice.

It is advisable to wash any fleece before putting it through a drum carder. Washed fleece cards more easily and will not leave a sticky residue of grease on the drum and teeth of the carder. Allow the wool to dry thoroughly before carding, as wet wool can damage the carding cloth.

A drum carder has two turning drums covered with carding cloth. The smaller, or infeed, drum catches the fiber and transfers it onto the larger drum. Most drum carders have a belt to drive the mechanism. There are usually two positions for the belt and it should be left in the unstretched position when not in use. Some drum carders allow the adjustment of drum placement. The drums should be adjusted so that the teeth of the two drums are as close as possible without actually touching. Follow the manufacturer's instructions when determining the distance between the teeth of the two drums.

## YOU WILL NEED

- drum carder
- washed fleece or locks
- doffing stick or metal awl

Drum carder (photo courtesy of Ashford Handcrafts, Ltd. NZ, manufacturers of textile equipment)

1 Tease open all locks before carding. Place the teased locks on the intake tray. Cover the tray evenly with locks to cover the entire drum.

2 Feed the locks into the infeed drum by turning the handle on the drum carder in a clockwise direction.

3 Rest your hand lightly on the locks in the tray so they aren't pulled too quickly and tangle.

## Technique

A hand carder or dog slicker brush can be used to brush the fiber down as it transfers onto the drum. This allows more fiber to fit on the drum and produces a fuller batt. If the fiber begins to stay on the infeed roller or not stick down to the large drum, the drum is full.

**4** Continue feeding fiber onto the drum, making sure it distributes equally. Keep turning the handle until the large drum is covered and full to the top of the metal teeth.

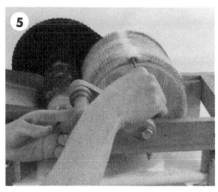

**5** Remove the fiber from the drum using a doffing stick, knitting needle, or metal awl. Slide the doffing stick under the fibers on the open strip of the drum.

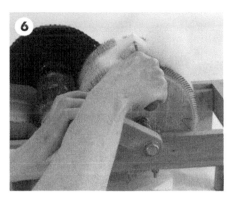

**6** Gently lift the doffing stick up and toward the right of the drum. The fibers will pull up and separate naturally.

**7** Lift the batt up off the drum and turn the handle slowly counterclockwise.

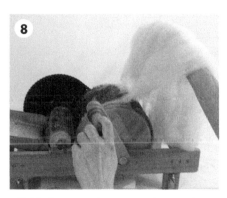

**8** Lift the entire batt up and away from the drum.

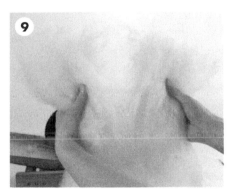

**9** Split the batt in half lengthwise and spread the fibers apart. Run each half of the batt separately through the drum carder again.

## Technique

Working in small sections across the drum will be easier than attempting to remove the fibers in one piece across the width of the drum.

The drum carder should be cleaned between carding runs of different types of fiber or colors. To clean the carder, use a hand carder or dog slicker brush. Hold the brush over the drum and turn the handle counterclockwise. Pull the brush up frequently to pull fiber away from the drum. Clean the infeed drum with the same method. Also remember to take the tension off the belt if the drum carder will not be in use. Oiling the drum carder may also be necessary. Follow the manufacturer's directions for maintaining the drum carder.

## Blending Colors and Fibers

Combining different types of fibers or different colors to achieve a custom blend can be done by hand, with combs, hand carders, or on the drum carder. Blending can be used to add specialty fibers to wool, mix different breeds of wool together, or combine different colors of wool to create a one-of-a-kind fiber batt.

When blending different breeds of wool, consider the compatibility of the characteristics of each breed. Think about the project for which the blend will be used. Do you need more elasticity and loft? Add a breed of wool with greater crimp, such as Delaine Merino, to the mix of wools. What if the project needs to be very sturdy and durable? A mixture of coarser wools such as Norwegian, Pelsull (Pelssau), and Icelandic might be the perfect combination.

Beautiful blends can be made by adding specialty or embellishment fibers such as silk, manmade fibers, or other animal fibers that felt. Remember that many of the embellishment fibers do not felt. A greater percentage of wool should be included in the blend for greater ease in felting and so that the nonfelting fibers will have enough wool surrounding them to achieve a firm felt. If the blend is being used as a top layer of embellishment, less wool is required, as the wool present will adhere to the wool in the other layers.

Blending can also be used to develop custom colors. Blending two different colors of already dyed wool can produce a color with more depth than wool dyed with a single color. For example, blending blue and yellow wools to achieve green will produce a mix of wool that the eye sees as a variegated green and cannot be accomplished as easily from dyeing. These blended colors will combine to create a much more striking felt.

If only a small amount of fiber needs to be blended, this can be done by hand. You might need a color for a small needle-felting project that you don't have in your stash. Don't rush out and buy more wool, combine what you have already. For example, if purple is needed, use red and blue mixed together to make purple.

## YOU WILL NEED

- drum carder
- washed fleece or locks
- doffing stick or metal awl

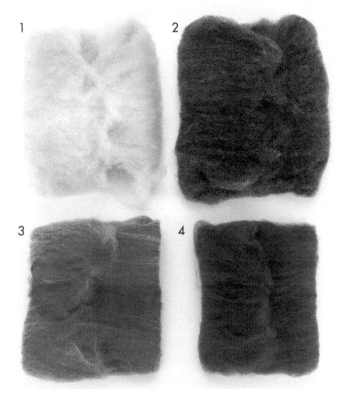

Examples of blended batts as compared to a Polwarth batt. Polwarth batt (1), Moorit + Corriedale batt (2), mixed breed 56s + silk top batt (3), Merino + banana fiber batt (4)

**1** Take a small tuft of red fiber and a small tuft of blue fiber and stack them on top of each other.

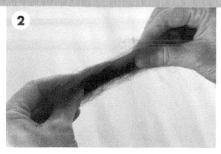

**2** Hold each end of the stack of fibers (fibers running longitudinally) between your thumb and first finger.

**3** Pull the fibers apart and stack them back together. Also, turn the pile of fibers over in your hands, split in half, and restack in opposite directions to mix the two colors of fiber as much as possible.

## Caution

This method works only for small amounts of fiber and is inefficient for larger batches of fiber.

**4** Keep pulling the fibers apart and stacking them back together again until the two colors are well blended.

Blend larger amounts of fiber using hand carders. Determine the percentage of each type or color of fiber to be mixed. This can be done by eye or by measuring specific units by weight or by length if using roving. If specialty fibers are to be mixed with wool, load a thin layer of wool, then a layer of specialty fiber, and then another layer of wool on to the carder. Remember not to overload the carder. Then card the fibers together as described on page 29. It is easier to blend already processed fiber than to attempt blending with raw locks.

The most efficient way to blend various fibers is with the drum carder. Loading the drum carder with a thin layer of wool first before adding a specialty fiber will assist in removing the batt from the drum after it is full. The blended fibers will need to be run through the drum carder several times, resulting in a more even blend.

Experiment by making different blends with a variety of fibers and then felting a small sample. Keep track of the amounts blended so that the results can be repeated. Developing your own blends of fiber is fun and will give you even more flexibility and options in felting.

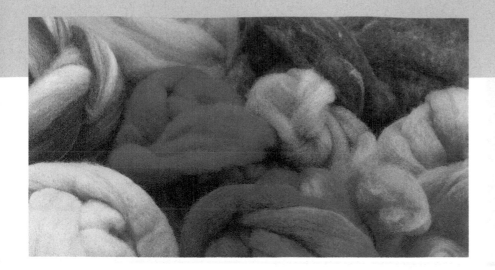

## DYEING

Dyeing is a combination of art and science. The dyes that work best with animal fibers are called acid dyes. The acid refers to the use of vinegar, citric acid, or acetic acid as a fixative or setting agent in setting the dyes. Heat or steam is also required to set acid dyes so that the resultant dyed fibers are wash fast. Dyeing fiber can be a very simple process and allows the versatility of developing your own colors.

Different types of fibers, and even different breeds of wool, accept dyes differently. Some fibers accept dye at lower temperatures than others. If a variety of fibers are in one dye pot, the fibers that require higher temperatures to dye may not have as much color as other fibers. This is because the fiber that dyes at a lower temperature takes up most of or all the dye before reaching a high enough heat for the other fiber to dye. Different fibers can certainly all be dyed at one time but be aware that the resultant colors produced will not be the same.

Wool can also be dyed with food dyes such as Easter egg dyes, icing dyes, and even unsweetened drink crystals. Natural dyeing is another alternative for dyeing wool. Natural dyes provide subtle coloring that is hard to obtain with manmade dyes. Another option to consider when choosing a color scheme is the use of the natural colors of the wool without dyeing.

Wool can be dyed before the fiber is used for felting or a piece can be felted and then dyed. The advantage to dyeing an already felted piece is that there is no danger of loose fibers becoming matted during the dye process. Many times, fiber needs to be carded after dyeing due to excess agitation during dyeing.

This technique is one way of dying wool. The results are not exactly repeatable as each set of wool dyed is distinctive and multicolored. For a solid color roving, either purchase the wool already dyed and carded or use the dye pot method of simmering wool in one color dye. Remember that any utensil or tool used for dyeing should not be used for the preparation of food once it has been used in the dyeing process.

## YOU WILL NEED

- large plastic covering for work surface
- paper towels
- citric acid, acetic acid, or white vinegar
- textile detergent or liquid dish detergent
- wool (one 12oz./350-mL mixture of dye covers approximately 3 to 4 oz./ 80 to 113 g of wool)
- powdered acid dyes in a variety of colors
- dust mask or respirator mask
- rubber gloves
- measuring spoons
- containers for mixing dyes (glass measuring cups work well)
- mixing spoon
- 12 oz. (350 mL) squeeze bottle
- plastic wrap
- large dye pot (stainless steel or enameled steel) with lid
- vegetable steamer basket
- stove or heat source

1 Make a soaking solution for the wool. Mix 1 gallon (3.8 l) of room temperature water, 2 or 3 drops of textile detergent or liquid dish detergent, and 6 tablespoons (89 mL) of citric or acetic acid in a bucket. For vinegar, mix 1 cup (250 mL) per gallon (3.7 l) of water. Hard water may require more acid.

2 Put the wool in the soaking solution and gently press down until the wool is submerged. Avoid agitating the wool. Let the wool soak for 30 minutes.

3 Cover the work surface with plastic.

4 Heat one cup (250 mL) of water to near boiling and pour into the dye-mixing container.

5 Place the cup of hot water on a damp paper towel. Any loose dye particles will be caught by the moisture in the paper towel.

6 Wearing rubber gloves and a dust mask or respirator mask, add ½ teaspoon (2.5 mL) of acid dye to the hot water and stir to dissolve. Keep the mask on until the dye is completely dissolved.

7 Pour the dye into the squeeze bottle and fill to the top with cold water. Close the bottle tightly. Rinse out the mixing cup with water.

8 Repeat steps 5–7 with as many colors of dye as desired. To save time, calculate the total amount of water needed and heat at one time. Allow the dye to cool.

9 Spread a 3' (91 cm) piece of plastic wrap on the table.

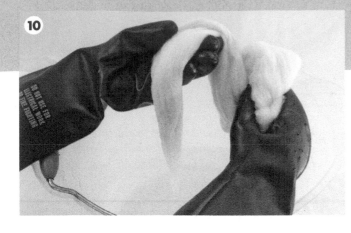

**10** Take the wool out of the soaking solution and drain the soaking solution back into the bucket. Gently press the wool between your hands but do not wring the wool.

**11** Place the wool on the plastic wrap. Arrange the roving so that all parts are close together.

**12** Squirt the chosen colors of dye over the wool. Wearing gloves, press gently down on the wool to make sure the dye soaks into all the wool.

**13** Cover the wool entirely with the dye. Flip the wool over to make sure the other side is completely covered with dye. Avoid large puddles of dye; use just enough dye to cover the wool.

**14** Wrap the colored wool in the plastic wrap. Wrap the wool packet with another layer of plastic.

**15** Repeat steps 10–14 to dye as much wool as needed.

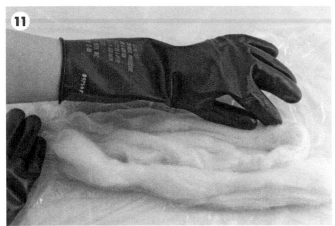

## Storage

Soaking solution can be saved in an airtight container for up to a month at room temperature and be reused. Leftover dye can be stored in the refrigerator in a closed, well-marked container for up to a month. The dyes will start to break down fairly quickly and will result in less vibrant colors the longer the dye is stored. Try to make just enough dye for the amount of wool needed.

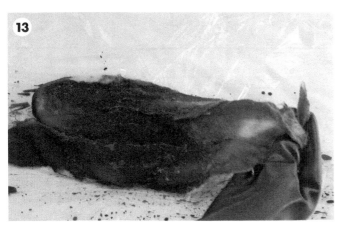

**16** Fill the dye pot with 1" (2.5 cm) of water in the bottom; place the vegetable steamer open in the bottom of the pot.

**17** Put the pot on the heat source and lay all the plastic-wrapped wool packets in the vegetable steamer. Put the darker colored packets at the bottom and the lighter colors on top in case of any leakage.

**18** Put the lid on the pot and turn on the heat source. As soon as the water starts to boil, turn on the timer. Steam the packets for 30 minutes.

**19** Remove the pot from the heat source and remove the lid. Let it cool completely.

**20** Transfer the wrapped packets to an area near the sink covered with plastic. Wearing gloves, remove the plastic wrap from all the wool and place it on the plastic-covered work surface. It should be completely cool.

**21** Fill the sink with room temperature water. Add 2 or 3 drops of textile detergent or liquid dish detergent but do not mix or make suds. Textile detergent attracts loose dye, keeping it from reacting any further with the wool.

**22** Gently place one color of wool in the water and submerge completely. Let the wool soak for 5 to 10 minutes.

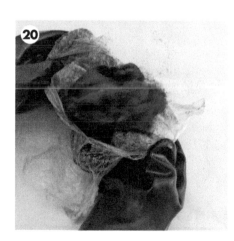

**23** Drain the water from the sink, keeping the wool away from the drain. Take the wool out of the sink and place back on the plastic-covered work surface.

**24** Refill the sink with clear, room-temperature water. Submerge the wool and let it soak for 5 to 10 minutes. If the water still shows residual dye from the wool, continue to rinse until no dye is present in the water.

**25** Spin the excess water out of the wool in the washing machine on the spin cycle.

**26** Hang the wool to dry.

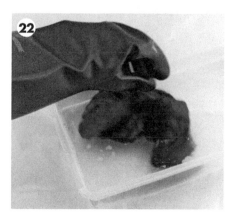

## Variations

Dye can be applied randomly on the wool, or certain portions of the wool can be colored with different colors of dye to produce a roving with blocks of color. Remember that mixing two colors from the opposite sides of the color wheel will mix to become a muddy brown.

## Safety Precautions

Safety should always be considered first whenever dyeing. Loose dye powder should be contained at all times. Whenever dye powder canisters are open and there is loose dye powder in the work area, a mask should be worn. Wipe down all surfaces with a damp paper towel to pick up any loose dye powder. Gloves should be worn at all times to prevent dye from soaking into the skin. Care should be taken with hot or boiling water and with steam to prevent burns.

Dyeing with food dyes is a simpler process and requires fewer safety precautions. Food dyes have less wash fastness and may fade in the sun. However, food dyes for wool used in needle-felting projects work quite well. The process still requires use of an acid such as vinegar, acetic acid, or citric acid before or during dyeing. Kool-Aid unsweetened soft drink mix has acetic acid already mixed in. Experiment with the Kool-Aid to see whether extra vinegar or citric acid is needed. Kool-Aid can even be used to dye wool in a jar in the sun, a process similar to making sun tea.

Small amounts of wool can be dyed very easily with food dye in a plastic bag in the microwave oven. Soak the wool in the acidic soaking solution, place the wet wool in a plastic baggie, pour the dye solution into the baggie, and press gently to spread the dye through the wool. Place the open baggie in a microwave-safe bowl and microwave on high for one minute. If the water still has dye present, microwave for another minute. Once the dye bath is exhausted (and the water is clear), let the wool cool. Rinse the wool if necessary and then dry.

To dye larger amounts of wool with food dyes, try using a large dye pot to simmer the wool in the dye bath. Be aware that silk does not take food dyes well and will not be wash fast. To maintain the brightness of the color in the wool, it is best not to rinse the wool. Wool that is to be used for wet felting will need to be rinsed and the brighter colors will be less vibrant. If the wool is used for needle felting only, washing or rinsing isn't necessary. Kool-Aid unsweetened soft drink mix is flavored and has a very strong odor especially when multiple packets are used. If you are sensitive to strong odors, wear a dust mask or respirator or avoid using flavored drink mixes.

*Rainbow Sprite Woolie Wog Goblin by Kasey Sorsby of Tanglewood Thicket Studio, needle-felted entirely with wool dyed with Kool-Aid and Wilton's Icing Dye. Goblin's hair is hand-dyed silk.*

**1** Fill the pot two-thirds with water and bring to a simmer. The exact water amount does not matter but make sure there is enough water to cover the wool.

**2** Add at least ½ cup (118 ml) of white vinegar.

**3** Stir in one to five packets of Kool-Aid per 1 oz. (28 g) of fiber depending on the darkness of the fiber desired. Teaspoons of gel icing dye can be substituted. Use a tongue depressor or craft stick to transfer the gel dye from the container to the dye pot. The deeper the shade of color required, the greater amount of dye required.

## Variation

Different colors can be achieved by mixing different packets of color or different gel dye colors. Pastel tones can be obtained by removing the wool before the dye bath has exhausted or by using less dye.

**4** Place the wool in the dye bath and submerge gently. To achieve a vibrant color, let simmer until the water is clear, signaling that the dye bath is exhausted.

**5** Drain the wool and let it dry. If the wool is to be used for wet felting, rinse as explained when dyeing with acid dyes (page 38).

Comparison of 1 oz. (28 g) of wool dyed with 1 packet of cherry Kool-Aid and 1 oz. (28 g) of wool dyed with 5 packets of cherry Kool-Aid.

Natural dyeing can be done with a variety of plants. Many natural dyes require a mordant to dye successfully. A mordant is a part of the chemical process of dyeing that binds or fixes the color to the fiber. Natural dyeing is usually done by brewing the plant matter in a large pot of water, adding the mordant, and then adding the fiber and simmering the dye pot. A multitude of plant materials can be used in natural dyeing. Some that are commonly used are onionskins for yellow, walnut hulls for browns, sweet woodruff or birch bark for pink, tea for tans and browns, and purple cabbage, for colors such as pink, purple, or yellow depending on the mordant used.

Needle-felted figures by Teri Canepa, wool dyed with goldenrod flowers, onionskins, birch twigs and bark, woodruff roots, choke cherry bark, and walnut hulls.

All wool is not white. A wide range of wool colors is available due to the variations of the natural colors in different sheep breeds. Many breeds, such as Icelandic, have a wide range of natural wool colors in black, brown, gray, and white. Blue-faced Leicester sheep produce some beautiful variegated wool. Exploring the range of colors available from the natural wool colors can provide a subtle monochromatic felt that can be very striking. Try using natural colors from a variety of wool breeds as well as other animal fibers such as alpaca, llama, or angora. Natural-colored wool is a great resource when looking for a more organic color to use as hair on dolls or to create pieces inspired by nature such as rocks, bark, trees, or animals.

Wall hanging made with 38 different animal fibers, from sheep, alpaca, and angora goats, needle felted onto a wet-felted base, by Zed.

Making a felt project with undyed wool and then dyeing the felt avoids any problems caused by agitation of the wool fiber during dyeing. An already felted piece could be dip dyed, painted with dyes, or dyed in a large vat or pot. Gradations of color can be achieved with dip dyeing by placing the entire piece in the simmering dye pot and then gradually lifting the felt out of the dye. The parts of the felt left in the dye bath the longest will be the darkest.

For painting dyes on wool, the felted piece needs to be wet, or it will not soak up the dye well. Dye will just sit on the surface of the dry felt and not soak through the entire thickness. It helps to press the dye into the wool to make sure it penetrates the full thickness. It isn't possible to create intricate patterns or thin lines by painting dye on felt. Because of the unevenness of the surface, the dye generally soaks in irregularly and fine designs will be lost. To achieve one solid color, dye the felted piece in a large dye bath. Make sure the felt is wet before placing in the dye bath and allow plenty of room so the entire piece is surrounded by dye. The felt should not be folded in on itself to prevent areas being blocked from the dye.

Other processes such as shibori can also be effectively used on felted items. Shibori is a Japanese term for a

process of binding cloth and then dyeing it. Where the fabric is bound, the dye is blocked, which allows patterns to be made on the fabric. The closest Western equivalent is tie-dyeing. Shibori can be a simple process but is a technique that can create complex patterns and intricate designs.

Mixing colors is a fun aspect of dyeing. Most suppliers who sell dyes also carry color wheels, which are inexpensive. A color wheel will provide guidance during the dye-mixing process and help to prevent mistakes. The color wheel shows which colors to mix together to achieve the desired color. Color mixing can be a scientific process or can be more of a happy accident. Both methods of mixing are valid. You can either keep specific records of your experiments, or you can experiment and achieve unexpected results.

The study of color is a continuous learning process. Each time that dyes are mixed, you can learn more about color. Yellow, red, and blue are primary colors, which means they can't be mixed from any other color. Mixing yellow and red yields orange, yellow and blue becomes green, and red and blue gives purple. Orange, green, and purple are known as secondary colors. Tertiary colors are mixed by combining secondary and primary colors that are adjacent on the color wheel. In dyeing, the primary colors are often magenta, turquoise, and yellow. Suppliers that sell dye usually mark the primary colors. By purchasing a set of three primaries and black, you will be able to mix most colors.

Horst created this garment first by creating a top out of white wool. He then attached roving of pre-dyed wool onto the lower portion of the piece. He completed the garment by over-dying it, coloring the base white to blue.

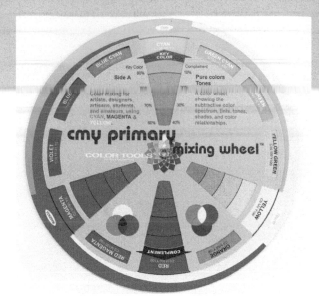

Colors on opposite sides of the color wheel are called complementary. If blue is used as the dominant color in a project, consider adding a small amount of orange as a highlight. Complementary colors used as accents add a nice pop of color that will draw the eye.

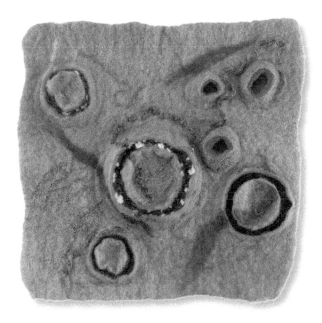

Hue is the word that denotes color, such as navy or turquoise. The value of a color is the relative darkness or lightness of the hue. A tone is a color that has been grayed by adding a mixture of black and white; a tint is a color that has been lightened by adding white; and a shade is a color has been darkened by adding black. Cool colors are on the blue to green side of the color wheel, and warm colors are from yellow to red. Warm color schemes often benefit from using cool colors as shadows or accents and vice versa.

Other terms that are used in color theory relate to color schemes. A monochromatic color scheme means using one other hue in a composition with black and white. For example, a piece made with a range of pink to medium-value red to dark red would be considered monochromatic.

Another straightforward color scheme is called analogous. Analogous colors are ones that are right next to each other on the color wheel. For example, if yellow is the dominant color, an analogous color scheme could also include yellow-orange, orange, and yellow-green.

Most color wheels will show the various color schemes and experimenting with different colors is always enjoyable. Many people have a tendency to use only a few colors that they prefer instead of using the full range of colors available. Expand your color horizons and try mixing dyes for a full spectrum of beautifully colored wool to use in your projects.

## INSPIRATION AND DESIGN

Inspiration can be found in all sorts of unlikely places. Perhaps the rusty surface of old machinery catches your eye. Or maybe you love the texture of tree bark. Take the time to look closely at your surroundings and to see beauty in the ordinary objects of everyday life. Go out and take a walk. What captures your attention? Nature can be a constant source of inspiration. Observe the way a flower petal attaches to its stem or the movement of the leaves in the wind. Even surrounded by a city, inspiration is all around you. Perhaps the many layers of posters and graffiti on an old building interest you, or even the texture on a manhole cover. Look for different color schemes or a specific pattern. See how many shades of orange you can find on your walk. For figurative work, take photos of faces and body types or study a book on anatomy. For animal figures, find a book that shows a variety of breeds of the type of animals that you like or visit an animal shelter or zoo. Think about how you can use these ideas in your felting projects. Don't forget to take a camera or a sketchbook to capture the essences of what inspires you.

(continued)

Consider keeping a studio journal to keep track of inspirational photos, ideas, and sketches for projects, magazine photos that catch your eye, collages to try out a new color scheme, and even to-do lists. A studio journal can be anything you want it to be; it can be a sketchbook, a loose-leaf notebook, or even a file on your computer. It could contain ideas of projects to be done in the future or a book of inspirational photos. The journal could include sketches, instructions for a new technique, or motivational quotes. Don't feel that you have to keep a beautiful, perfect journal. It is a tool to be used for inspiration and planning; there is no need to show it to anyone else. You can look back through it when you need an idea for a new project.

When beginning to plan a felting project, it is helpful to spend a few minutes thinking about the design of the project. Elements and principles of design provide guidelines that will give a composition or project a more satisfying overall look and feel. Learning about design principles will give a structure to follow when planning a particular piece. Strictly adhering to these principles is not always necessary. As an artist you can take creative license when designing, but understanding the basics will certainly improve your ability to create a felting masterpiece.

The elements of design are the pieces of the composition that are put together using principles that help develop a work of art that is pleasing to the eye. Elements of design include line, shape, form, color, value, and texture. The principles of design consist of the focal point or center of interest, harmony, balance, scale or proportion, and rhythm.

One of the more important points to remember about the principles of design is placing the focal point, the part of the piece that draws the eye. Using the rule of thirds to place the focal point prevents the look of a bull's eye with the focal point directly in the center. Divide the composition into thirds both horizontally and vertically. Where the lines intersect is a good area to put the focal point providing a more interesting and less static design.

Another important aspect of design is to have enough variety in the placement and choice of elements so that the piece remains visually stimulating. Avoid a chaotic look but use repeating shapes that are slightly different from each other for more appeal. For example, if the piece has lines, have you included lines of different thickness? Is there a mixture of solid and broken lines?

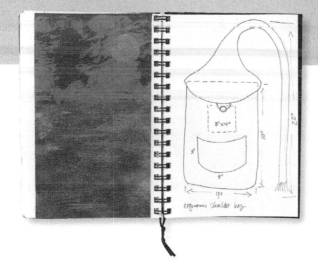

Work a design out on paper first to save time and supplies. Sketching a few options before committing to the final design will help in determining an appropriate size and what felting process will be the best alternative to use. Don't worry if you can't draw, these sketches are not meant to be works of art. The sketch will assist in working out any design flaws before felting begins.

Everyone has the potential to be creative. All children are creative, and the creativity is still there inside you. It may take work to find it and practice to keep being creative, but you can do it. There are numerous online sources and books about creativity, and I urge you not to give up on that inner child who wants to come out and play. Think of your first attempts at creative design as playing and just have fun; the creativity will follow. Creativity comes back with time and practice. You can learn how to see things creatively.

When designing three-dimensional items such as clothing, bags, or hats, make sure to consider form and functionality. No matter how beautiful the item, if it isn't functional, it won't be used as frequently. A bag or purse should be fairly simple to open and close; the shape of the bag should allow for easy access to items inside; and most people prefer to have at least one pocket included in the bag design.

# TRADITIONAL
# WET FELTING

Wet felting is a fairly simple and straightforward process. People of all ages can quickly learn to wet felt and will soon be able to make many projects easily. Felting can also be used for more complex projects and to master the art of felting can take years of practice. The versatility of wet felting allows you to be able to make anything, from a simple square of felt up to a complex, seamless felt garment. The possibilities are endless.

Many people like to jump in and try felting without experimentation first. If you do so, your project might not come out exactly as you planned. Experimentation is important when beginning to felt. With just a small investment of fiber and time, you will gain the knowledge and confidence to complete your planned project. Making small pieces of flat felt teaches you about the shrinkage rates of various fiber types, how the number of layers will affect your project, how the direction of fiber layout causes the felt to shrink differently, how embellishments felt into the wool, and many other issues that affect the outcome of your project. Remember to jot down a few notes to go with the samples to save time later. Making samples is very useful especially when planning a larger and more complex project. By making a small square of felt first, you will save yourself from disappointment and the feeling that you've wasted the fiber. Wet felting is an organic process resulting in imperfect edges and fibers that migrate. It takes practice to achieve straight edges and designs that are "perfect." As your felting skills develop, you will be better able to control your outcomes.

On opposite page: Gaillardia, wet-felted, mixed breed wool, silk noil, silk top, and Wensleydale locks

## EQUIPMENT AND SUPPLIES

The tools needed for wet felting are very basic and you may already have them around your home. The essentials needed are wool, soap, water, and something to agitate the wool, such as bubble wrap or a sushi mat. You can buy equipment made specifically for felting, but if you are just starting out, it is most economical to use what you already have available. As your skills improve and you develop a preferred method of felting, your needs may vary, and you may want to invest in other pieces of equipment. The list here is extensive and gives many options, but you don't need every piece shown. Felt makers are very inventive in their equipment choices, and many times all equipment needs can be met at the local hardware or home store.

### Wet-Felting Equipment

Most of these items can be found around the home. Old towels can be used for rolling felt, soaking up excess water, and rolling finished felt to remove as much moisture as possible. Keep a pair of sharp scissors handy to cut the felt to remove a resist (page 80) and to trim edges to make them straight. Plastic bags can be used to cover your hands while rubbing the felt. A bag can also be used to cover a power sander to prevent water from getting into the sander. Round plastic lids that are made to cover food storage containers can be used for rubbing soft felt. A measuring device such as a yardstick, ruler, or measuring tape is needed to determine the shrinkage rates of the felt.

Equipment for rolling includes bubble wrap (1), rubber shelf liner (2), nonslip rubber rug pads (3), bamboo blinds (4), woven rush rugs (5), or pool covers (6). Bubble wrap is especially good for fulling a nuno-felted project. Either the small or bigger bubble-type wrap can be used. Bubble wrap can also be used to make resists. Tape smaller sections of bubble wrap together with duct tape if a bigger piece is needed. Pool covers can be used for rolling, and since they come in large sizes, they work well for larger projects such as clothing or rugs. Pool covers are usually blue and come in 5- to 16-mm thicknesses. The less expensive 5-mm thickness works just fine for most projects. Pool covers can be found at pool supply stores.

A bamboo blind can also be used for rolling. It provides a greater agitation force and should be used for fibers that are slower to felt or projects that need aggressive fulling. Rubber shelf liner or nonslip rubber rug pads can be used to roll or used for resists. Due to their textured surface, these provide more agitation force but are not as rough as a bamboo blind and will speed up the rolling process. Woven rush rugs come in various sizes and can be found in home stores. The rug provides less agitation when rolling than the bamboo blind but more than bubble wrap and works for most projects. It also provides a good surface for the felt when using a power sander.

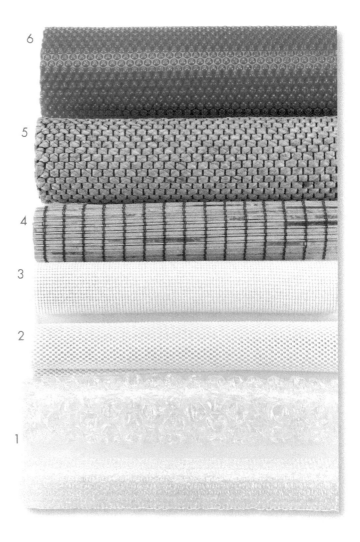

The middle of a rolled bundle of felt needs support and several options are available including a pool noodle (1), a dowel rod (2), or PVC pipe (3). A pool noodle works well for the center of the rolling bundle especially when using bubble wrap. Due to its softer surface, it has more give, so less force or agitation is applied to the felt. The pool noodle can be cut easily to make a less cumbersome size. A dowel rod or piece of PVC pipe can also be used for the center of the rolling bundle. These have a harder surface than the pool noodle and will provide greater force to the felt when rolling. To tie the roll and keep everything in place, use old nylon stockings or elastic ties.

Mosquito netting or tulle is used to cover dry fibers when wetting down and for the beginning process of rubbing during felting. The netting prevents wool fibers from moving and holds designs applied on the surface of the fibers in place. Often curtain netting can be found at thrift stores and can be substituted for tulle or mosquito netting.

Various devices can be used to apply water to your fibers. Plastic spray bottles (1) work but may take more effort than necessary if the spray is very fine. The force of the spray can also cause movement of the applied design. The ball brause sprinkler (2) is good for nuno-felt projects as the gentle spray won't disturb thin layouts. A water-soaked polyester sponge (3) can be used to apply water through netting and force the air out of the wool at the same time. Water can even be applied with an improvised device such as a jar with a lid that has holes in it.

(continued)

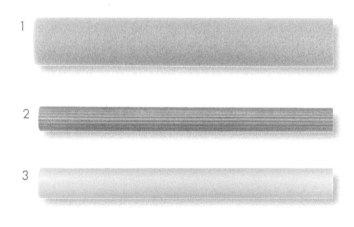

Plastic sheeting is invaluable in keeping the work area dry. It is inexpensive and can be purchased in rolls found in most painting sections of hardware or DIY stores. Plastic comes in various thicknesses, and the thicker varieties will also work to make resists. Plastic can also be used to make templates and be used for flipping wet-felt projects.

A glass or metal washboard (1) is great for fulling. Washboards provide a rough surface that works well for spot fulling on items such as slippers and hats that need to be sized and fit correctly. Sometimes you can find washboards in a thrift store, but often they need to be ordered online. A good substitute for a washboard is a hard plastic-ridged microwave tray (2). Other fulling tools include a grooved rolling pin, a meat tenderizer tool (3), ridged vinyl stair tread, or even a rubber dish drain mat. For lighter felt or rolling cords and beads, a finer ridged surface works best. Ridged plastic shelf lining (4) or a bamboo sushi mat (5) work well for rolling cords and beads. The Turbo Felting Board (6) accelerates the felting/fulling process and is especially helpful for making beads and cords.

Flat resists are used when making three-dimensional forms, and many materials will work for making a resist. Foam packing material (1) works well. It can be purchased in rolls from packing supply companies and comes in thicknesses of ⅟₃₂″ to ½″ (0.8 to 12.7 mm); ⅛″ to ¼″ (3 to 6 mm) foam works the best. Check with local retail stores to see if they have unwanted packaging material that they normally throw away. Craft foam (2) is similar to foam packing material and can be purchased at discount or craft stores. Another product that makes good resists is floor underlayment (not shown), which is used under laminate flooring. It comes in three types, standard foam, foam/film combination, and modified/upgraded. The standard foam padding that is ⅛″ (3mm) thick is the least expensive and works fine. Floor underlayment comes in big rolls and is a great size for the larger resists needed for seamless garments. Cardboard can be used for a resist but degrades quickly once the project is wetted down. Use duct tape to cover your cardboard resist and it will last longer.

Three-dimensional resists such as balls or balloons can also be used when making a felted 3D item. For spherical shapes, there are many options of balls available including toy balls, therapeutic inflatable balls,

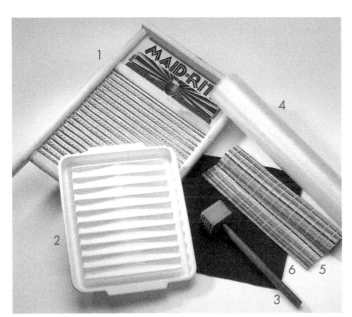

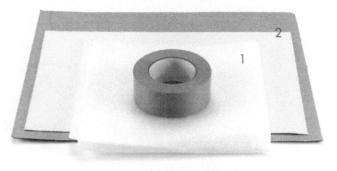

or balloons. A vase could be made over a bowl, plastic tub, or even, with care, a glass vase. Upholstery foam can be stacked, glued, and shaped to whatever form is needed by cutting with an electric knife.

A kitchen scale or postal scale (1) is used to weigh fiber. Weighing the fiber allows better estimates for fiber layout and getting equal amounts of wool to cover the project. A plastic brush (2) is used to rough up the surface of prefelt to make sure that the fibers are loose enough to felt into the project. A salad spinner (3) is a good tool to remove excess water from a felted project. The plastic kinds are inexpensive and work well when you don't want to spin out a small project in the washing machine. A small power sander (4) can be used to speed up the felting process. The sander needs to be the type that just vibrates and doesn't have a belt or orbital movement. The sander will be used without sandpaper. Do not use a sander that has a vacuum attachment and holes on the bottom of the sanding surface. This type of sander may suck water up into the body of the sander and be an electrical hazard. There are rubber attachments made now specifically for felting that are used in place of sandpaper, but they aren't absolutely necessary.

Hat blocks are available in various shapes and sizes and aid in forming and shaping to a specific form. Hat blocks can be made from plastic, wood, or foam. Improvised hat blocks, such as a bowl or crumpled plastic bags, can be used as well.

Shoe lasts are used to shape and block slippers and boots. Lasts come in different sizes and can be expensive, especially if more than one size is needed. To make an improvised shoe last, wrap your foot in a plastic bag. Then cover the bag with duct tape. Take off by cutting very carefully through the duct tape and removing your foot. You can stuff the duct tape form with plastic bags and then repair the cut with more tape.

## Wet-Felting Supplies

The most important supply needed for wet felting is wool. There are many types of wool as noted in the wool and fiber section. The types of wool most often used for wet felting include Merino, Gotland, Corriedale, Falkland, Blue-Faced Leicester, Pelsull (or Pelssau), Polwarth, Romney, Finn, and Icelandic. Many additional types of wool can be used for wet felting. Most other animal fibers have the ability to felt, but goat, llama, and alpaca fiber felts more readily than others.

Wool can be purchased in many formats including fleece (1), roving (2), top (3), or batts (4). It can be natural or dyed in a wide variety of colors. Choose the wool that best suits the project and in a quantity slightly larger than what you estimate is needed.

Many felt makers have a preferred soap to use when felting. Any kind of liquid or bar soap will work. Choose a soap that is gentle on your skin, especially if you will be felting frequently. Olive-oil soap is a good choice as it keeps your hands from drying out and can be made into a soap gel. To make a soap gel from bar soap, chop up or grate the soap and put into a container of water. The soap will dissolve and become gooey. Then add this soap mixture to water for the soapy water used during felting.

Vinegar is needed in the final stages of felting to return the wool to its natural pH. Wool has an acidic PH and adding soap causes the pH to be more alkaline. Soaking the felt in a vinegar and water solution brings the wool back to its normal pH level.

Commercial prefelt (1) is made from a carded web of wool put through a large felting machine with

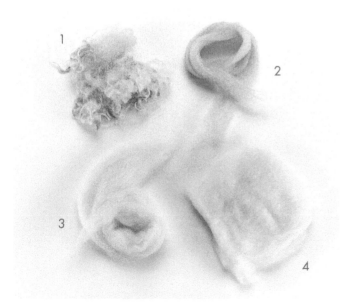

thousands of felting needles. Prefelt, available in white or dyed in a variety of colors, can be used singly or in layers in place of laying out fibers individually, or added as embellishments. A variety of die-cut prefelt shapes (2) are also available. If you have a die-cut machine that cuts fabric, you can cut your own prefelt shapes. You can easily make your own prefelt (3) following the instructions on pages 60 to 68.

Embellishments in felting are limited only by your imagination. Silk in all its forms creates a wonderful enhancement to felt. The sheen of silk contrasts nicely with the duller wool sheen. Silk does not felt in its own right, but its fibers will get caught up in the wool as it felts. Since the silk doesn't shrink, beautiful organic patterns develop as the wool shrinks pulling the silk with it. Other embellishments can be added such as wool locks, novelty yarns, wool yarns, preyarn, pencil roving, ribbons, and thread. Embellishments can also be added after the felting process, including machine stitching, hand stitching, beading, or other surface design.

## TECHNIQUES

There are many methods of wet felting and everyone has their favorites. This section shows you several different methods and offers a variety of tips to try. The more methods you try, the more likely you are to find what works best for you and the fibers you choose. Read through all the instructions first before beginning so that you have a basic understanding of the

process and everything you need at hand. The photos in this section show different colored fibers to better differentiate the layers of the fiber layouts and are not necessarily how a specific project would be completed. The sequences for the steps in wet felting are not set in stone, especially for the felting and fulling stages. Many people begin rolling the felt before the pinch test and may alternate various methods of fulling. There is no right or wrong way to felt. Choose the methods and sequence of steps that work for you, your project, and the fiber used.

### Basics

To begin, you will learn to make a flat piece of felt and the fundamentals of wet felting. If this is your first attempt at wet felting, choose wool that felts easily, such as Merino. After making several projects with a fast-felting wool, try other coarser wools to see and feel the difference in how the coarser fiber felts. It is good to practice making a sample before attempting a specific project.

Many people are unable to buy their supplies locally and end up purchasing online. This can be difficult if you don't understand what you're buying. How much is one ounce of wool or 100 grams? Is that enough to make a bag, a scarf, or a hat? Each of the techniques in this book list approximately how much wool is needed by weight. Wool is often more economical if purchased undyed and in bigger quantities. You should always buy more wool than you think you need, as it is very frustrating to run out of supplies in the middle of your project.

### Set Up

If you have a dedicated space for felting, it is wonderful to be able to leave projects and not have to put everything away if you haven't completely finished. If not, you'll need to prepare an area in which to work each time you begin.

## YOU WILL NEED

- plastic to cover work surface
- two pieces of plastic 16" x 16" (41 cm x 41 cm)
- ½ oz. (14 g) of wool roving in chosen color
- scale (optional)
- lukewarm, soapy water
- spray bottle, ball brause sprayer, or sponge
- plastic bag (optional)
- netting or tulle
- old towels
- access to hot and cold water
- bubble wrap, woven rush rug, bamboo blind, or other rolling device
- ties or old nylon stockings
- washboard or other corrugated surface (optional)

One ounce (28 g) of mixed breed wool roving compared to four ounces (113 g)

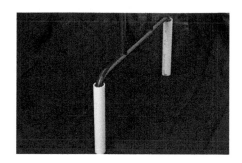

1 Set up your felting area close to a water source or use buckets/dishpans to keep water close at hand. Put a large piece of plastic over the table to prevent any water damage. On top of that, place one 16" x 16" (41 cm x 41 cm) piece of plastic. Have the other tools and supplies close at hand.

2 The table should be at a height that is comfortable for you to work. Continuously leaning over for wool layout, rubbing, and rolling is hard on your back. The table should be high enough for you to stand and work comfortably without having to bend. Use cut pieces of PVC pipe to raise the height of your table as needed.

## Separating Fibers

Pulling the fiber from the roving can take a little practice. It is actually quite easy once you get the feel of it. There are two different methods that are widely used, and it is a matter of preference which method you choose. The second method listed may be easier for someone with an arthritic or other hand condition.

## Entire Hand Method

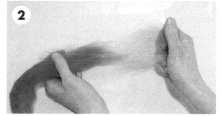

1 To begin, pull off a small, thin piece of fiber from the wool roving. Hold the roving between your fingers and the side and base of your thumb.

2 Gently pull off a small piece of fiber. Do not jerk or pull quickly, ease the fibers out slowly.

3 Remember the staple length of the fiber you are using and have your hands far enough away from each other to accommodate that fiber length.

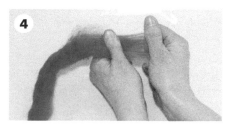

## Technique

To make the roving easier to handle, pull off a piece of roving about 6" to 8" (15 to 20 cm) long. Split the roving lengthwise in two parts and then split each of those two parts lengthwise again. The result will be four pieces of roving that are not as thick and will allow more control of laying out thin layers of fiber.

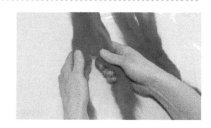

4 If the fiber length is 6" to 8" (15 to 20 cm) and your hands are 3" to 4" (7.6 to 10 cm) apart, you will be pulling on each end of the same fibers, making it nearly impossible to separate out the fibers.

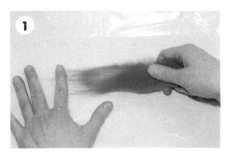

**1** Put the end of the piece of roving on the table. Place your finger near the end of the fiber and push down against the fiber into the table.

**2** Gently pull the roving away from your finger.

**3** To make a row of fibers, place the end of the roving next to the first piece of fiber. Overlap the fiber slightly and press your finger down at the end of the fiber. Pull the roving away.

## Technique

Placing your finger at the very tip end of the fiber and pulling will leave the least amount of fiber on the layout.

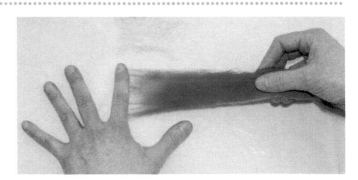

Putting your finger farther away from the end of the fiber will leave more fiber.

Thinner or thicker layers can be more easily achieved with this method as it gives a more reliable result.

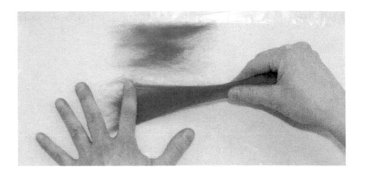

### Layout

Laying out the fibers is one of the most important steps in making an even piece of felt. The time and effort you put in on this step will improve the end result greatly. Always pull the fibers apart and don't cut them. Cutting the fibers alters the ability of the wool to felt together evenly. The methods of layout shown here use wool in top or roving form as it is the most common preparation available. Batting is simple to use; just tear off the amount needed to the correct shape. Batting can be used in a single layer or multiple layers depending on the thickness required for the particular project. Projects that have edges and seams and use batting are not as tricky as with roving as the fibers are not all laid in the same direction allowing easier attachments for seams.

### Time Saver

If you plan on making two items of the same type, lay both items out at once, and then you can roll both at the same time.

**1** Draw a 10" x 10" (25 cm x 25 cm) square in the middle of the plastic with a waterproof pen to make a template for layout. Pull a small amount of fiber from the roving using the method you prefer. Lay the small piece of wool at one corner of the sample square on the plastic. Keep pulling small pieces of wool off the roving and laying them in a row, overlapping each piece of wool slightly so an even layer of wool is created.

**2** Continue laying out another row of wool pieces, overlapping the prior row. The layers should be thin and fine. It is easier to add more wool if needed, but it is difficult to take excess wool away.

**3** Complete the first layer of wool filling in the area of the square drawn on the plastic.

(continued)

### Technique

When making a piece with a specific shape other than a square, draw the shape on the project-sized plastic with a waterproof marker. Lay out your fibers according to the drawn shape.

**4** Check the first layer to make sure there are no large gaps or holes. Add small pieces of wool to cover any holes.

**5** Add a second layer of wool over the first. Lay the fibers at a right angle from the first layer. If you place all the layers of the fiber in the same direction, the piece will shrink more in that direction. An odd number of layers will often result in uneven shrinkage in the direction of the most layers.

## Technique

Leave the corners of the overlaid fibers empty, and when it is wet down and the edges are folded in, there will be less bulk in the corners. The finished layout will have fibers extending out approximately ¼" (6 mm) from all edges of the template but no fiber extending over the corners.

**6** Add one more layer. Always place fibers in the opposite direction or at a 90-degree angle on subsequent layers. Adding more thin layers of fiber will achieve a more even piece of felt than adding just one or two thick layers. Different projects may require a different amount of layers depending on the desired thickness of the resultant felt.

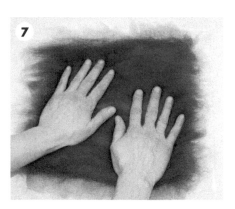

**7** Check to make sure that the stack of fiber is even. Press the fibers down gently with your hands. Close your eyes and trust your hands. You will be able to feel uneven spots when pressing down.

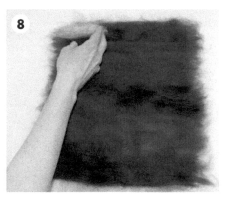

**8** Add more fibers to the spots where there is less wool. Many times the edges are a trouble spot when it comes to uniformity. Check to make sure that the edges have the same amount of fiber as the center sections.

## Technique

For larger projects, it is often useful to weigh the fibers before lay out. Divide the weight by the number of layers needed. Separate the fibers by weight for the needed layers. Each layer will now have the same amount of fibers and will be more even.

### Wetting Down

The next step is to wet down the fibers. Wool has a lot of air in it; this is called loft. The fibers just laid out may be 1" to 2" (2.5 to 5 cm) thick but when wet down it may be less than ⅛" (3 mm) thick. Some projects such as rugs may even be over a foot (30.5 cm) thick before being wet down. There are many implements used to wet down felt (see equipment and supplies, page 54). Use what you have available. Some felt makers cover the wool with netting before wetting; others don't. If you have never felted before, it is easier to start using netting. Once you've felted a few times with netting, try it without and see which you prefer. Soap serves as a wetting agent and a lubricant helping the wool fibers to absorb water and tangle together more easily. Some wools felt better with more soap, while others felt more easily with less; so again, experimentation is the key. The wool should be completely wet, but there shouldn't be water pooling under the wool. Soak up any excess water with a towel.

## Technique

Soak a sponge in warm, soapy water. Place netting or tulle over the laid out fibers. Press the wet sponge down over the netting and fibers. Keep pressing the sponge down over the fibers to remove all the air from the wool and completely dampen the wool.

## Technique

Hot water can cause the outer layers of the wool to felt before the inner layers. Beginning with cooler water slows the process and allows all the layers to felt together more easily.

**1** Begin by using lukewarm, soapy water.

**2** Sprinkle or spray water over the wool starting in the center and working toward the edges.

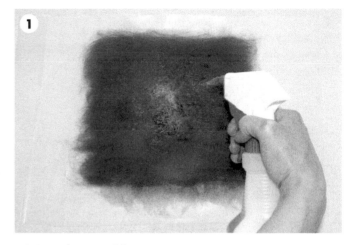

**3** Use your hand to press the air out of the wool and make sure that the soapy water penetrates all the layers. Dry fiber will still have air pockets in it, and the wool will look puffy in spots.

*(continued)*

**4** Continue sprinkling water and pressing down with your hands until all the wool is wet through and flattened. Soak up any excess water with a towel or sponge.

## Technique

If you don't use netting to cover the wool when wetting down, the wool may stick to your hands as you press the wool down. To prevent this, apply soap to your hands. If the wool is still sticking to your soapy hands, you can put a plastic bag over your hand.

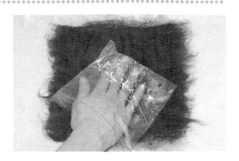

**5** Once your wool is completely wet, begin folding the edge fibers in toward the center.

**6** Fold over any stray fibers onto the top of the wet wool. Do not fold the stray fibers under as it will disturb the edge and will result in edges that are less straight. A project that has embellishments or a design will need to have those added after the edges are folded in.

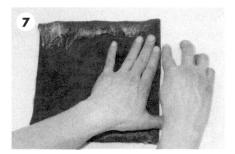

**7** Straighten the folded edges by running your fingers along the edge and pressing down the fold.

## Technique

If there are still puffy areas in the wool that are not completely wet, place another piece of 16" x 16" (41 cm x 41 cm) plastic on top of the wool, flip it over and apply water to the back of the wool as in steps 2–5.

### Felting

This step begins the process of matting the fibers together. Start with gentle movements and don't be overly aggressive at the beginning. A light touch will not disturb the fibers and will keep any design from moving as much. Again, some felt makers use netting for this step, and others don't.

**1** Begin gently rubbing your hands over the wool fibers.

**2** If the wool sticks to your hands and moves, you will need to either use a plastic bag over your hand or netting over the wool.

**3** Rub gently over the entire surface of the wool.

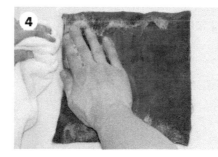

**4** Soak up any excess water with towels periodically through this process.

**5** Carefully rub the edges of your felt to keep them as straight as possible. The fibers at the edge need more attention as they will migrate away from the rest of the fibers if they are not frequently pushed back toward the rest of the center fibers.

(continued)

## Caution

If you use netting, pull the netting up off the wool frequently to make sure that the fibers haven't migrated through the holes in the netting and attached to its surface. Peel the netting away slowly and carefully to avoid excess movement and pulling up of the fibers.

## Technique

Start slowly and gently; too much movement early on can cause thin spots in your felt due to the fibers shifting. Remember that felt shrinks in the direction that it is rubbed. For wobbly edges or bulging corners, rub those areas inward.

**6** After rubbing the entire surface of the wool, the felt needs to be flipped to the other side. Put another piece of plastic on top of the wool so the wool is sandwiched between two layers of plastic.

**7** Holding all the layers together, carefully flip over the entire sandwich. If you are using netting, remember to remove the netting before flipping the piece over.

## Technique

Two pieces of netting also work to sandwich the felt, but care will need to be taken to prevent the netting from felting to the wool.

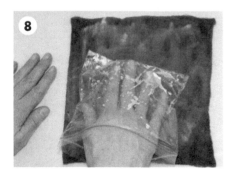

**8** Take off the piece of plastic that is now on the top. Gently rub the entire surface of the wool through the netting, if you are using it, or with your plastic-covered hand. As the wool begins to felt, you will feel that the fibers are less likely to move under your hand. Increase the pressure of your hands and continue rubbing.

**9** Check to see if the wool has felted enough by performing the pinch test (Pinch Test).

**10** If the felt passes the pinch test, move on to palming. If fibers are still loose continue felting until the felt passes the pinch test over the entire surface.

## Pinch Test

The pinch test is a method to determine if the felt is holding together enough to begin fulling. Pinch the fibers and pull up and away from the piece of felt. If the fibers pull loose, the piece is not felted enough.

If the fibers pull taut, making a tent shape, but hold together in a solid piece, it is time to begin fulling.

Perform the pinch test over different areas on the felt to make sure it is felted evenly. Pay special attention to the edges and areas with embellishments, designs, or different fibers. These areas may need extra felting/rubbing to make sure they are well felted. Early fulling attempts may cause distortion or creasing of the design or embellishments. After your felt has passed the pinch test, you have made prefelt. Prefelt is fragile and needs to be handled carefully. See the embellishment section for further information about prefelt (page 90).

## Palming

Palming is a step that is performed between the felting and fulling stages. Not everyone includes this step, but it is useful for making sure that the entire piece of felt holds together. It is easiest to perform palming in the sink.

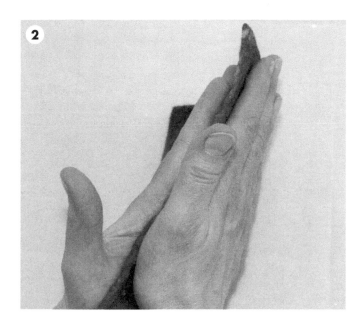

**1** Sprinkle the felt with warm to hot soapy water.

**2** Place the felt between your palms and press the felt tightly while vibrating your hands. To vibrate, make a jiggling or oscillating motion. You should not rub the felt, but instead, press your palms together.

**3** Palm all parts of the felt, moving from spot to spot in a consistent manner so you don't miss any areas.

## Fulling

Fulling is the process that hardens and shrinks the felt. Fulling has many variations, and it's up to you to decide which method works best for you. Specific projects and types of felting respond better to different methods of fulling. For the square of felt just completed above, a combination of rolling and throwing will work well. No matter which method of fulling you choose, check the felt frequently to see how it is shrinking and how firm it is becoming. It is often a matter of experience and personal preference as to deciding when fulling is complete. An accessory that will be worn or used will need to be fulled very firmly as compared to a wall hanging, which receives little wear. Pilling may occur when a piece has not been completely fulled. Pilling is the formation of little balls of wool on the surface of the felt. Stretch the felt frequently during the fulling process, especially items such as a scarf or wrap. Stretching will improve the drape of the felt. If the felt has minimal size change when stretched, it is probably completely fulled. If, when you stretch the felt, it gets bigger as you pull, more fulling needs to be done. Fulling can also be accomplished by other methods such as stomping, using a rolling machine, or putting it through the washer or dryer. The three methods described here are the most prevalently used.

## Rolling

Rolling is a very popular method of fulling. Rolling with bubble wrap can be used for very delicate projects, or more aggressive fulling can be achieved with a bamboo shade. The equipment used in rolling will determine the amount of agitation transferred to the felt.

**1** Lay the felt on your preferred type of rolling mat. If you are using bubble wrap, no plastic is needed under the felt. Place bubble wrap bubble side up. If you are using a bamboo blind or woven rush rug, place the felt between sheets of plastic. Make sure the felt is smooth and not wrinkled.

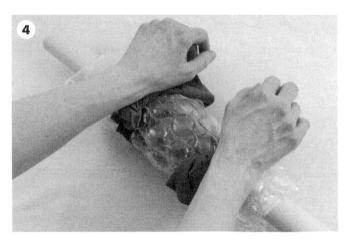

**2** Place a pool noodle or dowel rod at one end and roll all the layers around the noodle or rod.

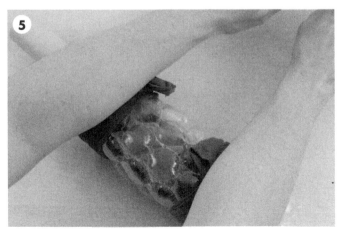

**3** Tie the wrapped roll together with elastic bands or old stockings.

**4** Roll the wrapped bundle back and forth on the table. Start with the roll at the palms or wrists.

**5** Roll forward with your forearms almost to your elbows and back to your wrists. This motion counts as one roll.

## Technique

Get in the habit of always turning the felt either clockwise or counterclockwise each time the felt is repositioned. Then you won't forget which direction the felt should be turned after rolling.

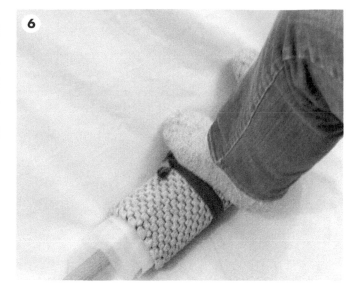

**6** Rolling can also be done with your feet while sitting in a chair.

**7** Roll back and forth 50 times. The amount of rolling required may differ with each project.

**8** Unroll the bundle and turn the piece of felt 90 degrees and flip the felt over. Straighten out the felt and remove any wrinkles.

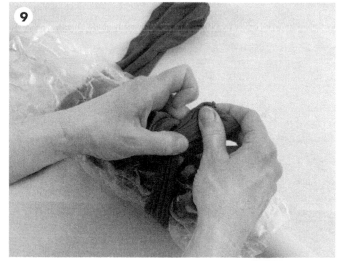

**9** Re-roll the bundle and refasten the bands.

**10** Repeat steps 7 to 9 and turning and flipping the felt 90 degrees after each 50 rolls. Turning the felt facilitates more even shrinkage.

### Throwing or Tossing

Another method of fulling is called throwing or tossing. This method does not full the felt as evenly as rolling. Start gently and work up to throwing harder as you progress. Perform throwing in the sink as it is a bit messy or throw onto a piece of plastic or into a dish pan.

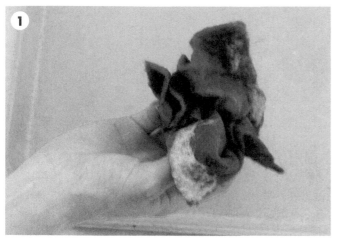

**1** Wad up your felt and begin by gently dropping it.

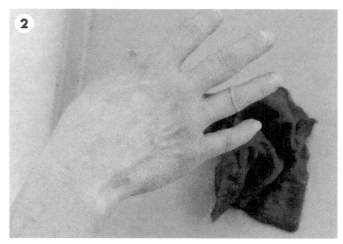

**2** Pick it up and move it around in your hands; wad it up and drop it again.

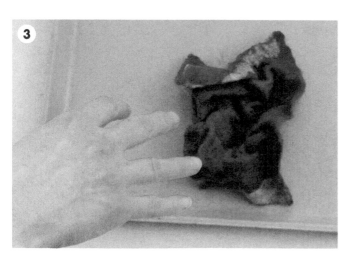

**3** As you feel the felt beginning to harden and shrink in your hands, you can begin throwing it against the sink or plastic-covered surface.

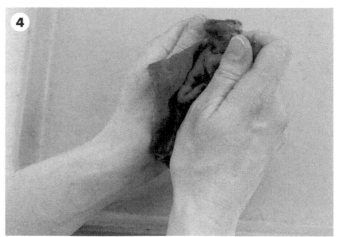

**4** Keep moving and kneading the felt around in your hands. Different parts of the felt need to hit the hard surface with each throw. Continue to throw more vigorously. Stretch the felt in between throwing and kneading. This is a great stress reliever.

## Fulling on a Washboard or Other Corrugated Surface

The third method of fulling is rubbing the felt against a washboard or other corrugated type surface. Use the washboard for spot fulling for items that need to be fitted like slippers or for hats and vessels that need to be shaped. Using the washboard in the sink works best to prevent excess messiness. Make sure to use plenty of soap on the felt to prevent any sticking to the washboard.

**1** Place the felt on the washboard.

**2** Use your hands to press the felt against the grooves on the washboard as you move the felt gently back and forth. Make sure to turn and move the felt around so that all portions of the piece are fulled evenly.

**3** If fulling a piece with embellishments, be careful as they can loosen and fall off if rubbed aggressively against the grooves. Rub the back side of the felt on the washboard to prevent this occurrence, or rub the embellished side of the felt on bubble wrap to make sure they adhere properly.

**4** Turn shaped or hollow objects inside out and rub the inside surface on the washboard.

## Technique

Place a piece of netting over the washboard to prevent fibers or embellishments snagging and catching on the surface of the washboard.

Remember the felt will shrink in the direction that you rub across the washboard. If the felt is too big in one area, rub that specific area in the direction you need it to shrink.

## Shocking

Shocking the wool can be combined with the fulling process to speed up the shrinkage of the wool. Shocking is alternating putting the felt in hot and cold water. Use two containers, one with cold water and one with hot or boiling water, and transfer the felt from container to container.

## Safety Precautions

Be careful with hot and boiling water to avoid burns. Use heavy black rubber gloves (the kind used for dyeing or handling chemicals) to handle the hot felt or wait until the felt and water cool sufficiently before handling. You can also use tongs to transfer the hot felt. Remember not to reuse these tongs for food or cooking.

## Rinsing

Once the felt is completely fulled to your satisfaction, rinse all of the soap from the felt. To return the wool to its natural acidic pH, soak your finished felt in water with a small amount of white vinegar. Use approximately ¼ cup (60 ml) of vinegar to one gallon (3.8 l) of water. After soaking the felt in vinegar water for a few minutes, rinse it again in clear water.

## Letting Felt Rest

If you need to leave the felt before it is completely finished, that won't hurt the felting process. If you only need to leave your project for a few hours, just leave it as is. If you have to leave it until the next day, rinse the soap out and leave the felt where it can dry. If left wet or in a small amount of water, the felt can mildew. When you are ready to restart the felting process, just rewet the wool and take up where you left off. Many times if the felting process is going slowly and not progressing as you wish, letting the wool rest and restarting later kick starts the process.

## Removing Excess Water

The felt will dry more quickly if you remove as much water as possible before blocking or leaving the piece to dry. One method of removing water is to roll the felt up into a dry towel and squeeze and roll the towel bundle. Another method is to put the felted piece into the washer and run on the spin cycle. If the piece of felt is small and there is only one piece, a salad spinner works well to remove any excess water. If you don't mind getting damp or if you're making felt with children, put the wet felt in a nylon stocking, tie up one end, take it outside, and spin it around your head as quickly as possible.

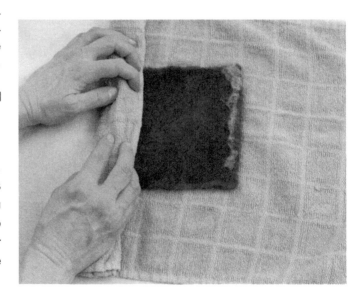

## Blocking

Many felting projects may need to be blocked. Blocking is a process in which the felt is held in a certain position and dried in that shape. Slippers, hats, bags, and vessels are all projects that benefit from blocking. Steam a felt item while blocking to change its shape. Use an iron on the highest steam setting and use bursts of steam on the felt to heat it up. Then stretch the part that needs to be lengthened or use a hard object such as a meat tenderizer tool to beat the felt into shape against the block or form. Wear gloves to avoid burning your hands when using steam.

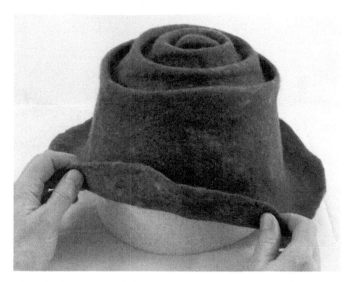

Hat blocks are available in various sizes and facilitate the completion of a certain size hat. A bowl can be substituted for a hat block if the correct size is available.

Wadded up plastic grocery bags can be used to stuff a felt vessel so it holds its shape while drying. Another option is microfiber cloths, as they will also soak up excess moisture.

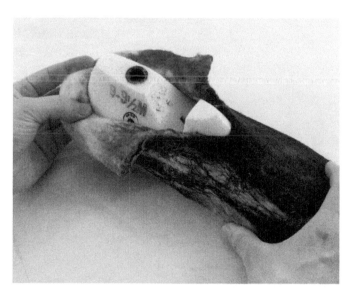

Shoe lasts are also available in various sizes for shaping of boots and slippers. A shoe last can be made from duct tape. You can also stuff the slippers with plastic grocery bags to maintain their shape while drying.

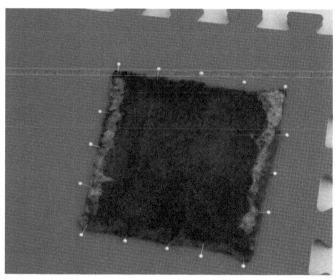

For flat pieces that need to be squared, pin opposite sides down to a foam flooring square, stretching the felt evenly as you pin each side.

## Sampling and Shrinkage

Making samples before you start a felting project is an important first step of wet felting. It helps to match a fiber to its appropriate project type. Perhaps you feel you don't have enough time to spend on sampling. The simple fact is that you will save yourself time and supplies if you do a few samples first. It doesn't take that long and you will learn whether or not the wool you have selected will work for the intended project. You will also determine how much shrinkage will occur, what the drape of the resulting fabric will be, approximately how much wool is needed, and whether the surface of the felt will be hairy or smooth, and you can experiment with color choices and embellishments.

To make a sample, use a set size and set amount of wool. An easy size is 10" x 10" (20 cm x 20 cm) with ½ oz. (15 g) of wool. Use a set number of layers when laying out the wool for the samples. An even number of layers is best so that shrinkage will be even in both directions. Follow the directions in the previous section to completely felt and full the sample. Keep track of how long the process takes. Full the sample completely until it no longer stretches out of shape. Measure the size of the fulled felt and compare it to the original size to determine the amount of shrinkage. One good thing about samples is the edges don't need to be kept straight.

Make a notebook of the samples of different breeds of wool. Note the wool breed, shrinkage rate, the number of layers, and amount of time needed to felt and full the sample completely. The sample book will be an invaluable resource to refer back to in the future and to share with other felt makers. Samples could also be made into small items such as coin purses, hot pads, cell phone holders, or anything else you desire.

Another type of sample is when you are considering buying raw fleece from a local source and you aren't sure whether the breed felts. You need a rough test to determine whether it will felt. Put a small amount of wool in your palm and lay another small amount in the opposite direction on top of the first. Put some soapy water over the wool and begin rubbing with your fingers. Fold the ends over and keep rubbing. Is the wool beginning to tighten up and hold together? Fine wool that felts quickly will felt in a couple of minutes. Run hot and cold water over the wool. Is the surface hard and smooth or loose and hairy? If the sample doesn't hold together after five minutes, it will not felt easily, and you should consider another option.

(continued)

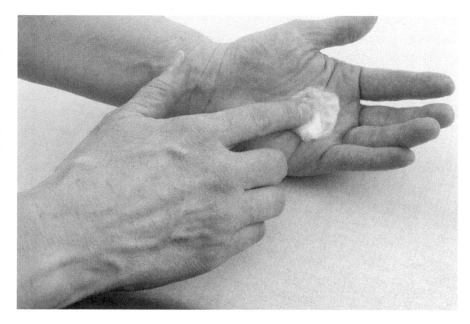

Understanding how to figure out shrinkage uses a simple math formula. The formula is based on a basic percentage decrease equation.

Percentage Decrease = Change in Amount ÷ Original Amount

or

Shrinkage Rate = Change in Size of Sample ÷ Original Size of Sample

For a percentage decrease, divide the change in size by the original size. If the sample started out to be 10" x 10" (25 cm x 25 cm) and ended up to be 7" x 6" (18 cm x 15 cm) the formula would be:

Percentage Decrease: $(10 - 7) \div 10$
or $(3 \div 10) = 0.30$ or 30%

Percentage Decrease: $(10 - 6) \div 10$
or $(4 \div 10) = 0.40$ or 40%

Average: $(30\% + 40\%) \div 2$
or $(70\% \div 2) = 35\%$

Therefore, the sample shrunk an average of 35%. As felting is an inexact science, finding the average from each direction gives a better indication of overall shrinkage. Now you know how much this particular wool will shrink if felted under the same conditions.

How do you figure out what size you need to start the project when you know the percentage it will shrink? Again you use the formula for percentage decrease.

Percentage Decrease = Change in Amount ÷ Original Amount

However, you don't know what the original size needs to be so the original amount in the equation will be y. You know that the change in size is 35% and that the final size will be 65% (100% – 35%) of the original. Therefore the equation should be:

$$65 = 35 \div y$$

To solve the equation:

Multiply each side by y
$$y \times 65 = y \times (35 \div y)$$

And the result is:
$$65y = 35$$

Now divide each side by 65
$$\frac{1}{65} \times 65y = \frac{1}{65} \times 35$$

And the result is:
$$y = \frac{35}{65}$$

Therefore, y equals:
$$y = 0.54 \text{ or } 54\%$$

To increase any amount by 54%, multiply by 1.54. Notice when you increase by a percentage, you multiply by a number greater than one.

The table below provides shrinkage rates and the number or percentage to multiply by to determine the resist or template size needed. Take the size you need at the end of felting and multiply it by the number in the second column.

| Shrinkage | Multiply this number by size needed at end of felting |
|---|---|
| 10% | 1.11 or 111% |
| 15% | 1.18 or 118% |
| 20% | 1.25 or 125% |
| 25% | 1.33 or 133% |
| 30% | 1.43 or 143% |
| 35% | 1.54 or 154% |
| 40% | 1.67 or 167% |
| 45% | 1.82 or 182% |
| 50% | 2.00 or 200% |

Example: To make a scarf that is 14" x 72" (35.6 cm x 182.9 cm) with a wool shrinkage rate of 30%, multiply the length and width by 1.43.

$$72" \times 1.43 = 103"$$

$$14" \times 1.43 = 20"$$

Lay out the wool 20" (50.8 cm) wide and 103" (261.6 cm) long so that the scarf after felting and shrinking 30% will be the desired size of 14" x 72" (35.6 cm x 182.9 cm).

This next section discusses a way to estimate the wool needed to make a project. For example, to make a rug, make a sample with the wool to be used and the number of layers that will be used in the rug (which could be 10 to 12 layers of coarse wool). Weigh the sample and measure the two sides. The amount of wool per square inch (or square centimeter) can now be determined.

Example: If the sample measures 6" x 6" (15.2 cm x 15.2 cm) and weighs ½ oz. (14 g), the ounces of wool per square inch are 0.0139.

$$6 \times 6 = 36; \text{ so for 36 square inches}$$
$$\text{it takes ½ oz. of wool}$$

$$0.5 \div 36 = 0.0139; \text{ so each square inch}$$
$$\text{takes 0.0139 oz. of wool.}$$

Now multiply this value by the square inches in the rug. To determine the square inches, measure each side and multiply these two measurements.
Example: To felt a rug measuring 36" x 50"

$$36 \times 50 = 1800;$$
$$\text{so there are 1800 square inches in the rug.}$$

$$1800 \times 0.0139 = 25.02;$$
$$\text{so 25.02 oz. of wool is needed to make a 36" x 50" rug.}$$

To convert the previous example above into the metric system, if the sample measures 15.2 cm x 15.2 cm and weighs 14.17 g, the grams of wool per square centimeter are 0.061.

$$15.2 \times 15.2 = 231.04; \text{ so for 231.04 square}$$
$$\text{centimeters it takes 14.17 grams of wool.}$$

$$14.17 \div 231.04 = 0.061; \text{ so each square centimeter}$$
$$\text{takes 0.061 grams of wool.}$$

Now multiply this value by the square centimeters in the rug. To determine the square centimeters, measure each side and multiply these two measurements.

Example: To felt a rug measuring 91.4 cm x 127 cm

$$91.4 \times 127 = 11,607.8; \text{ so there are}$$
$$\text{11,607.8 square centimeters in the project.}$$

$$11,607.8 \times 0.061 = 711.92; \text{ so 711.92 grams}$$
$$\text{of wool is needed to make a 91.4 cm x 127 cm rug.}$$

If a project uses a resist, remember to double the number since there will be two sides. For a more complex project, such as a garment, measure the front, back, and sleeves separately. Then add those numbers together at the end of the calculations.

## Using Resists

A resist is used in wet felting to make a hollow, seamless three-dimensional felt object. The resist blocks the inside surfaces of the piece from felting together. The material used for a resist can vary but needs to be waterproof. Packing foam, plastic, bubble wrap, floor underlayment, and even duct tape–covered cardboard will work.

The resist is easier to feel inside the wool when it has a thickness of at least ⅛" (3 mm). With very thin plastic, it is hard to feel the edge of the resist, and a ridge may form because the wool wasn't wrapped tightly enough around the hard-to-detect edges.

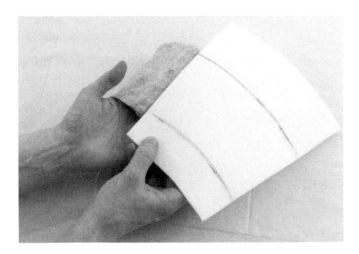

A resist can be open or closed. A closed resist is one that is completely covered with wool and no part of the resist remains showing after fiber layout. The closed resist has no loose fiber edges so all the fibers felt together evenly in one mass. The closed resist will need to be cut out during the felting process. Advance planning in deciding where the opening is cut is essential for a good design. With an open resist, a portion of the resist remains uncovered. The wool edges at the open end of the resist have a tendency to shift since they are not surrounded by other fibers. Extra attention must be paid to those open edges so that they will be even and straight. An open edge of felt doesn't shrink as much because it has no wool pulling against it like the remainder of the felt does.

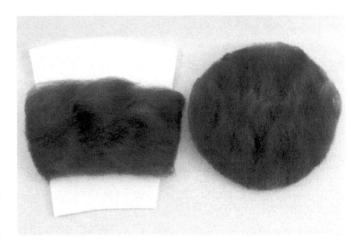

Resists can be any shape, but care should be taken with acute angles. Very sharp points will push through the wool so corners should be rounded. Sharp inner angles should be rounded and opened out as much as possible; otherwise excess wool in these areas may cause binding. Due to the versatility of shaping wool, one resist can be formed into many different shapes.

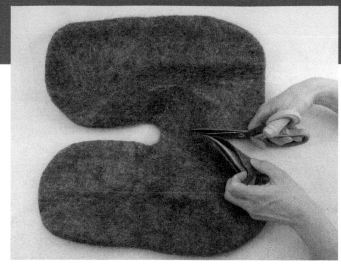

The most common felt items made with a resist are hats, bags, vessels, clothing, slippers, and mittens. The line drawings of resists shown here are examples of various shapes that could be used. Resist shapes are only limited by your imagination.

Embellishments can be applied on the outside of the wool when using a resist or on the inside. If the design will be on the outside, remember to apply the embellishments first, then wool, then the resist, more wool, and then last the embellishments.

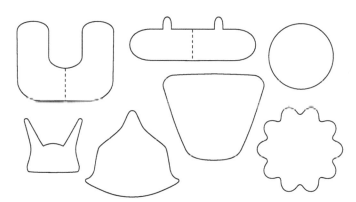

Illustration by Nanci Williams

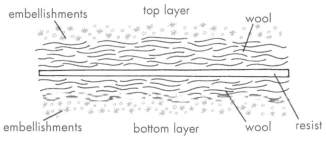

Illustration by Nanci Williams

For application of the design on the inside, next to the resist, first lay down the layers of wool, then the embellishments. Cover the embellishments with the resist. Next lay down the embellishments on the other side of the resist, then the wool layers.

## Time Saver

Make a pair of slippers or mittens on one resist. It saves time and the slippers or mittens will be more even since they were formed at the same time. Cut straight across right through the resist to open, cutting the pair in two. The resist can be repaired with duct tape and used again.

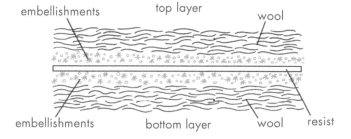

Illustration by Nanci Williams

There is more than one method of covering a resist. Some felt makers feel the edges can be wrapped more tightly by applying one layer of wool at a time, wetting down the layer, flipping the resist over, and folding the edges in. Then the other side of the resist is covered with wool and wet down, and the resist is flipped over again. Each layer is applied and wet down separately, wrapping the edges tightly each time until all layers are completed. The other method of covering the resist is described in the step-by-step process below.

Begin with an easy resist shape such as a circle. Depending on how the felt is cut open to remove the resist, a bag or a beret can be made. A diameter of 12"–14" (30.5–35.6 cm) is a good size resist for either a beret or a small bag using wool with a 30%–35% shrinkage rate.

## YOU WILL NEED

- plastic to cover work surface
- two pieces of plastic 6" (15 cm) bigger than project size
- foam larger than 14" x 14" (35.6 cm x 35.6 cm)
- 12" to 14" (30.5 to 35.6 cm) plate or 6" to 7" (15 to18 cm) string with pen attached
- waterproof marker
- scissors
- 2 to 3 oz. (57 to 85 g) of fine to medium-fine wool roving or batt in chosen color (batt is shown in the sample photos)
- embellishments (optional)
- lukewarm, soapy water
- spray bottle, ball brause sprayer, or sponge
- plastic bag (optional)
- netting or tulle (optional)
- old towels
- access to hot and cold water
- bubble wrap, woven grass rug, bamboo blind, or other rolling device
- ties or old nylon stockings
- 2" to 3" (5 to 8 cm) circle template from cardboard or foam
- craft knife
- washboard or other corrugated surface (optional)

1 Cut a 12" to 14" (30.5 to 35.6 cm) circle out of foam to make a resist. Use a plate to draw around or use 6" to 7" (15 to 18 cm) string with a pen attached to draw a circle.

2 Use a project-sized piece of plastic, trace the resist circle on the plastic with a permanent marker.

**3**

**4**

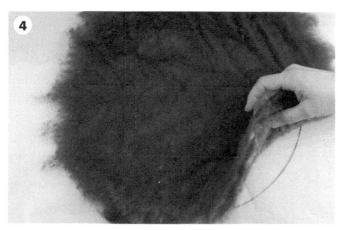

**5**

**6**

Reminder

Split the total amount of fiber in two even parts before layout so each side will have an even amount of fiber.

**3** Decide whether the design/embellishments will be on the outside of the wool or on the inside next to the resist. Place the design accordingly. The photos will show placement of the design on the inside next to the resist.

**4** Lay out three to four layers of fibers. Allow the fibers to extend beyond the circle drawn on the plastic by about 1" (2.5 cm). Remember to alternate the fiber direction in each layer. Also place the embellishments as the top layer during this step.

**5** Wet down the fibers.

**6** Rub the center section gently to begin felting. Do not rub the outer fibers that overlap the circle.

**7** Once the fibers begin to hold together or form a skin, place the resist over the wet felt lining up with the circle on the plastic template.

(continued)

**7**

## Technique

Place any embellishments on the resist before folding the wool over if embellishments are on the inside.

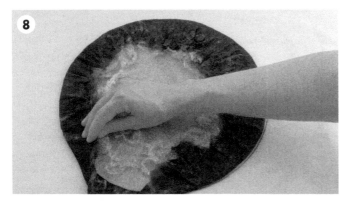

**8** Wrap the excess fibers sticking out past the resist over the resist carefully. Make sure to pull the fibers tightly around the edge of the resist. See technique below if fibers are thick at the edges.

**9** Lay three to four layers of wool over the resist. Keep the fibers from overlapping the resist so that the edge areas won't have more layers than the rest of the circle.

**10** Wet down all the fibers and begin rubbing to felt.

## Technique

If the fibers are very thick at the edges, wet down just the center section of the fibers only leaving the edges dry. When step 8 is performed, wrap the dry fibers around the resist. If there is too much fiber, pull some dry fiber out at the bulky section. Then wet the edge fibers and wrap as in step 8.

**11** Once the fibers begin to hold together in the center, begin working on the wool around the edge of the resist. Make sure that all stray edge fibers have been folded over to the other side. The edge will feel baggy and need to be rubbed in an inward direction. Gently run your fingers on either side of the edge of the resist pushing in toward the center of the resist.

**12** Continue rubbing on both sides of the resist, flipping it over frequently and working the edges until the wool is holding together fairly well.

**13** Begin rolling the felt-covered resist. Roll 50 times and then reposition the felt 90 degrees and turn it over to the other side.

**14** Repeat step 13 until the felt has been rolled in all directions.

**15** Check the edges to make sure that they pull tight against the resist. If not, rub edges as in step 11.

**16** Keep rolling until the felt passes the pinch test and the resist begins buckling inside the felt.

**17** Cut the felt to remove the resist.

(continued)

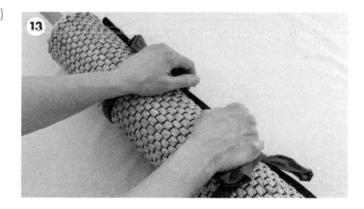

**18** If making a beret, cut a 2" to 3" (5 to 7.6 cm) diameter circle out of the center of the felt. Cut a small slit with a sharp craft knife. Be careful not to cut through the resist. Finish cutting the felt with a pair of scissors around a circular template.

**19** If making a bag, cut out the resist according to the illustration at left. Cut the front piece completely away. Cut only the top half of the semicircle on the back piece, leaving it attached at the straight edge. This piece will become the flap closure. See photo under the illustration.

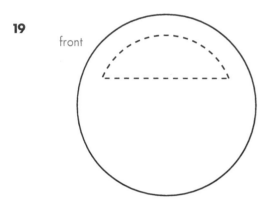

front

Cut front first. Cut along dotted lines and remove piece.

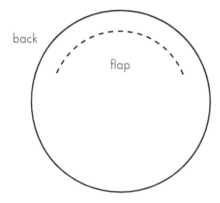

back

flap

Cut along dotted line and fold flap through cutout in front piece.

Illustration by Nanci Williams

## Technique

The hole is cut smaller than needed because the opening will grow bigger as fulling is completed. Holes in felt always get bigger because the wool pulls away from the hole.

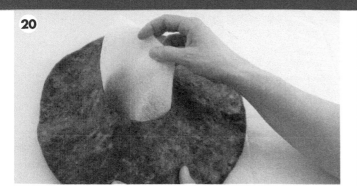

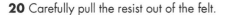

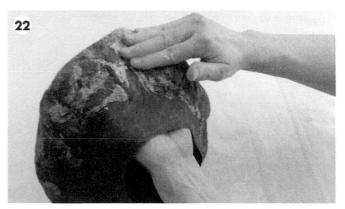

**20** Carefully pull the resist out of the felt.

**21** Immediately after cutting, get the cut edges soapy and rub in the direction of the cut. Keep rubbing the edges until they are firm and there is no loose wool noted.

**22** Check the inside of the felt to make sure it is well felted and embellishments are well attached. If not, get your hands soapy and rub the felt between your hands until it is well felted inside.

**23** Check the felt in the area that was at the edge of the resist. If a ridge has formed, hold onto the felt on each side of the ridge and pull gently, wiggling it apart and carefully stretching the wool.

**24** Turn the felt inside out and rub the ridged area over a washboard or corrugated surface. Be cautious with any embellishments and avoid catching them on the washboard. Keep the felt ridge perpendicular to the ridges on the washboard when rubbing. Keep rubbing around the entire circle where the ridge has developed until the ridge is smoothed out.

**25** Continue fulling, stretching, and shocking (page 74) the felt until it is completely fulled.

**26** Stretch and steam the felt as needed for fitting if making a beret. If the cut edge of the beret is too small, steam and stretch the edge until it fits.

**27** Block as needed and dry thoroughly.

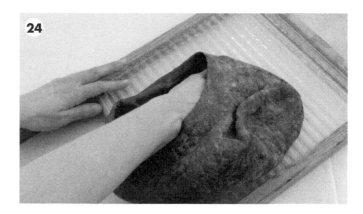

## Using a Hand Sander

A small hand-held sander can be used to speed up the felting process. Avoid sanders with belts, rotating parts, or vacuum attachments with holes in the bottom of the sander. The sanders that work best are usually called palm or triangle sanders, although a bigger sander will also work. When using the sander for felting, remove the sandpaper. A fitted rubber or plastic shoe with ridges can be purchased for the sander but isn't necessary.

Caution and safety should always be considered when using an electrical appliance around water. The sander should be plugged into a GFCI (ground fault circuit interrupter) type outlet. In the United States, these types of outlets are usually found in the kitchen or bathroom. A portable GFCI plug can be purchased and used in a three-wire outlet that includes a ground wire if no GFCI outlets are available. Don't allow water to pool around the felt. Soak up excess water with a towel. Stand on a rubber mat or wear rubber-soled shoes when using the sander. Cover the felt with plastic or use a plastic bag over the sander. Avoid long periods of sanding as the vibration from the sander can cause nerve damage. Hearing protection should be used if the sander is used frequently.

The sander can be used for most types of wet felting including nuno felting. If a resist is being used, be careful with the edges to avoid sanding a ridge at the edge. Use a textured surface under the felt to provide greater agitation when sanding. Try this method after you understand the basics. It helps to know what the felt feels like at various stages under your hands before you start to try and speed the process up.

## YOU WILL NEED

- plastic to cover work surface

- woven rush rug or bamboo blind

- two pieces of plastic at least 6" (15 cm) larger than project

- enough wool and embellishments for chosen project

- lukewarm, soapy water

- old towels

- electric hand or palm sander

**1** Lay out the project on plastic over top of a ridged surface. A woven rush rug works well.

**2** Wet out the project but soak up as much excess water as possible before using the sander.

**3** Cover the project with a large piece of plastic. The plastic should have at least 6" (15 cm) of overlap on all sides of the plastic.

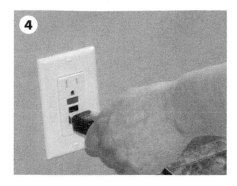

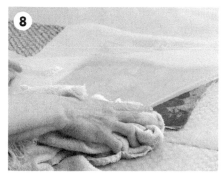

**4** Plug the sander into a GFCI outlet.

**5** Turn on the sander and place it at one corner of the project. Don't apply pressure to the sander; just allow the weight of the sander and vibration to begin felting.

**6** Pick up and move the sander, overlapping the last spot where the sander was placed.

**7** Pick up and move the sander over the entire surface of the felt by picking it up and putting it down in overlapping rows, sanding in each spot for 5 to 10 seconds.

**8.** Repeat step 7 several times over the entire surface of the felt. If water seeps out from under the plastic, soak it up with a towel.

**9.** Pull the plastic back and soak up excess water with the towel. Recover with plastic.

**10** Hold all the layers together and flip the felt over to the other side.

**11** Sand the other side as in step 7.

**12** Once each side has been sanded at least twice, begin moving the sander over the plastic without lifting the sander.

**13** Turn the felt two more times, sanding each side thoroughly and applying more pressure as time progresses.

**14** Perform the pinch test. If the felt passes the pinch test, begin fulling. If the fibers still pull apart, sand each side several more times until the felt passes the pinch test.

## Caution

Don't rub the sander over the surface to start. Too much movement will shift embellishments or cause the design to migrate.

## Embellishments

Felt can be embellished in a myriad of ways. Once the basics of wet felting are understood, experimenting with different embellishments is exciting and fun. There are so many techniques and wonderful specialty fibers to include in the felt that a lifetime could be spent exploring all the possibilities.

This section only touches on the basics of embellishments to get you started. Again, experimentation is the key. Ask yourself "what if?" What if I combined silk fiber and alpaca? What if I added spikes to this vessel? What if I used prefelt to make a bag? There are infinite combinations, and the fun is in the journey. Don't limit yourself.

## Prefelt

Prefelt is felt that has not been fulled. It still has enough loose fibers that it will still attach to loose wool or to other prefelt. Prefelt can be used in a variety of ways and not necessarily just as an embellishment. Prefelt can be used as the base of a project and then further embellishments added, which decreases the time needed to lay out the project.

Prefelt is either manufactured or can be made at home. Manufactured prefelt is made on an industrial needle-felting machine. It is available in yardage (or by the meter), precut sizes, or in die-cut shapes. Numerous colors are available, or prefelt can be purchased in white and dyed as needed.

To make prefelt, follow the instructions in the basics section (page 60) and stop before fulling. Be careful when rinsing prefelt as it is fragile and can be pulled apart easily. Fill the sink with water and place the prefelt in the water. Drain the water from the sink and press the water out of the prefelt. Roll the prefelt in a towel to remove excess water and dry flat. The prefelt can be used while still wet but it does not cut well. The number of layers used to make the prefelt is determined by how you plan to use it. If you need prefelt for an embellishment, two layers are usually plenty. When prefelt is used as the base of a project, three to four layers of wool will be needed. Stack prefelt on top of each other and felt together to form a sturdier felt or for design purposes.

Prefelt can be cut into whichever shape is required either as an embellishment or for the entire project. To help prefelts stick to each other, use a prefelt brush or wire brush to loosen the fibers enough so the prefelts will felt together easily. Needle felt the areas where prefelts cross

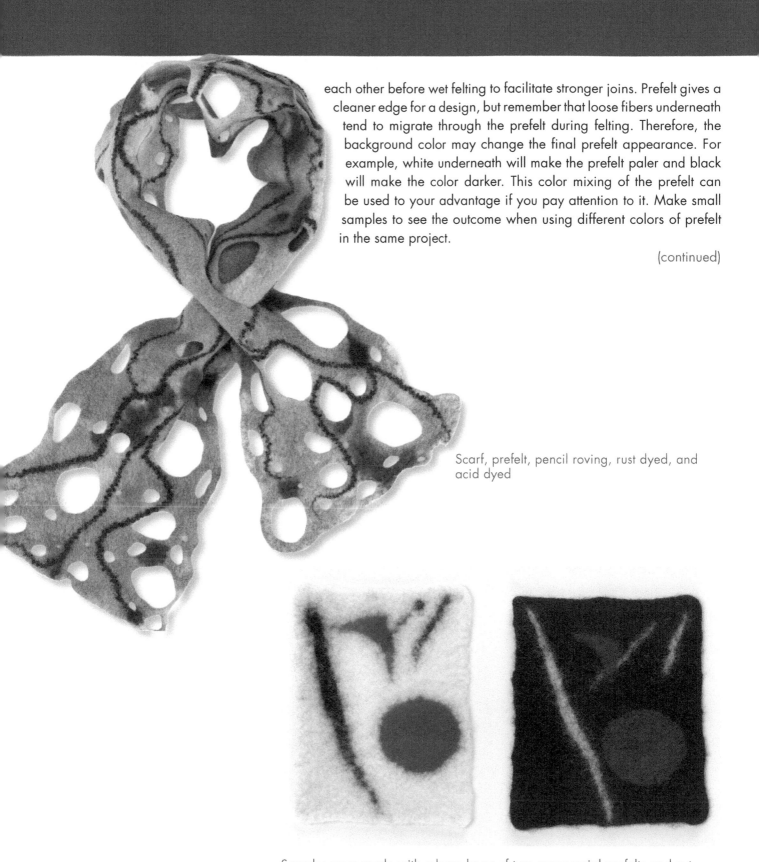

each other before wet felting to facilitate stronger joins. Prefelt gives a cleaner edge for a design, but remember that loose fibers underneath tend to migrate through the prefelt during felting. Therefore, the background color may change the final prefelt appearance. For example, white underneath will make the prefelt paler and black will make the color darker. This color mixing of the prefelt can be used to your advantage if you pay attention to it. Make small samples to see the outcome when using different colors of prefelt in the same project.

(continued)

Scarf, prefelt, pencil roving, rust dyed, and acid dyed

Samples were made with a base layer of two commercial prefelts and cut prefelt shapes on top. As you can see, the prefelt on the surface is affected by the color underneath.

To start using prefelt, make a small sample piece combining fiber and cut out prefelt shapes.

## YOU WILL NEED

- wet felting supplies
- ¼ to ½ oz. (7 to 4 g) fine wool
- prefelt cut in shapes

**1** Lay out the wool fibers in a 6" to 8" (15 to 20 cm) square with 3 to 4 thin layers.

**2** Wet down the fiber and rub gently.

## Technique

The base fiber will migrate less if it is wet down and slightly felted before applying prefelt.

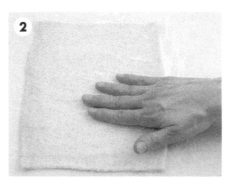

**3** Brush the back of the prefelt pieces with a prefelt brush or wire brush. This raises the fibers to help in felting tightly.

**4** Put a small amount of extra soap in the area under the prefelt shapes.

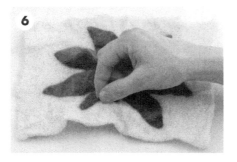

**5** Apply prefelt shapes and press them into the wet felt underneath. If prefelt does not get completely wet, spray lightly with warm, soapy water.

**6** Felt and full as usual, paying special attention to the prefelt and making sure it is well attached before beginning aggressive fulling.

## Attachments and Inclusions

A variety of felt pieces can be made to attach to a felt item during the felt-making process either to embellish or to add further functionality. Cords can be made by rolling a length of wool roving with soapy water to felt a strong ropelike structure. Cords are often used for a shoulder strap or handle for a bag, a loop closure, or ties on a garment. Cords can also be split and then rejoined or split into multiple ends. A cord can be curled into a spiral, then fulled and blocked to maintain the spiral shape.

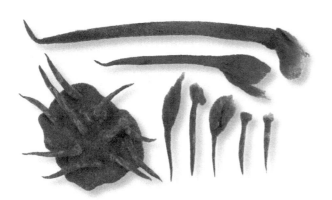

Spikes are simple to felt, and when attached, enliven a hat or a bag. If a cord or spike is to be attached to a felted piece at least one end must be left dry. The dry end will then be used to attach the piece to the project during the rubbing and felting process.

A similar process is used to make felt beads. Like glass cane making called millefiori, the felt is put together in different colored layers and rolled lengthwise. Once felted very firmly and dried, the felt roll can be sliced to make beads.

Another bead-making technique is to roll little balls of wool in your hands, working them down to hard felt beads. These are great for making jewelry but could also be felted into the surface of a wet-felted piece as an inclusion. Other types of inclusions could be glass marbles, shisha mirrors, buttons, polymer clay pieces, or even pebbles. The inclusions can then be partially revealed by cutting the felt.

If the inclusion is surrounded by a different color of wool before felting and then cut out after felting, a colorful crater in the felt is created. The crater can be formed in the layers of felt or can protrude from the felt. Accomplish this by tying at the base of the inclusion before fulling.

Making cords and beads can be very time consuming and tricky if attempted with coarse wool. Using fine wool with a short staple length will save time and frustration. Short fiber Merino in batt form works well for this type of project. It will provide a very smooth, fine surface with no hairiness. The Merino is extremely easy and quick to felt and is well worth the price.

## Method 1

Making cords is simple, but patience is required to achieve an even, smooth cord.

This first method of making cords is most often used for one-color, longer cords.

**1** Use a full roving if a thicker cord is needed. Use split roving for thinner cords. If batting is used, roll it up lengthwise to desired thickness. Shrinkage will occur in thickness and in length.

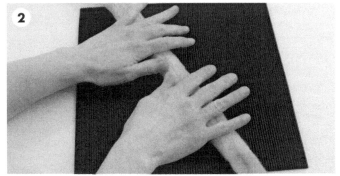

**2** Roll the entire length of wool by rolling gently back and forth across the corrugated surface without getting the wool wet.

**3** Keep dry felting until wool holds together well.

**4** Spray lightly with warm, soapy water and continue rolling with light pressure only. If the cord is to be connected to a project later, such as a cord for a bag, remember to leave one or both ends dry.

## Time Saver

The more air forced out of the wool before wetting, the less time will be needed for rolling later.

Heavy pressure at this point may cause cracks and furrows to develop in the cord.

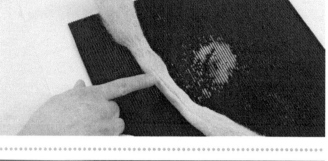

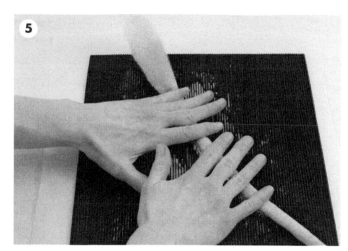

**5** Continue rolling on corrugated surface and increasing pressure as the wool hardens. Roll at a diagonal to achieve a stronger cord.

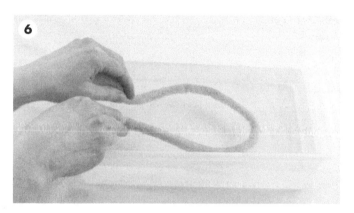

**6** Dunk the cord in hot water and continue rolling.

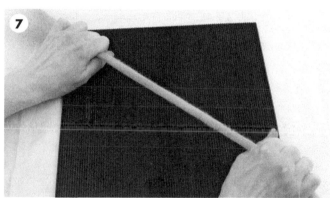

**7** Gently stretch the cord lengthwise in between rolling.

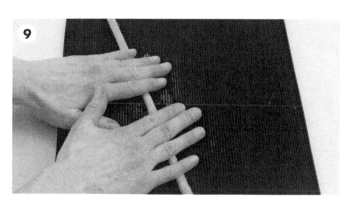

**8** Shock the wool by dunking in alternating hot and cold water.

**9** Continue rolling on the corrugated surface with heavy pressure until the cord is completely fulled. Rinse the cord thoroughly and let dry.

## Technique

Try a short cord to start and measure before and after to determine the shrinkage rate.

## Method 2

This second method is used to make millefiori-type beads with a spiral design. It can also be used with one color to make a solid cord or bead.

**YOU WILL NEED**

- wet-felting supplies
- corrugated surface
- fine wool roving or batting in a variety of colors
- prefelt in a variety of colors (optional)
- white glue (PVA) (optional)
- craft knife

**1** Lay out one layer of wool in a long rectangular shape. The length should equal the final length of the cord, and the width will determine the thickness of the cord. If the fibers are arranged lengthwise, the cord will shrink more in length.

**2** Layer different colors on top of each other. The colors will create the spiral effect when bead is cut. Make these layers slightly thinner than the bottom, outside layer so the outside layer will completely cover the roll.

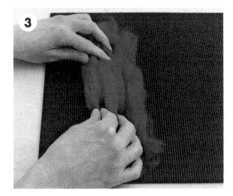

**3** Carefully roll the layers of wool together lengthwise while pushing as much air out of the roll as possible.

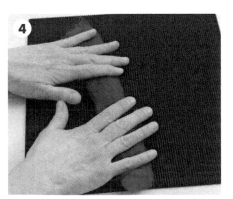

**4** Keeping pressure on the roll to prevent air coming back into the wool and wool rebounding, roll the log of wool across the corrugated surface. Continue dry rolling to remove as much air as possible.

## Technique

Simplify the process by using a stack of different colored prefelt or batts. For your first cord, keep it simple and use two colors.

Add additional tufts of outer color wool if any thin spots are evident.

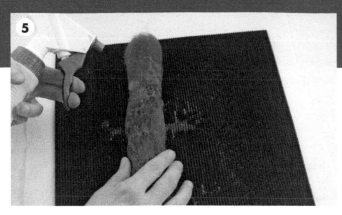

**5** Spray lightly with warm, soapy water and gently roll with light pressure.

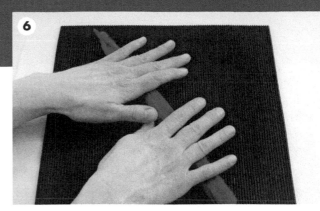

**6** Continue rolling and increasing pressure as the wool hardens.

**7** Dunk the cord in hot water and continue rolling. Stretch the cord lengthwise in between rolling.

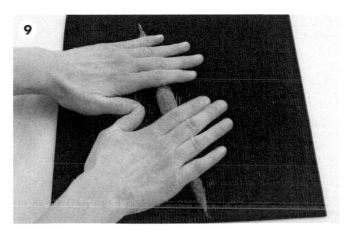

**8** Shock the wool in alternating hot and cold water.

**9** Continue rolling with heavy pressure until the cord is completely fulled.

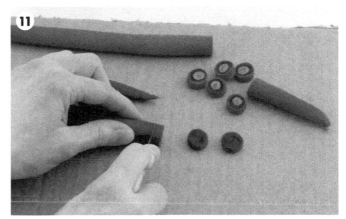

**10** Rinse and let the cord dry. Roll the cord in a towel to alleviate as much moisture as possible. Due to their density, cords may take longer to dry than flat felt.

**11** Slice into beads with a sharp craft knife.

## Technique

For a very durable and hard bead, mix up a solution of half white glue and half water. Soak the cord in glue solution and then let dry before slicing.

## Method 3

The third method for cords and beads makes a bull's eye type pattern in the bead.

**YOU WILL NEED**

- wet-felting supplies
- corrugated surface
- fine wool roving or batting in variety of colors
- prefelt in variety of colors (optional)
- white glue (optional)
- craft knife

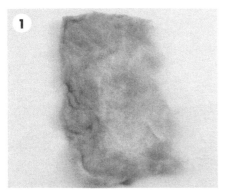

**1** Lay out one layer of wool in a long rectangular shape. Prefelt can be substituted for one layer of wool. This color will be the center of the bull's eye.

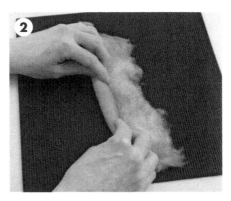

**2** Roll the wool lengthwise.

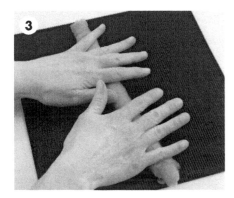

**3** Dry felt by rolling on corrugated surface.

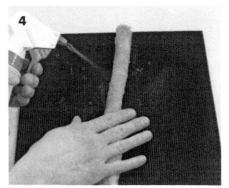

**4** Spray lightly with warm, soapy water and roll lightly.

**5** Lay out a second layer of contrasting wool in the same rectangular shape or use a different color of prefelt.

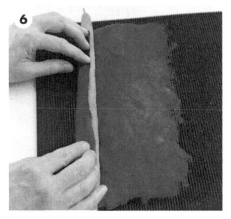

**6** Roll the wet cord up in the second layer of wool or prefelt, wrapping it completely.

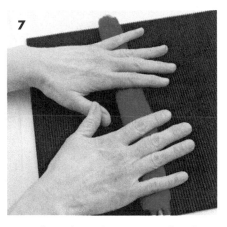

**7** Roll gently on the corrugated surface. Spray lightly with water as needed.

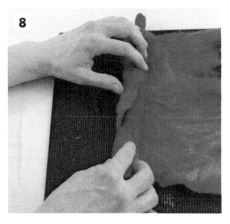

**8** Keep adding layers of wool in different colors until the desired thickness and pattern of colors is achieved.

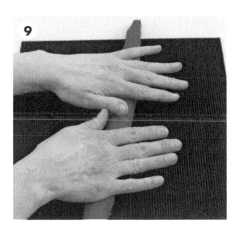

**9** Roll gently on the corrugated surface increasing rolling pressure gradually.

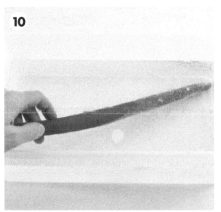

**10** Once the felt cord begins to harden, dunk in hot water.

**11** Continue rolling on corrugated surface with more pressure. Stretch lengthwise in between rolling.

**12** Shock cord, alternating with hot and cold water.

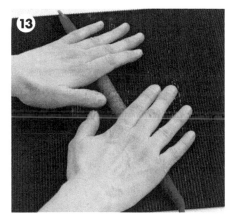

**13** Continue rolling until cord is completely fulled. Rinse and let dry.

**14** Follow instructions in the second cord-making method for finishing beads.

## Wired Cords

Wired cords can be attached to other felt items and bent into a shape that will be retained. This process only works with a certain type of pipe cleaner called a tinsel stem or glitter stem. The regular chenille pipe cleaners are too slick.

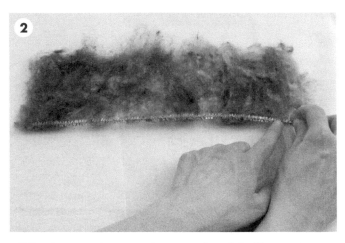

**1** Lay out a small amount of fiber the length of the pipe cleaner.

**2** Put the pipe cleaner at the very edge of the fiber and wrap the wisps of fiber carefully around the pipe cleaner.

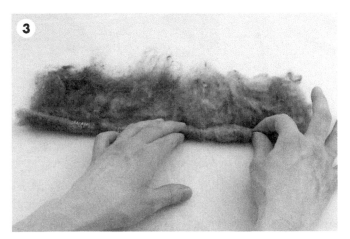

**3** Gently roll the pipe cleaner and fiber to completely cover the pipe cleaner.

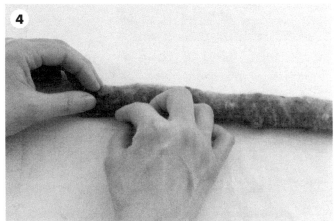

**4** Make sure that the ends of the pipe cleaner are well covered. The ends may be bent over to prevent the sharp end sticking out.

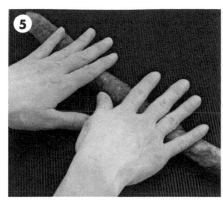

**5** Dry felt by gently rolling on the corrugated surface.

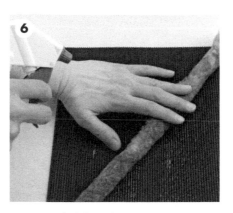

**6** Spray lightly with warm, soapy water and gently roll to attach the fiber to the pipe cleaner. Leave one or both ends of the fiber dry if the cord will be attached to another project.

**7** Keep rolling gently on the corrugated surface.

**8** Watch the ends of the pipe cleaner closely to make sure it doesn't break through the wool. Add more wool where needed.

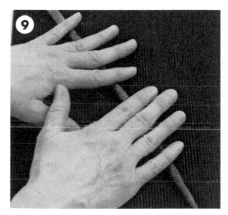

**9** Continue rolling the cord on the corrugated surface, applying more pressure as the felt begins to harden.

**10** Dunk the cord in hot water.

**11** Continue rolling the cord with more pressure.

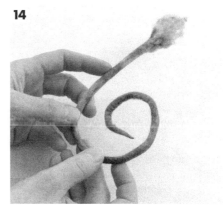

**12** Shock the cord, alternating between hot and cold water.

**13** Continue rolling on the corrugated surface until the cord is completely fulled. Rinse the cord thoroughly.

**14** Bend the cord to the desired shape and let dry.

## Spikes

Spikes are fun embellishments for a hat or a bag. One larger spike could be used, or a group of smaller spikes applied. If a group of spikes need to be all the same size, pull off equal amounts of wool to begin for the number of spikes required.

### YOU WILL NEED

- wet-felting supplies
- corrugated surface
- fine wool roving in chosen spike colors (one spike takes only a small pinch of fiber)

**1** Use a small amount of wool for a small spike. Increase the amount for larger spikes. Larger spikes need to be fairly thick and short to be able to support their own weight if the spike is to stand up from the surface of the felt.

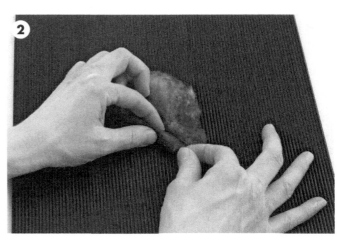

**2** Roll up the spike from one end, leaving the bottom end fluffy and dry.

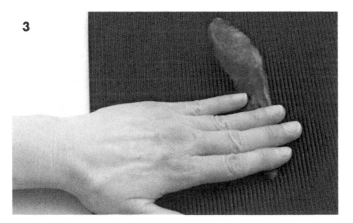

**3** Gently roll the pointy end of the spike over the corrugated surface.

**4** After dry rolling and ridding the spike of air, spray the pointy end lightly with warm, soapy water. Avoid getting the loose fibers at the bottom end wet.

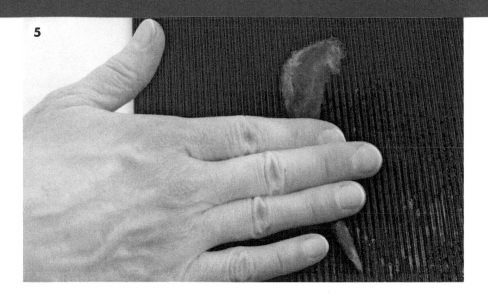

**5** Roll the pointy end of the spike on the corrugated surface.

**6** Hold the dry end of the spike and dunk the pointy end of the spike in hot water.

**7** Continue rolling on the corrugated surface until the spike is hardened and fulled. Spikes can be shaped in a bent position by concentrating fulling and rubbing on one side to shrink that side more than the other.

### Attaching Cords and Spikes

Attaching cords and spikes is a fairly simple process. The dry end that wasn't felted is used to attach it to a project as it is being felted. Make all the cords and spikes in advance so that they are ready to attach once the project has reached the soft felt stage. This sample shows spikes being attached to a square of felt. If a cord is being attached to a bag for a handle or another area that will receive pressure with use, make sure to reinforce the area with extra wool around the cord attachment.

## YOU WILL NEED

- wet-felting supplies
- premade cords or spikes with at least one end with dry, loose fibers
- felt project wet down and partially felted-ready for cord or spike attachment

**1** Spread the loose fiber ends of the spike out evenly around the spike.

**2** Place the spike on the partially felted wet surface in the appropriate spot with the fiber spread out over the felted surface.

**3** With soapy water on your hand, gently stroke the dry fibers getting them wet and pressing them to the felt surface.

**4** Gently rub the attaching fibers for a few minutes to make sure that they are felting to the surface.

**7**

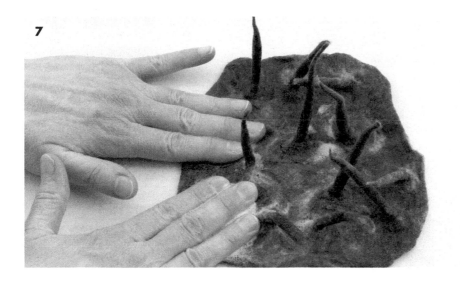

**8**

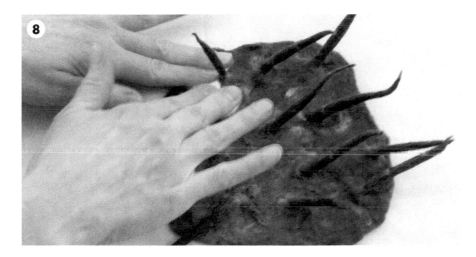

**9**

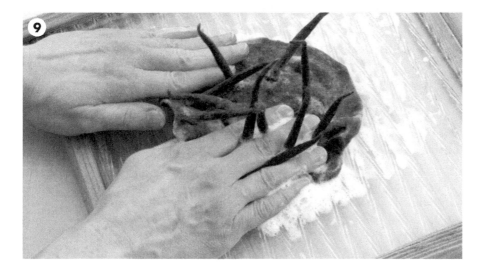

**5** Add more soap if the fibers are slow to attach.

**6** Add the rest of the spikes to the wet surface of the felt by following steps 1– 5.

**7** Once all the spikes are partially attached, begin rubbing with more pressure around each spike.

**8** Work methodically to make sure that all the spikes are felted in. Start with the spikes pointing up and after rubbing each spike, point it downward so you can see which have already been felted.

**9** Once the spikes are well attached, continue to full the piece as usual. Most methods of fulling will work with spikes as they are soft enough to roll. Check the spikes often when fulling to make sure that they do not felt down to the surface of the felt.

## Balls

Round felt balls or beads are an easy project. They can be used to make jewelry and buttons or as inclusions in other pieces of felt.

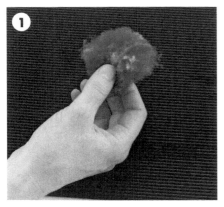

**1** Pull off a small amount of fiber.

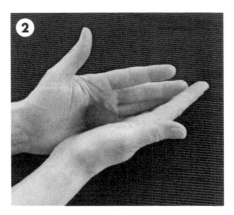

**2** Wrap the fiber into a ball shape and begin rolling it in your hands.

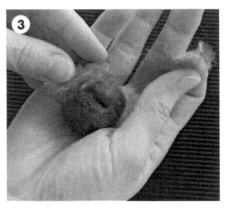

**3** If there are uneven spots or fissures in the wool, cover them with small wisps of wool and continue dry rolling in your hands.

**4** Once the ball begins to firm up, dunk it in hot, soapy water.

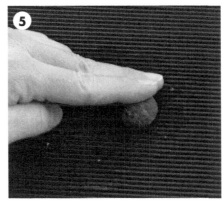

**5** Continue rolling the ball in your hands and over the corrugated surface. Increase the pressure applied as the felt begins to harden.

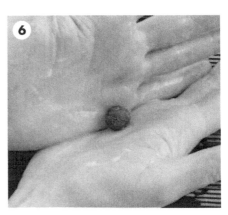

**6** Keep rolling until the ball is completely hard.

Inclusions in felt can give texture or provide an unexpected glimpse of color or shine to the surface design. The example shown here is a flat piece of felt with several different inclusions. Remember that the inclusions will cause the felt to shrink differently and samples should be made to determine shrinkage.

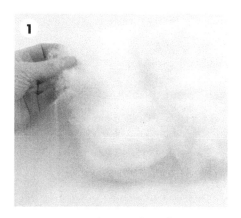

**1** Lay out two layers of wool or use batting.

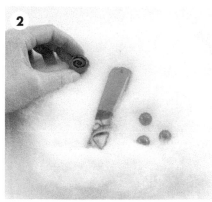

**2** Place the inclusions in appropriate spots.

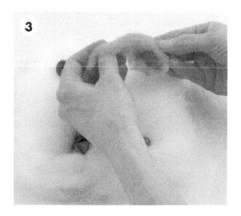

**3** To have different colors show after cutting and removing an inclusion, wrap the inclusion in a different color of wool.

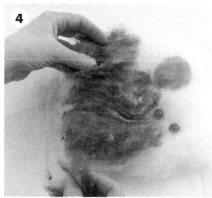

**4** Cover the inclusions with two layers of wool. Extra wool may be needed around each inclusion to ensure full coverage.

**5** Wet down the wool and begin to gently rub and felt. Care must be taken around each inclusion to make sure that the felt is shrinking around the inclusion. Make sure to rub around the base of each inclusion to ensure that the layers of wool on each side felt together.

(continued)

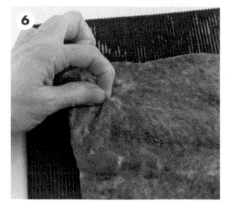

**6** Once the felt passes the pinch test, fulling can begin.

**7** Rolling does not work well as it causes too much shifting and pressure on the areas of felt surrounding the inclusions. Instead, use techniques such as kneading and rubbing on a corrugated surface so that you can feel the inclusions and make sure they are not shifting excessively. Check the bottom surface frequently to make sure the felt is not developing holes around the inclusions from the friction of the rubbing surface.

**8** Shock the wool, alternating between hot and cold water, and stretch in between fulling sessions.

**9** Continue fulling until the felt is hardened.

**10** Rinse and dry the felt.

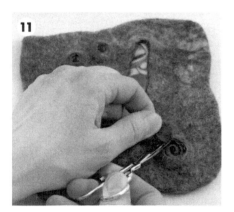

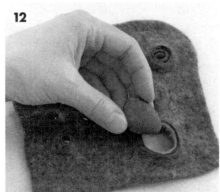

**11** Use embroidery scissors or a craft knife to carefully cut the surface of the felt to show the inclusion. If you want to leave the inclusion in place, cut only a small hole that is smaller than the diameter of the inclusion.

**12** To make a crater, cut about a third of the way down on the inclusion re-moving the top layer of felt and tak-ing out the inclusion. Inclusions could also be left in the felt for texture or to embellish further with techniques such as hand stitching.

## Other Fibers

Most of the specialty fibers described in the chapter about fiber and wool will work in wet felting. The most important thing to remember when adding specialty fibers or yarns to projects is to cover them with tiny wisps of wool to make sure they will adhere to the surface. Most of the specialty fibers do not have felting capabilities and must be caught up in the wool fibers, or they will pull free. Even wool nepps and slubs need to be covered with wisps of wool since they do not have enough free fibers to felt to the surface easily. The samples here are to show you how various fibers look when applied to the surface of wool and wet felted.

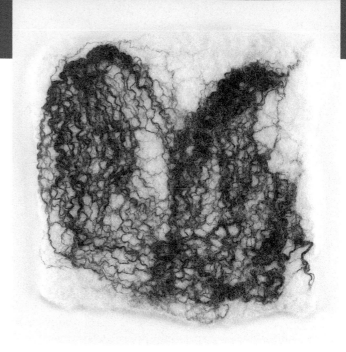

Silk top is a beautiful addition to felt and, when applied in small amounts to the surface, it will catch easily in the wool as it felts. All silk products accept acid dye well and produce vivid colors.

Silk cap felts in easily as it is thin and fine. It gives a lovely sheen to the surface of the felt.

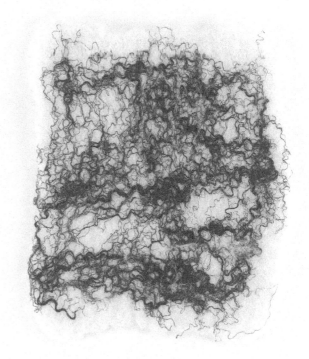

Silk throwsters waste (page 23) is stiffer than silk top and will need small wisps of wool to help it adhere to the wools surface. If a large amount is used, sandwich the silk between two thin layers of wool.

(continued)

Silk hankies are quite similar to caps in how they adhere to the wool during felting. They rarely need extra wool to adhere to the surface.

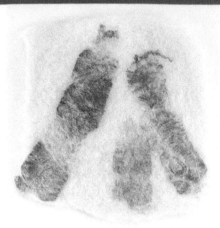

Silk carrier rods need to be separated into thin layers and anchored down with wisps of wool.

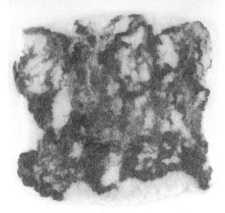

When applied to felt, silk noil provides a beautiful organic texture and shine. Spread thinly over the wool fibers, silk noil needs only small wisps of wool to lock it into the felt.

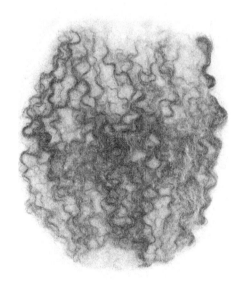

Nylon top fibers need only small wisps of wool to anchor them down when felting.

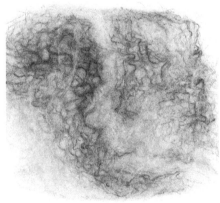

When applying loose Angelina fibers to the surface of felt, use a bit more wool to lock the fibers down to the felt as the Angelina fibers are a bigger diameter and don't catch easily in the wool.

Fake cashmere will not felt on its own but if spread thinly over the wool surface, it will felt in readily. Larger amounts of fake cashmere need to be covered with wisps of wool to anchor them in.

## Caution

Plant-based products need to be dyed with fiber reactive dyes. Compare the colors of the fake cashmere, Tencel, banana, and SeaCell felted samples. All were dyed with black acid dye. The plant-based fibers did not accept the dye like the fake cashmere.

A thin layer of Tencel needs only small wisps of wool to anchor it down when felting to the surface.

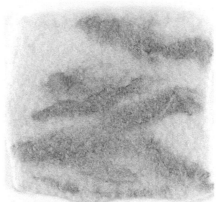

Banana fibers are fine, so they felt to the surface of the wool easily in light layers with minimal wisps of wool to anchor them down.

Applied lightly to the surface of the wool, SeaCell fibers felt in easily with thin wisps of wool to assist in anchoring them down.

Flax top requires wisps of wool to cover and anchor it during felting. It provides a pleasing organic design when felted.

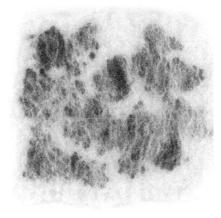

Wool nepps can be used to form a bumpy texture on the surface of felt, but because they are so well felted, make sure to cover them with a fair amount of wool to lock them into the felt. If you don't, you will end up with nepps everywhere.

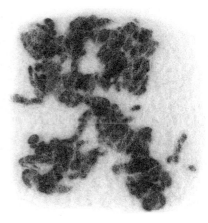

Wool slubs should be felted like nepps and are good for adding texture.

(continued)

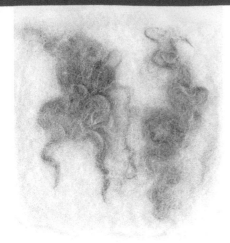

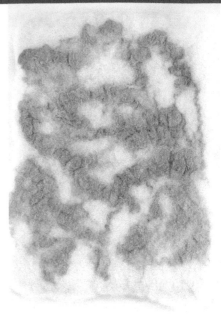

Wool locks of curly, longhaired breeds can be felted completely to the surface of felt or just the ends felted down. Wool locks do not usually need wisps of wool to cover them to be able to felt in. However, if the base felt is a very fine, quick-felting fiber and the lock is coarser wool, it would be advisable to use fine wisps of wool to lock down the coarser fiber.

To felt just the ends of a lock to the surface, work the lock in as if it were a spike. Felt one end down and lift and move the free ends frequently to prevent them from accidentally felting in.

Cotton is a soft fiber, and small amounts adhere fairly well to wool; larger amounts will need wisps of wool to adhere the cotton to the surface of the felt. Its matte finish blends in with the wool.

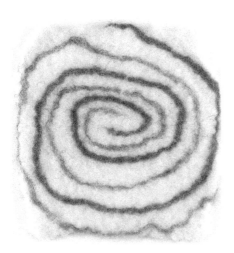

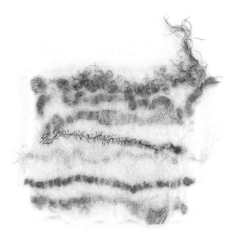

Pre-yarn also known as hahtuvalanka or plotulopi, felts in easily and rarely needs wool to anchor it down. Combined with prefelts, intricate designs can be formed in the felt.

Soy fiber is very similar to silk top in its sheen and weight of the fiber. It adheres easily to the wool in light layers and needs little extra wool to felt to the surface.

Any type of specialty yarn can be used but, remember that a yarn that isn't fuzzy will not felt in easily. For a knitting tape or smoother yarn, it is best to sandwich the yarn in between two thin layers of wool. If the yarn overlaps itself, it will not felt together at that junction. Extra wool should be added at overlaps. Make a felting sample first with the preferred yarn to determine how much wool is needed to anchor it down.

Other types of additions performed after wet felting is completed include machine embroidery, hand stitching, use of a needle-felting machine or hand-felting needles to add further embellishment, and other surface design techniques such as dyeing. The scope of this book doesn't allow an in-depth discussion of these techniques, but do experiment further on your own. Hand stitching through felt is a real pleasure as the needle slides so easily through the soft felt. Felt makes a wonderful base for machine embroidery as it needs no hoop for stabilization. Remember to make a thin felt for machine embroidery so it will fit under the presser foot of the sewing machine. Consider combining wet- and needle-felting techniques for further embellishment (see also page 132).

An assortment of pieces embellished with machine-stitching, hand-stitching, and machine-needle felting.

# NUNO OR
# LAMINATE FELTING

**N**uno felting, sometimes called laminate felting, is a relatively new type of felting invented by Polly Stirling and Sachiko Kotaka in 1994. In their experimentations with felting, Polly and Sachiko were looking for a way to make a lighter-weight felt for the sub-tropical climate of Australia. By combining a loosely woven fabric and felting in a layer of wool, nuno felting was born. Nuno, which is the Japanese word for cloth, is made by the wool fibers migrating through the weave of the fabric to form an entirely new material.

Nuno felting uses the same techniques as wet felting but care must be taken during the process to make sure that the wool fiber migrates through the weave of the chosen fabric. Natural fabrics such as silk or cotton are the best choice for nuno felting, but any fabric with a loose weave can be used.

Nuno felting produces a versatile fabric that drapes well and is lightweight. It tends to use less wool than wet felting, and the resulting fabric is thin but stronger than the same amount of wet-felted fabric. Nuno felt is also less likely to stretch out of shape. The other effect achieved in nuno felting is the ruching or wrinkling of the fabric after it is fulled. This wrinkled appearance develops due to the wool that is attached to the fabric that shrinks and pulls while the fabric stays the same size. Different types of fabric produce different ruching effects.

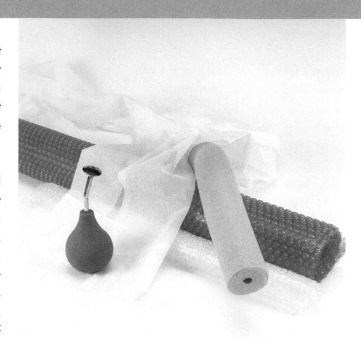

## EQUIPMENT AND SUPPLIES

If you have equipment and supplies for wet felting, you won't need to invest in much more for nuno felting. If you haven't tried wet felting yet, read through the equipment section in wet felting (page 54). The supplies needed are also similar except for the addition of loose weave fabric. Fine-grade wool works the best for nuno felting, as it is easier to get the fine-grade wool to migrate through fabric.

### Equipment

The equipment listed for wet felting is the same equipment used in nuno felting. The only difference is that nuno felting needs a lighter, gentler touch. Therefore, use tools that don't cause as much agitation. For rolling, use bubble wrap, a pool cover, or a rubber shelf liner with a pool noodle inside. Use the bubble wrap with the smaller bubbles to provide a smoother finish. Avoid items used for rough fulling, such as bamboo blinds or a washboard. If you prefer to cover the wool when wetting down the project, use a nylon curtain–type material instead of tulle. Tulle is more coarse and tends to catch the lighter pieces of wool used in nuno felting.

For water application, avoid using a spray bottle because it will shift the light layers of wool out of place. Instead, dribble water on with your hand or use a ball brause sprinkler, which emits less air with water application. The fabric can be wet down before applying the wool, which will make it easier to wet the wool down.

A power sander can be used with nuno felting to speed up the process. Refer to the wet felting equipment section (page 88) for specific information about the type of sander to use.

Nuno-felted shawl (opposite) by Ann McElroy

## Supplies

Nuno felting requires loosely woven fabric and fine-grade wool. As in wet felting, there are many ways to embellish nuno felting. Because nuno felting is so much lighter, care should be taken to apply only light layers of embellishment. Use finer fibers that need less wool to lock them into the felt. Silk, nylon, banana, or soy fibers are all good options.

Finer wool is needed when nuno felting so that the wool fiber's diameter is thin enough to pass through the chosen fabric. Coarser wool will be difficult to use as it will tend to felt to itself before it is able to pass through the fabric. Merino, Polwarth, and Cashmere are excellent choices for nuno felting. For better results, use the lowest micron grades such as 18 to 22 microns when first attempting to nuno felt. Other wool can certainly be used, but try experimenting with a small sample first before attempting a larger piece.

Prefelt can also be used for nuno felting. Commercial prefelt is generally made with Merino and will migrate well through fabric. Die-cut prefelt shapes provide a simple way to nuno felt and offer an easy way to design a pattern. If making the prefelt yourself, use fine wool and consider how thick the prefelt needs to be. Usually, one to two layers of wool are all that is needed for prefelt used in nuno felting.

A variety of fabric can be used with nuno felting, but natural fabrics work the best. Try blowing through a fabric to see if the air penetrates the weave easily. If so, it will be a good fabric for nuno felting. If the air doesn't penetrate the fabric, neither will the wool. Fabrics should be prewashed before nuno felting in case of shrinkage. One of the most popular fabric types to use is silk as the sheen of the silk contrasts nicely with the wool. Silk fabrics are differentiated by weight and measured in mommes (pronounced mummy) or mm. The momme is determined by the weight in pounds of a 45" by 100 yd. (114 cm x 91.5 m) piece of fabric, and the higher the momme, the heavier the weight of the fabric. Lighter-weight silk fabrics, 8 mm and less, are the best for nuno felting. The types of fabric that are more loosely woven are gauze, chiffon, organza, and the lighter-weight habotais (habutais).

Lightweight cotton fabrics also work well with nuno felting. The cotton has a more matte finish than silk fabric and tends to blend in more with the wool. Again, the important factor is the looseness of the weave. Cotton fabrics such as, gauze or voile work well.

Many lightweight man-made fabrics work with nuno felting, but if the fabric is very slick, it is difficult to get the wool to migrate through the fabric. The wool has a tendency to slide over the fabric instead of penetrating the fabric surface. When attempting to nuno felt with these types of fabric, experiment with a small sample first. Other types of fabric to try with nuno felting could be lace, organza ribbons, or even a devore (burned out) fabric blend.

A selection of fabric with a brief description is shown here. Other fabrics work but, the ones shown allow the wool to migrate through easily and will provide better end results for your first try. The momme measurements given are for the particular fabric shown. Most of these fabrics will come in a range of weights.

Silk gauze (4.5 mm)(1) is a very sheer and delicate fabric with a soft hand and a floating drape. Silk chiffon (8 mm) (2) is a sheer fabric with more texture and a heavier weave than gauze. It has a soft hand, stretches slightly, and will drape softly. Silk organza (5.5 mm) (3) is a very sheer, nearly transparent fabric with a stiffer hand and a crisp feel. It has a flat, smooth texture and is strong and durable. Silk habotai (or habutai) (5 mm) (4) has a soft hand with a smooth surface and is also known as china silk. It has a lustrous sheen and is available in a variety of weights. Bleached harem cloth (5) is a sheer fabric with a visibly loose weave. It is stiffer and smoother than the cotton gauze. Cotton cheesecloth, or scrim (6), is a very open weave fabric and is often irregular in weave. Cotton bubble gauze (7) is semi-sheer with a loose weave. It has a crinkly appearance as opposed to being smooth.

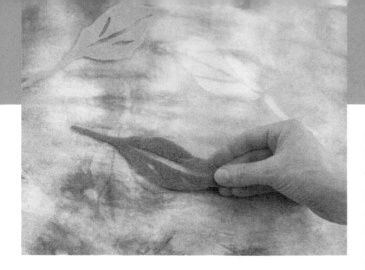

## TECHNIQUES

The techniques for nuno felting are very similar to wet felting. If you have already tried wet felting, nuno felting will be easy. If the basic techniques are the same for both, they are not repeated here. Refer back to the basic technique section in wet felting (page 60) for information about setup, separating fibers, palming, various fulling methods, and finishing felt.

The other techniques that have already been discussed in the wet felting chapter that can be used in nuno felting are the use of resists (page 80), a power sander (page 88), and prefelt and embellishments (page 90). Resists for nuno felting are usually used when making clothing or bags. The resist performs the same function as it does in wet felting, to prevent two surfaces from felting together while creating a three-dimensional project. A power sander is used in nuno felting just as it is in wet felting, to encourage the migration of wool through the loose-weave fabric. Start by sanding the side of the piece that does not have wool on it. Follow the instructions and safety precautions from page 88 and remember not to rub the sander over the surface of the felt. Pick the sander up and place it down when moving it to a new location on the felt.

Prefelt works very well with nuno felting; it allows for a more even, uniform design, and speeds up the layout process. With tighter-weave fabric, rough up the back of the prefelt with a brush so there are enough loose fibers to migrate through the fabric. Rubbing the fabric side will also encourage penetration of the fibers to adhere the prefelt to the fabric.

Embellishing nuno felt is very similar to wet felting.

Remember that embellishments that are not wool will not felt through the fabric. The embellishments must be on wool or have wool covering them to attach. The use of pencil roving (thin roving) or preyarn will provide many diverse design opportunities with nuno felting. Again, the key is to experiment. Try small squares of your chosen fabric with fine-grade wool and various embellishments. Nuno felting is an excellent choice for dyeing techniques such as shibori or even hand painting with dyes after the felting is complete.

### Basics

Each of the nuno-felted techniques shown here is a square sample. If you haven't tried nuno felting before, use a very open-weave fabric such as gauze and fine wool such as Merino. Once you've experimented with these techniques, try different fabrics and different breeds of wool.

Nuno felting takes a lighter touch than traditional wet felting. The process should be taken more slowly and with less force. Pressing harder and rolling faster will not speed up the process and may cause the wool to felt to itself before it adheres to the fabric. Take it easy and don't try and force the progression of the wool through the fabric.

### Layout

The layout of wool for nuno felting is similar to wet felting but in general much less wool is used. The strength of the resultant material comes from the fabric used rather than wholly from the wool. Therefore, only one or two very thin layers are necessary. The wool does not have to overlap always as it will felt to the fabric and doesn't need to cover the entire fabric surface. Big clumps of wool tend to felt together before adhering to the fabric. Lay out thin, fine layers instead. Avoid using fans or central air conditioning that will start up unexpectedly. Nor should you walk quickly past the felting table during the wool-layout process; the light wisps of wool can be blown out of place very easily. Gently pat the wool as it is laid down, and it will have less of a tendency to fly away. Wool can be laid out on only one side of the fabric or on both. The ruching effect achieved in nuno felting depends on how the wool is laid out as well as on the type of fabric. In general, the less wool used, the greater the ruching effect. To achieve even shrinkage in nuno felting, lay out two thin layers with the fiber in opposite directions. The other consideration with nuno felting is how to deal with the edges of the fabric. If the fabric already has a finished edge, such as when you use a scarf blank, the edge can be left alone. However, if unfinished fabric is used, the edges should be covered with wool to prevent raveling.

## One side

Nuno felting with thin layers of wool on one side of the fabric will give a very lightweight, softly draped result with an increased probability of a ruching effect on the fabric.

## YOU WILL NEED

- plastic-covered work surface
- painter's tape
- nylon curtain material
- 10" x 10" (25 cm x 25 cm) square of silk gauze (3 to 5 mm) for each technique
- ¼ oz. (7 g) or less Merino or Polwarth roving for each technique
- towels
- mild soap
- bubble wrap or pool cover
- pool noodle
- elastic ties or nylon stockings

**1** On the plastic covered work surface, make a 10" (25 cm) square with painter's tape in the center of the surface.

**2** Cover the surface with the nylon curtain.

**3** Lay out a thin, single layer of wool over the marked out square. Spaces can be left in between the wool, or the square can be completely covered. If the square is to be completely covered, lay out the wool as done in wet felting with the pieces overlapping over the ends of the prior row.

**4** Place the silk gauze square over the wool.

**5** Fold the nylon curtain over the square so it is sandwiched between two layers of curtain. Skip to the wetting down section to continue.

## Reminder

The wool will shrink in the direction in which the wool is laid out. If the wool is all placed in one direction, the piece will shrink in that direction.

## Laminate

Laminate nuno felting uses wool on both sides of the fabric. Putting wool on both sides of the fabric will produce a sturdier felt with less ruching effect. The resulting drape will be less but is good for projects such as bags, book covers, or a heavier wearable such as a jacket.

## Technique

Use two layers of wool on each side if the felt needs to be sturdier.

**1** Repeat steps 1–4 in one-sided nuno felting noted above.

**2** Lay out another thin layer of wool over the square of fabric. For more even shrinkage, place the wool fibers at a right angle from the layer underneath the fabric.

**3** Fold the nylon curtain over the square to sandwich the piece as noted above in one-sided nuno felting. Skip to the wetting down section to continue.

## Edges and Seams

There are several ways to handle the edges in a nuno-felting project. When using hemmed fabric, no special treatment is required. However, for raw-edged fabric the edges need to be covered with wool to prevent raveling. No-sew seams are possible with nuno felting by using the wool to hold the seam together. Seams can also be sewn first and then covered with wool so they are virtually invisible. Several options can be used when seams are necessary for a project.

Edge option #1 (1), edge option #2 (2), seam option #1 (3), seam option #2 (4), seam option #3 (5)

### Edge Option #1

Cover the raw edge of the fabric completely with wool. The edge can be covered on one side or both. Place the fiber perpendicular to the fabric edge with half of the fiber overlapping and then fold the fiber over the opposite side of the fabric.

### Edge Option #2

Fold the edge of the fabric to the back. Iron the fold if a completely straight edge is required. Put a small amount of wool between the folded edges of the fabric. Cover the raw edge of fabric with wool.

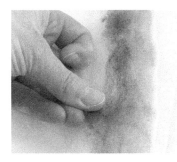

## Technique

For long seams, as in a garment, use safety pins to hold the seam together until it is well felted.

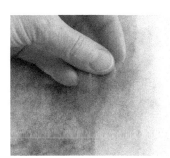

### Seam Option #1

Cover the first piece of fabric with a light layer of wool; make sure the wool covers all the way to the edge. Overlap the second piece of fabric edge to make a seam. Lay out another light layer of wool over the seam.

### Seam Option #2

Butt up the edges of the two pieces of fabric and layer wool underneath and on top of the seam. Both edges of the fabric should be well covered, and the fiber should be placed perpendicular to the seam. More wool will be needed in the seam area with this method.

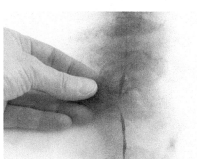

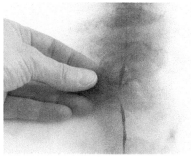

### Seam Option #3

Sew a seam on a partially nuno-felted piece, trim the seam edges, and then cover completely with wool. Once the felting is finished the seam is nearly invisible.

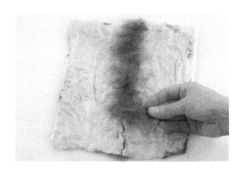

## Wetting Down

Nuno felting needs to be wet down thoroughly as is done in wet felting. One difference is in how vigorously the water can be applied. Spray bottles do not work well as the spraying action will move the small amount of wool around and disturb the design. Another consideration is the temperature of the water. Cool or cold water should be used during nuno felting. The coolness of the water helps to slow the felting process and allow the migration of the fibers through the fabric. Use of hot water at the beginning may cause the wool to felt to itself before it adheres to the fabric.

**1** Sandwich a sample between two layers of the nylon curtain.

**2** Take a ladle or cup of cool soapy water and gently dribble the water over the back of your hand as you press down on the wool. A sponge dipped in soapy water can also be used to wet down the wool and fabric.

**3** Gently press down so that the wool and fabric become completely wet and all the air is pressed out of the wool.

**4** Soak up any excess water with a sponge or towel.

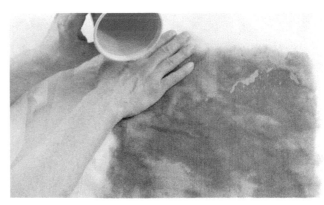

## Technique

Several samples can be laid out at one time, wet down, felted, and fulled at the same time.

If the sample has wool on both sides of the fabric, wet down one side, flip over, and wet down the other side to make sure all the wool is wet.

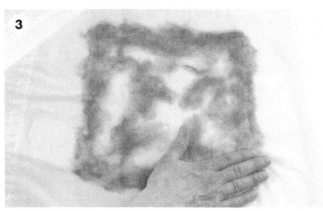

### Felting

Several different methods can be used for the soft-felting stage of nuno felting. Try the various options to see which method you prefer. Rolling the nuno felt is probably the simplest method and produces a smooth, even result. The use of a power sander cuts down the effort expended and speeds up the process. Rubbing the fabric side also helps to coax the wool fiber through the fabric. If wool is used on both sides of the fabric, the felting can be performed just as in wet felting.

### Rolling

Rolling in nuno felting is performed as described in the wet-felting techniques section (page 52). The main difference is to use a more delicate approach.

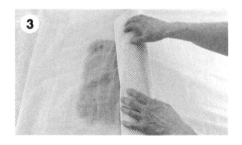

**1** Place bubble wrap, rubber shelf liner, or a pool cover bubble side up on the work surface.

**2** Sandwich the wet-down wool and fabric between the nylon curtains or between very thin plastic such as plastic wrap and place on top of the bubble wrap. The nylon curtain or plastic helps to prevent the design of wool from being disturbed before it has a chance to adhere to the fabric.

**3** Roll everything together loosely around a pool noodle and begin rolling with very light pressure.

**4** Unroll and check the felt frequently to avoid wrinkling and shifting.

**5** Reroll and gradually apply more pressure during rolling.

**6** Check for migration of fibers (see below) and continue rolling until the fibers have migrated through the entire surface of the fabric.

**7** Progress to fulling.

## Checking Migration of Fibers

To check to make sure that the fibers are migrating through the fabric, blot a portion of the fabric side on a towel. Hold the fabric up to the light at a slight angle and look closely for wool fibers on the back of the fabric. If the fibers are present over the whole surface, fulling can begin. If the fibers are not on the back surface, try rubbing on the back side of the fabric to encourage more penetration. Continue felting until fibers are present on the back side of the fabric. When the wool is placed on both sides of the fabric, use the pinch test (see page 68) to determine if fulling can begin.

## Power Sander

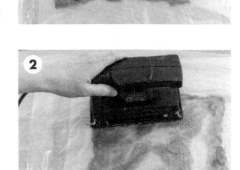

Using a power sander speeds up the process during nuno felting. Read through the directions and safety precautions in the wet felting section before beginning.

**1** Place a pool cover or woven rush rug on the work surface. Cover this with plastic and place the wet-down sample wool side down on the plastic. The sample can still be sandwiched between the nylon curtains. Cover with more plastic.

**2** Place the sander down on one corner of the sample and sand for 10 to 15 seconds.

**3** Pick up the sander and place it down on the next spot on the sample. Hold for 10 to 15 seconds.

**4** Continue picking up and placing the sander back down in a new position until the entire sample has been covered. Do not rub the sander over the sample.

**5** Cover the entire surface at least twice with the sander.

**6** Check to see if the fibers are migrating through the surface of the fabric. If so, turn the piece over and sand the other side.

**7** If the fibers haven't migrated, continue sanding on the nonwool side until the fibers migrate through the fabric.

**8** Progress to fulling.

## Rubbing

Rubbing can be used during nuno felting but should be done first on the fabric side without wool. Again, the point is to get the wool fibers to migrate through the fabric.

**1** Place the wet-down sample wool side down on the work surface and remove the top layer of nylon curtain.

**2** Gently rub the surface of the fabric. Use either your bare hand or put a plastic bag over your hand.

**3** Rub over the entire surface of the sample.

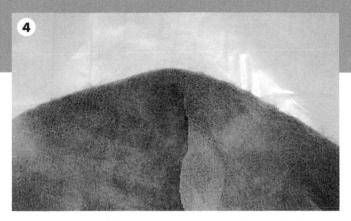

**4** Check to see if the fibers are migrating through the fabric before rubbing on the wool side.

**5** Rub gently on the wool side after the fibers have migrated through the fabric.

**6** Progress to fulling.

## Fulling

Once the wool fibers have migrated through the fabric, perform the pinch test. If the wool has adhered over the entire surface of the fabric and doesn't pull away with the pinch test, the process of fulling can begin. There are several ways to perform fulling, but the process is more delicate than for wet felting. The options for fulling in nuno felting are rolling, dropping, rubbing against the surface of bubble wrap, rubbing the felt against itself, kneading, or a combination of these methods. At this point, warm water can be added to speed up the fulling process. To get rid of cold water in the felt, blot with a towel. Do not wring the felt. Add warm water and begin fulling with your preferred method.

With each of these fulling methods, start gently and gradually add more force and agitation. Gently stretch the felt in between fulling. As the felt becomes completely fulled, there will be little give when stretching the portion of the fabric covered with wool. To test if fulling is complete, hold a section where the fabric is covered with wool between both hands and gently stretch. If the felt is completely fulled, there will be minimal give in the material.

## Rolling

When fulling with rolling, use more pressure and change from bubble wrap to using shelf liner or rug liner material to give more agitation. The felt can also be rolled upon itself or around a dowel rod. Rolling will give a more even surface and provides controlled fulling over the entire area of the felt at one time.

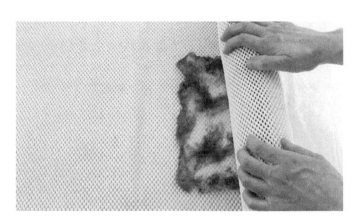

## Rubbing

Rubbing the felt against the surface of the bubble wrap or rubbing it against itself is another method of fulling. When rubbing against itself, the fulling will be more random, and the surface and shape will be less even.

(continued)

To have the most control of the final shape and surface, fold the piece evenly and rub against the bubble wrap. Unfold and refold frequently, straightening the edges each time the piece is unfolded.

## Kneading and Dropping

Kneading and dropping are fulling methods that are usually performed together. For random shrinkage and a less controlled outcome, knead the felt upon itself and drop on to a hard surface. Keep randomly wadding up the felt, kneading, and dropping. For a more controlled outcome, keep the felt neatly folded and drop gently onto a hard surface. To knead, fold the felt, roll it up, and squeeze gently. Keep unfolding and refolding throughout the process. Straighten out the felt, checking frequently for wrinkles or folded-over edges.

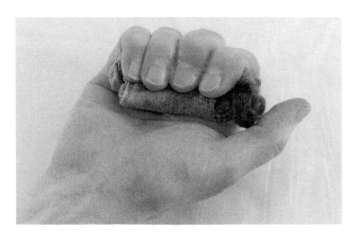

## Sampling

Experimenting and sampling is just as important with nuno felting as it is with wet felting. To determine shrinkage, use the same formulas as used in wet felting (page 78). Shrinkage in nuno felting will differ due to many various factors including the fabric used, the type of wool used, the amount of wool used, and the method of felting and fulling. When using less wool, there will be more shrinkage. When making a sample before beginning a larger project, make sure you consider all these factors and the sample is made with all these factors considered and done the same way as the project.

Another reason to make a sample is to find out whether or not the fabric will allow the fiber migration necessary for nuno felting. Loosely woven, natural fabrics are likely to nuno felt well. However, if the fabric type is unknown, it would be simpler to try a small sample first before embarking on a project where the fibers might not migrate through the surface. Due to their slippery surface, some manmade fabrics do not nuno felt easily.

Keep the samples in a notebook with other felting samples as a good resource for future felting projects. Remember to jot down the shrinkage rate, type, and amount of wool used, and any other important factors. The sample squares could be sewn together into patchwork designs. Use the patchwork designs to make a notebook cover, bag, pillow covering, or even a wall hanging.

The following photos show nuno-felted samples of some of the typical fabrics used. The wool used for each sample is 18-micron Merino, and the fabric samples were all 10" x 10" (25 cm x 25 cm). One layer of thin wool was applied in one direction for each sample, and each piece was felted and fulled by rolling, rubbing, kneading, and dropping. The samples all shrank more in the direction that the fiber was laid out, and the ruching was more even because the wool was laid out in one direction. The fabric was dyed and the wool was left white to provide a clearer contrast.

Cotton bubble gauze (1) allows easy wool penetration after only 100 rolls. The shrinkage was 45% with soft ruching. The resultant fabric has a fairly soft drape. Bleached harem cloth (2) is a stiffer fabric than the cotton bubble gauze but has a similar end result as the bubble gauze. The wool migrates easily and is seen on the opposite side after 100 rolls. The shrinkage rate was 49%, and the fabric looks nearly identical to the bubble gauze nuno felt. Cotton cheesecloth or scrim (3) nuno felts very quickly because it has such a loose weave and visible holes in the fabric. The wool migrated easily and was seen on the reverse side after only 50 rolls. The shrinkage rate was 60%, and there was no ruching of the fabric. The cheesecloth is so loose and soft, the individual strands were pulled tighter, but the entire surface remained smoother without ruching.

This fabric was a scarf found at a thrift store and has unknown fabric content. Due to the variance in weave in the fabric, the wool penetrated easily through the transparent section but tended to slide over the patterned areas without migrating through. Fibers began showing on the opposite side of the fabric after 150 rolls and, with a little extra coaxing (rubbing), the fibers did migrate. The felt shrunk 48% and the ruching was greater in the transparent areas than in the patterned sections.

Silk gauze (4.5 mm) (1) shrinks quite a bit when wet down; so if a specific size is needed, wet down before cutting. After 200 rolls, the fibers could be seen on the opposite side of the fabric. Once fulling began, the edges had a tendency to roll in and felt to each other quickly so check often when fulling. Forty-nine percent shrinkage occurred, and the resultant fabric was still quite sheer, with minimal ruching and a soft drape. The wool fibers began migrating through the silk chiffon (8 mm) (2) after 200 rolls. As the weave is slightly tighter, it took more rolls

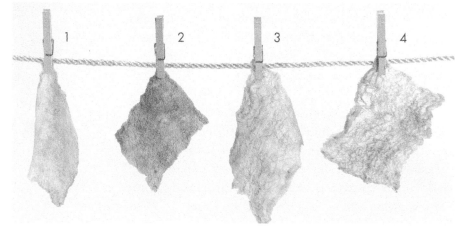

to completely penetrate the fabric's surface. The wool showed a very even migration through the chiffon making for a more even ruching effect with smaller wrinkles than the stiffer silks. Shrinkage was 56%, and the edges tend to roll and felt together easily. The fabric after felting is soft but doesn't drape as well as the silk gauze. Silk habotai (5 mm) (3) is a slightly stiffer fabric than the chiffon and gauze, and the fibers did not migrate as evenly through the fabric. Fibers were seen on the nonwool side of the fabric after 200 rolls. The shrinkage rate was 38% with more ruching and a drape that was slightly stiffer. Silk organza (5.5 mm) (4) allows the wool fibers to migrate easily and took 150 rolls before fibers began to appear on the opposite side of the fabric. The shrinkage rate was 48% with lots of ruching and a fairly stiff fabric with much less drape than the other silks.

Laptop sleeve, nuno felted with Merino and 8-mm silk scraps, overdyed and hand embroidered with wool thread.

## Mosaic or Collage

Basic nuno felting is often done with one piece of fabric, and the wool is laid out to cover the fabric partially or entirely. However, the fabric can be cut into smaller pieces, or pieces of various fabrics can be nuno felted together with the wool holding the fabric parts together to make one large piece of nuno felt. This type of nuno felting has been called a variety of things including mosaic, collage, and even stained-glass nuno felting. The felting techniques are the same as for standard nuno felting, but there must be enough wool between the fabric pieces to make sure that they will become one piece of felt.

The following step-by-step instructions show three methods of nuno felting with smaller pieces of fabric. These are small samples, but the same process can be used for any nuno-felting project. There are many ways to nuno felt, and there is no wrong way as long as it works. Keep experimenting once you understand the basics.

Collage nuno felting is made in a similar way to making a collage out of paper and art supplies. The word collage is derived from the French word colle, which means to paste or glue. With nuno-felting collage, the single surface is the wool, which acts as the glue, and the materials to be glued will be pieces of fabric. Pictorial designs can be made, but the edges will be softened. Shrinkage and ruching should also be considered when developing the design. In addition, the color of the wool and the fabric combined will affect the end color of the felt.

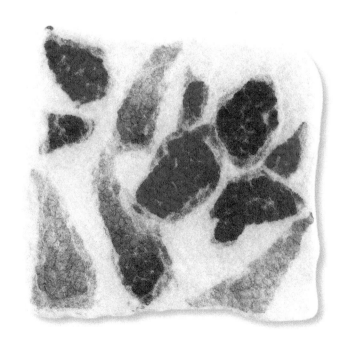

1 On a plastic-covered work surface, draw a 10" x 10" (25 cm x 25 cm) square with a waterproof maker or painters tape. Cover the marked square with a 20" x 20" (50 cm x 50 cm) piece of plastic.

2 Lay out two layers of wool at right angles to each other to cover the marked square.

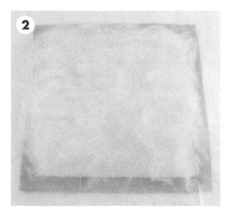

3 Place various pieces of fabric on the surface of the wool in the desired pattern or design. Place the fabric so all the edges are on the wool.

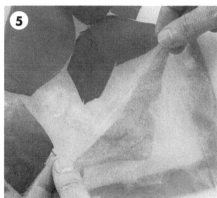

4 Check to see if any of the fabric pieces overlap. Either move the overlapping pieces so that they are separated or add a small amount of wool between the over-lapping edges.

5 For any fabric that is more difficult to nuno felt such as tighter woven or slick fabric, put a small amount of wool to cover the edges.

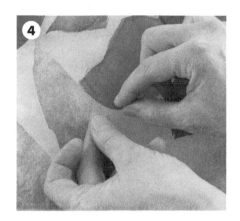

6 Wet down, felt, and full as directed in the basics nuno-felting section (page 114).

Mosaics are usually made from small pieces of glass, ceramic, or stone forming a design and held together with mortar or grout. A nuno-felted mosaic is made up of pieces of fabric with wool as the mortar or grout. The fabric pieces can be any size, not necessarily all small, but again, when developing a design, consider shrinkage; i.e., how the wool will affect the edges of the fabric, color mixing, and ruching.

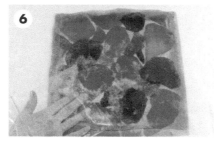

**1** On a plastic-covered work surface, draw a 10" x 10" (25 cm x 25 cm) square with a waterproof maker or painter's tape. Cover the marked square with a 20" x 20" (50 cm x 50 cm) piece of plastic.

**2** Lay out a variety of different fabric pieces in the marked square. Pieces can overlap as desired.

**3** Apply thin layers of wool over the fabric pieces. Cover the "seams" well where the fabric edges overlap or touch. The entire fabric surface does not have to be covered but all the fabric edges should be well covered with wool. The wool can be all one color or a variety of colors depending on the design desired.

**4** Cover the fabric and wool with another piece of plastic and flip the sample over. Remove the top layer of plastic.

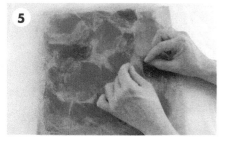

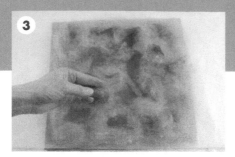

**5** Apply small wisps of wool over the edges of the fabric pieces. Put a small wisp of wool between any overlapping pieces of fabric. Take care to avoid shifting the design.

**6** Wet down and rub gently over the edges and seams to begin coaxing the fibers through the fabric.

**7.** Felt and full as usual. Check frequently to make sure that the various pieces haven't shifted and that all the edges have enough wool to hold the pieces together. More wool can be added if necessary before felting and fulling is complete.

The stained-glass nuno-felting technique is comparable to real stained glass. Instead of glass pieces, sections of fabric are used. The wool is used to bind the fabric edges together as leading lines do in stained glass. The most important factor in this process is making sure that all the edges of the fabric are well covered with wool on both sides so that the resultant felt will hold together. Pencil roving works very well for lead lines, but regular roving can also be pulled apart in long, thin lengths and used the same way. Using fabrics with a looser weave will make this process easier as only small areas of the fabric will be covered with wool, and it needs to migrate through the fabric easily for good adherence. This is a more complex method of nuno felting requiring some experience to complete successfully. The pieces tend to shift easily and can pull loose while fulling if not adhered well. Repairs can be made with needle felting if any of the lead lines pull loose from the fabric. Add more wool along the lines, needle felt to reattach the fabric and then rewet and felt again.

## Variation

Open spaces can be left without fabric if so desired to form a lattice pattern.

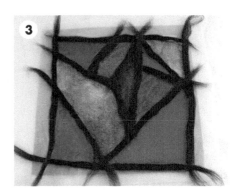

1 On a plastic-covered work surface, draw a 10" x 10" (25 cm x 25 cm) square with a waterproof maker or painter's tape. Cover the marked square with a 20" x 20" (50 cm x 50 cm) piece of plastic.

2 Lay out the selected fabric pieces over the marked square. Butt all the edges up together.

3 Cover all the edges and seams with pencil roving or thin pieces of roving lengths. Allow the roving pieces to extend beyond the borders of the fabric.

4 Cover with another piece of plastic and flip the sample over. Remove the top piece of plastic.

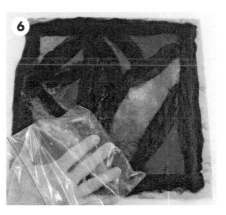

5 Cover the seams and edges of the fabric on this side with more lengths of roving. Align them with the roving on the opposite side. Fold in roving pieces from the opposite side. Check carefully to make sure all the fabric edges are well covered.

6 Wet down and rub gently over the wool lines. Take care when rubbing to avoid excessive movement or shifting of the fabric away from the wool.

7 Felt and full as usual. Check the piece frequently to make sure that the design hasn't shifted.

## Technique

Use two pieces of flat Styrofoam or foam insulation board to sandwich nuno-felting projects for flipping a larger project. Place the bottom piece of board before laying out any wool. This method will help to keep designs in place with less shifting.

# NEEDLE FELTING

Needle felting, also called dry felting, is a recent innovation developed from the manufacturing process of felting wool, plant-based fibers, and synthetic products into large flat pieces of felt to be used commercially. The first patent for needle felting was dated in the late 1850s and was for an industrial machine with 150 to 200,000 needles. These types of needle-punch machines are still in use today making nonwoven flat felt from wool as well as other fibers for a large variety of commercial and industrial purposes such as shoe felts, automotive insulation, carpet backing, filters, linings, and even tennis ball covers.

In the early 1980s, David Stanwood began using a single barbed needle to make multicolored wool felt balls which he then wet felted. During a felt-making party at his house, David showed this process to Ayala Talpai. Ayala went on to further develop the use of an individual felting needle for sculpting wool and wrote the first book about needle felting.

Felting needles can be used in many different ways including sculpting wool into three-dimensional shapes or figures and making two-dimensional wool paintings and can be used in combination with wet felting. A wet-felted piece can be shaped using needle felting; fine details can be added or embellishments can be secured in place before wet felting. Repairing wet-felting trouble spots is another function that felting needles perform well. Needle felting strengthens seams and joins; more wool can be needled to cover thin spots or holes; and wool socks can even be repaired with a felting needle.

Needle-felting machines are one of the latest developments that provide greater versatility and speed when making two-dimensional felted items. The needle-felting machine, sometimes called the embellisher after one of the first models available, looks like a sewing machine without thread or a bobbin. There are numerous brands of needle-felting machines on the market that use from one to fifteen needles at a time. Some sewing machines can be converted into needle-felting machines with the appropriate attachments.

## EQUIPMENT AND SUPPLIES

The basic equipment needed for needle felting is only a single barbed needle and some wool. There is much more equipment available, but only a minimal investment is needed when beginning to learn to needle felt. The equipment listed here shows the different tools that are available to needle felters. Start with the basics, try different techniques, and gradually add more tools to your arsenal as needed.

The supplies used in needle felting are nearly the same as the ones used for wet felting and nuno felting. Even fibers that don't wet felt well can be needle felted, especially with a needle-felting machine. Certain wool breeds needle felt better than others, and experimenting with different fibers will help you to determine what works best for you.

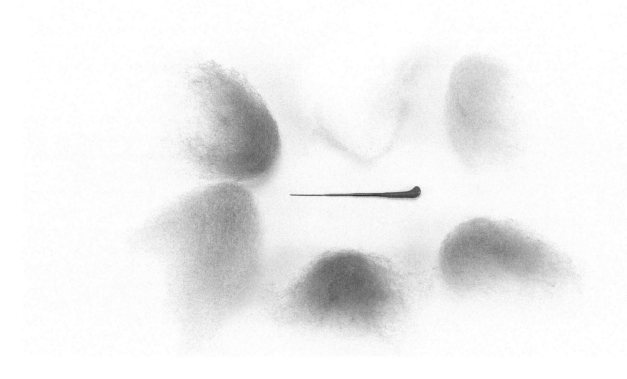

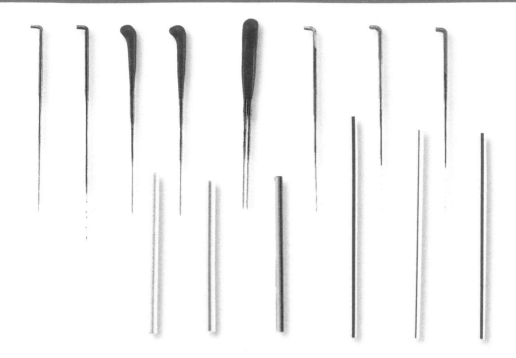

## Equipment

The most important piece of equipment in needle felting, and the only tool that is strictly necessary, is the needle. However, there are other tools that will help speed the process and also protect you from accidental needle sticks.

Felting needles are available in a variety of brands. They are made from carbon steel with a very sharp point. Needles come in a variety of gauges and blade styles and can have a variety of barb placements and depth. Further discussion about felting needles is included in the basic

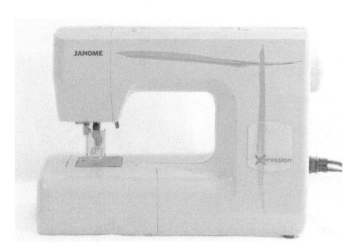

techniques section (page 138). Often, needles are color coded, but unfortunately there isn't one single system of coding. A yellow-coded needle from one company may be a completely different needle from a yellow needle from another. Buy needles that are marked for gauge and blade style so you know what needle you are buying. Needles often come in sets with a variety of gauges and blade styles. When first beginning to needle felt, buying this type of set allows you the opportunity to try different needles for different types of projects and to see which size and type you prefer.

Needle-felting machines come in a variety of brands. Check with your local sewing machine dealers, as many will carry the same brand of needle-felting machine. The brands are all fairly similar, although some machines will have more needles in the head than others. The heads that hold the needles should allow for single needles to be replaced without having to replace the entire head when a needle is broken. Some brands also offer a guide that allows yarn to be fed through so that the yarn can be easily felted on to the surface of the project.

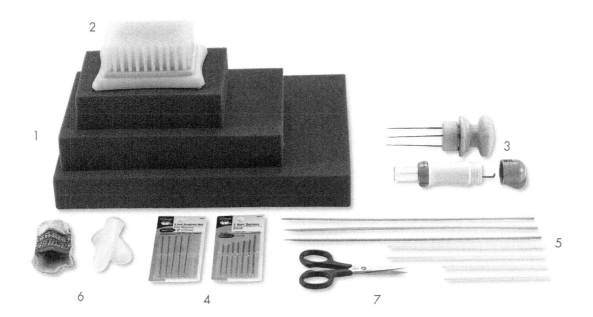

Foam pads (1) are used in needle felting so that the wool being felted is placed on the pad instead of being held in your hand and to provide support for a two-dimensional felt piece. This makes it less likely for a needle to poke all the way through into your hand. Many different types of foam pads are available, and some are denser than others. Dense upholstery foam will work, as will a stack of interlocking foam floor pads. Different sizes of felting pads are available and can be fit to the size of felted items being made. Pads should be 2" to 3" (5 to 8 cm) thick for the best protection. Brushes (2) are also made to needle felt against. These seem to work best when needle felting wool to a base fabric.

Multineedle holders (3) come in a variety of shapes and sizes. These holders allow the use of more than one needle at a time. Using several needles at once speeds up the needling process and allows more surface area to be covered per poking action. Look for handles that allow the needles to be changed in and out easily. A handle could be made from polymer clay by shaping the clay around the ends of the needles and then baking. However, if a needle was broken, it could not be replaced.

A darning needle or a doll needle (4) is used in needle felting for pulling already needled wool back out to reshape if the original shape isn't as desired. Darning needles are large blunt needles with a big eye and can be found with sewing supplies. Doll needles are extra long needles with long eyes and are found with doll-making supplies.

Popsicle sticks or bamboo skewers (5) can be used when shaping long, thin tubular wool shapes. These items can usually be found with kitchen or candy-making supplies.

## Caution

Use two foam pads, one for lighter colored wool and one for darker wool. Stray bits of wool from the pad have a tendency to adhere to the item as it is being felted. The stray wool won't show as much if a lighter colored wool item is needled only on the pad used for light colored wools.

Finger Gloves or finger guards (6) can be worn to protect against accidental needle pokes. The Finger Gloves were originally designed by a crafter to protect fingers from hot glue but will also protect fingers from sharp needles. Finger guards are usually used by wood workers and are more bulky but will also protect fingers from needle pokes.

Embroidery scissors (7) are useful for snipping fuzzy fibers still showing after finishing needle felting the surface. Scissors are also handy for cutting shapes out of prefelt for embellishment or clothing.

## Supplies

If the only tool required for needle felting is a felting needle, the only supply required is wool. Other supplies that work well with needle felting are core wool, wool locks, prefelt, preyarn, and other types of fiber for embellishment. When machine-needle felting, use a background or substrate to support the wool and other fibers. This could be a partially wet-felted piece, a fulled recycled sweater, flannel, or other soft fabric.

Any type of wool can be used for needle felting especially with two-dimensional works. Three-dimensional sculptural needle felting works best with shorter and coarser wools. Finer and longer fiber takes longer to needle felt and has a tendency to show needle holes more. Other fibers such as alpaca, llama, and camel down all needle felt well.

Core wool is the wool used in the middle of a three-dimensional needle felted item. It doesn't necessarily have to be different wool from the outer layers, but many felters use less expensive white wool as the core and then cover this with the more expensive dyed wools. Many of the down or meat breeds work well for core wool. They are less expensive, needle felt easily, and maintain a spongy quality when felted.

Wool locks are usually used in needle felting for embellishments. The locks can be used as hair for dolls, fur for animal figures, or embellishments on wool paintings. Locks come in a variety of colors or can be dyed to the desired color.

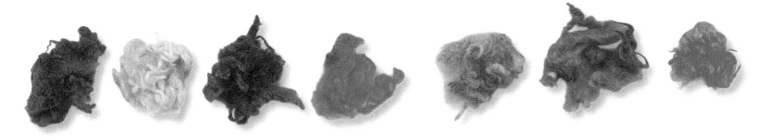

A variety of other fibers can be used for embellishing needle felting. The softer finer fibers such as silk, banana fiber, or soy fiber can either be blended in with the wool or needled on to the surface of the wool. Angelina fiber blended in with the wool gives shiny glints through the matted surface of the wool. The heat-fusible type of Angelina can be fused together with an iron and makes beautiful wings for fairies or dragonflies. The wings can then be needled into a figure with small amounts of wool to hold them in place.

Prefelt can be used in several ways with needle felting. Use prefelt for clothing when making figures. Cut out the shape required and then needle directly to the doll. The prefelt needs to be needled over its entire surface to shrink and make it firm. With two-dimensional needle felting, prefelt shapes can be cut out and needled to the wool surface. Remember that the prefelt will shrink as it is needled.

Care must be taken with heavier or stiffer fibers to prevent needle breakage. Avoid nepps or slubs as they tend to break needles.

A variety of fabrics and fibers can be used with machine needle felting. Most felters use fabric as the background or substrate for a wool painting. The most commonly used fabrics are silk, wet-felted wool, fulled sweaters, flannel, and other soft fabrics such as velvet or velour.

## TECHNIQUES

Master the basic techniques of needle felting and then begin exploring the endless possibilities of how wool can be shaped with a barbed needle. Whether you want to sculpt the wool into three-dimensional figures, make wool paintings, or learn to use your needle-felting machine, the opportunities to create with wool are limited only by your imagination.

The techniques shown here can be combined in different sequences to achieve different effects. Experiment with the basics and find out what works best for you. Needle felting is a forgiving craft because wool can be added or even taken away if it hasn't been needled in too tightly. Play with the wool and see where it takes you.

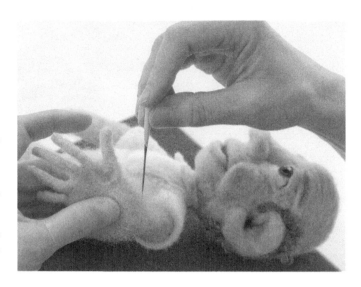

### Basics

In this section, you will learn about felting needles, how they work, the parts of the needle, and safety precautions. Different needle techniques will be explained and how each of these procedures can be used for differing effects. Samples are shown of how different breeds of wool react to needle felting and also how different needles affect the same type of wool.

### Needle Sizes and Features

Felting needles are an amazing tool considering their size. Almost any fiber can be felted with these barbed needles. Different needles have different purposes and using the correct needle with the appropriate fiber will make all the difference in a needle-felted project. Take a little time to learn about the felting needle so that you know which needle will work the best for what you are felting.

Detail of needle-felted wall hanging with a variety of fiber types by Zed

## Anatomy of a Felting Needle

Felting needles are made to fit in large industrial machines and not specifically to be used in the hand. The crank and shank of the needle are made to fit into slots in a large needle loom, and the barbs are designed for different industrial applications. Innovations continue to be made in blade styles and barb placements.

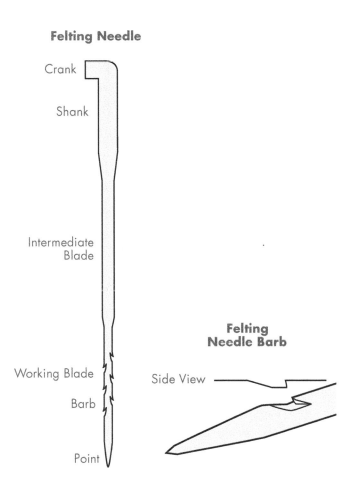

**Felting Needle**

Crank

Shank

Intermediate Blade

**Felting Needle Barb**

Working Blade

Side View

Barb

Point

Illustration by Nanci Williams

The L-shaped hook on the end is called the crank. This is the portion that fits into a needle loom and helps hold the needle in place. The larger portion of the needle that is attached to the crank is called the shank. The shank also helps to hold the needle in place in a needle loom. The blade of the needle is conical, triangular, or star shaped. The triangular blade has three sides, and the star blade has four. Star blades have more barbs as there are more surfaces for the barbs.

The intermediate blade doesn't have any barbs on it and thus causes no felting action. Only the lower quarter to third of the blade has barbs. It is called the working portion of the blade. All the felting action occurs in the area with barbs.

The barbs are indentations in the blade that catch fibers as the blade is poked into the fiber mass. The fiber is then pushed into the mass and entangled with other fibers, causing them to felt. Barbs can be placed in different positions on the blade and come in different shapes and sizes. The blades can have a different number of barbs; the more barbs, the quicker the felting action. Some needles can have edges without barbs. This allows easier penetration into denser felt.

The point of the needle is very sharp so it can easily penetrate wool or other fiber. It is unfortunately quite easy to poke yourself with a felting needle, and care should always be taken to keep the point away from your hands. The point and the working portion of the needle are very thin and the most vulnerable to breaking.

## Safety Precautions

Felting needles are sharp and should always be handled with care. Needle felting is not recommended for children under the age of ten. All children should have adult supervision when using felting needles.

## Sizing of Needles

Felting needles are sized by their diameter. This is called the gauge of the needle and is defined as the number of needles that fit in a square inch; the higher the gauge, the finer the needle. Needle gauges range from 12 to 42. Most needle felters use needles in the 36- to 42-gauge range shown here, but coarser needles can be used for inserting hair on a doll or for coarser wool.

In general, start with a coarser or lower gauge needle and work to a finer or higher gauge needle. Coarser fiber will felt better with a coarser needle. Coarse needles also work well for attaching two parts together. Finer fiber felts best with a higher gauge needle. Finer needles are also used for adding detail and for the final smoothing of the wool's surface.

Some needle felters use a variety of needle gauges when working on a project. Others prefer to use only one size needle throughout a project. Try different sizes of needles to see what works best for you and the wool you prefer. If many different grades of wool are used, a variety of needle gauges will provide a needle that is suited to each grade of wool.

It is difficult to determine the size of a felting needle by sight. If the felting needles are not color coded when you buy them, use nail polish or enamel paint to color code the needles on the handles. Mark an index card with the colors and corresponding gauges. Store the card with the needles for easy reference.

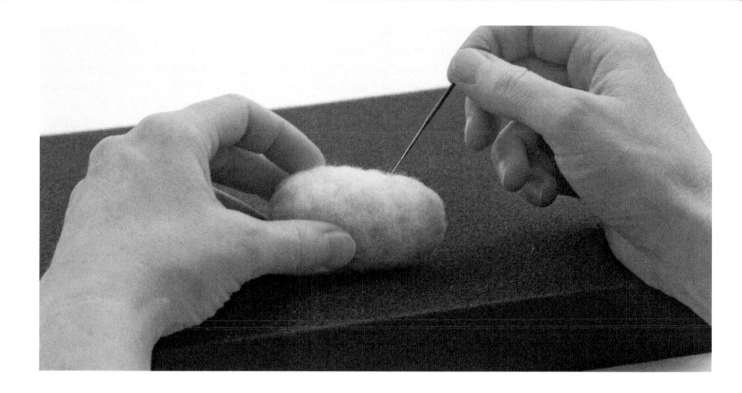

## Handling and Care

Felting needles are thin, and the working portion of the blade where the barbs are located can be broken if force is applied along the length of the needle. When poking the needle into the wool, always poke the needle in and out at the same angle. When the tip of the needle is in the wool, avoid pushing the shank of the needle from side to side. Push the needle in and then pull it straight out without changing the angle direction.

To hold the felting needle, grip it lightly like holding a pen to write. Avoid holding the needle tightly as your hand will tire easily. Poke the needle in and out of the wool fairly gently—vigorous jabbing isn't necessary. The needle only needs to be poked in as deep as the barbs on the blade. Deeper jabbing will be needed for attaching parts or making deep indentations, but in general, only the bottom third of the blade is used.

Be aware of your posture and body mechanics while needle felting. Avoid sitting in a hunched position. Position your chair so that you can place your feet flat

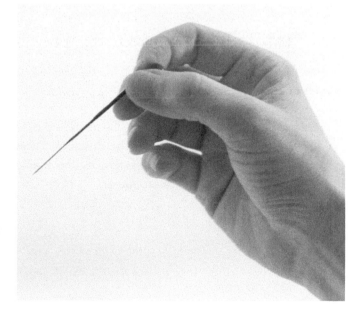

(continued)

on the floor and your forearms can rest comfortably on the work surface. Support your lower and upper back with a high chair back or pillow. Take breaks frequently to stretch your arms, shoulders, and upper back. Needle felting is a repetitive motion that can cause injuries such as carpal tunnel syndrome, but appropriate precautions and posture will help to prevent this occurrence.

When using needles for a project, many needle felters store spare needles by poking them part way into the felting pad. Care should be taken to avoid bumping the needle shaft as the tips can snap off. Store needles in a suitable place when not in use. Use a small plastic straw to hold the needles; store them in a plastic tube or in the edge of a small piece of corrugated cardboard. Felting needles will eventually become dull and need to be replaced. If the needle has been used frequently over a long period of time and doesn't seem to be working as well, try a new needle.

Always pay attention to the project when needling is occurring. If your attention drifts, you are more likely to poke yourself. Always be aware of the location of the tip of the needle and keep your hands and fingers out of the way. Handle the felting needles as you would a sharp kitchen utensil, and if you get distracted, put the felting needle down.

If you share felting needles with others, the needles should be disinfected after use. Needles can be disinfected with a solution of part bleach and part water. Dry the needle thoroughly after disinfecting before reuse.

## Samples

Experimenting and sampling with needle felting is quick and easy. When using individual needles, roll up a ball of the sample fiber and try out different needle gauges to see which works best for that particular fiber. Take another small tuft of fiber and needle it to the surface of the first ball. By trying different needles, you can determine which is the quickest and most effective. The resultant needle holes left in the fiber surface will also be visible.

With machine needle felting, it is a good idea to test a variety of fibers to see how easily they felt and also which substrates or backgrounds work best. Many fabrics will distort and buckle when other fibers are needled into the surface. A small sample square will show how the fabric will react.

## Wool Breeds and Other Fiber

Most fibers can be needle felted, although the shorter, coarser fibers are easier and quicker than fine, long staple fibers. Most needle felters have a preferred fiber for dry felting, but by trying a variety of wool breeds and other animal fibers, you can determine which you prefer for different types of projects.

Look at the chart of wool breeds in the All About Fiber (page 14) for information about wool micron counts and staple length. The following samples show each of these wool breeds needle felted, with a description of the needle gauge that was the most effective, the time required to felt, and a description of the resultant surface.

Blue-Faced Leicester wool felted fairly easily with 38- to 42-gauge needles. It took seven minutes to form the moderately firm shape that held together well. The surface of the felt was slightly uneven but moderately smooth.

Corriedale wool took seven minutes to needle felt into a firm shape. The wool felted easily, and the 38- to 40-gauge needles seemed the most effective. The resultant surface was fairly smooth.

Falkland wool was more difficult to needle felt and took 10 minutes to form a moderately firm shape. The 38 triangle or star needles proved to be the most efficient and caused the greatest compression of the fiber. The surface of the felt was uneven and it was hard to get a smooth surface.

Finn wool needle felts quickly to a firm shape in 6 minutes. The lower gauge needles, from 32 to 38, provide the best compaction. The surface is consistent and fairly smooth.

Gotland wool felts quickly to a firm shape and took 5 minutes to form an oval shape. Lower-gauge needles, from 32 to 36, felt the fibers together easily, while higher-gauge needles are not as effective. The felted surface is hairy but has a nice sheen.

Icelandic wool felted easily with 36- to 38-gauge needles, but the 32 gauge was ineffective. It took 5 minutes of needle felting to form a moderately firm shape with a fairly smooth surface.

(continued)

Merino wool (18-micron top) was difficult to needle felt, especially with lower gauge needles. The 42-gauge needle provided the best compaction, but it took 12 minutes to form a soft shape. The surface was uneven and showed needle holes easily.

Norwegian C1 wool felts quickly to a firm shape in 4 minutes. The most effective compression was attained using the 38-gauge needle. The felted surface was moderately smooth.

Pelsull (Pelssau) wool is similar to the Norwegian C1 and felts to a firm shape in 6 minutes. The 36- to 38-gauge felting needles provide the most effective needling action. The resultant felted surface is fairly smooth.

Polwarth wool felts fairly quickly with higher-gauge needles such as 38 to 42. The shape formed was still fairly soft after 6 minutes of felting but held together well. The surface is fairly smooth but does show needle holes.

Romney wool felts quickly to a firm shape in 6 minutes. The higher-gauge needles are ineffective, and the 36-gauge needle achieved the best compaction of the fibers. The surface of the ovoid, or oval shape, was fairly rough with visible needle holes.

Wensleydale wool felted fairly quickly—6 minutes with a 36-gauge needle. The higher-gauge needles did not achieve any compression of fibers and slid past the fibers without catching them. The form was moderately firm, but the surface was hairy and the long fibers are very visible wrapping around the shape.

Other animal fibers can be used for needle felting. The one most often used is alpaca, but other fibers will also felt, including llama and camel fiber. The following samples are needle felted and include a description of how the fiber felted, the gauge of the needle best suited to the fiber, and the resultant felted surface.

Alpaca fiber is more difficult to needle felt than wool. It took 11 minutes to form a soft shape. The higher-gauge needles do compress the fibers but very slowly. The 36-gauge needle was the most effective. The surface was uneven with visible needle holes.

Angora goat fiber was difficult to needle felt, as the fibers are very slippery. The only gauge needles that were effective were 40 to 42, and the resultant form was very soft although it held together fairly well after 13 minutes. The surface is very hairy and shows needle holes easily.

Camel fiber was fairly easy to needle felt but took 10 minutes to form a moderately firm shape. The 36 to 38 gauge needles were most effective with the camel fiber. The surface was hairy and uneven and tended to show needle holes easily.

Cashmere fiber was difficult to needle felt as the fibers are soft and slippery, and the only needle gauge that was at all effective was a 42 gauge. After 8 minutes of needle felting, the form was very soft and pulled apart easily. Even after felting in one area for several minutes, compaction was minimal. The surface was fuzzy and fluffy, and the needled areas did not hold together well.

Llama fiber felted fairly well with 36- to 38-gauge felting needles. It took 8 minutes to form a moderately firm shape. The surface was very rough and hairy.

Yak fiber wasn't difficult to needle felt, but after 8 minutes of felting, the fibers could still easily be pulled apart. Even if the same area was needle felted for several minutes, those fibers still would not hold together and took on their original configuration if pulled away from the form. The 42-gauge needle was the most effective, but the surface showed needle holes even with this higher-gauge needle.

| Fiber Type | Recommended Needle Gauge | Suitable Needle Felted Projects |
|---|---|---|
| Blue-Faced Leicester | 38 to 42 | Will work for 3D projects but better suited for 2D work as the result is fairly soft. |
| Corriedale | 38 to 40 | Works well for 3D projects, will also be suitable for 2D projects. |
| Falkland | 38 | Not suitable for 3D projects but will work well for 2D needle felting. |
| Finn | 36 to 38 | Works very well for 3D projects and would also add a nice heathery fiber for 2D projects. |
| Gotland | 32 to 36 | Works for 3D projects giving a shinier surface. Will work with 2D projects but doesn't blend in easily. Locks are good for hair on 3D projects or for embellishments on wool paintings. |
| Icelandic | 36 to 38 | Will work for 3D needle felting but better suited for use in 2D work. |
| Merino | 40 to 42 | The highest micron count Merino is not suitable for 3D work as the result is too soft. Use lower micron Merino batt for 3D projects. Works well for 2D projects and wool paintings especially in batt form. |
| Norwegian C1 | 38 | Excellent for 3D projects. Will work for 2D but is slightly coarse and wouldn't blend in well in wool paintings. |
| Pelsull | 36 to 38 | Works well for 3D projects and felts to a firm shape. Will also work for 2D applications although it is a coarser fiber and won't blend in as well as finer wools. |
| Polwarth | 38 to 42 | Will work for 3D project but the result may be soft or take longer to complete. Will work well for 2D projects and wool paintings. |
| Romney | 36 to 38 | Will work for 3D projects but has a fairly rough surface. Would work well for depicting close-cut animal hair. Will work for 2D projects, but is fairly coarse and won't blend in as well. |
| Wensleydale | 36 | Not really suited for 3D projects, but the locks are excellent for embellishment or curly hair. Will work for embellishments on 2D projects but won't blend in well with wool paintings. |
| Alpaca | 36 | Will work for 3D projects, but results will be fairly soft. Works well for 2D work. |
| Angora | 40 to 42 | Not really suited for 3D projects except as an embellishment. Will work for 2D projects and is a good source of bright white. |
| Camel | 36 to 38 | Will work for 3D projects, but the surface will be rough and hairy. Works for 2D projects but won't blend in easily in a wool painting. |
| Cashmere | 42 | Not really suited for formation of 3D projects. Will work in a 2D project but would work best when blended with other fibers to hold together well. Good source for bright white fiber. |
| Llama | 36 to 38 | Will work for 3D projects, but the surface will be rough and hairy. Will also work for 2D projects but will not blend in well in a wool painting. |
| Yak | 42 | Not really suited for 3D projects. Will work in a 2D project but needs to be needled into or mixed with a fiber that felts and holds together well. |

## Embellishments

The embellishments used in dry felting are diverse. Almost any soft fiber can be needle felted, although some fibers are more difficult using a single needle. Embellishment fibers will adhere better if felted into wool or one of the other animal fibers that felt, as they won't hold together well alone.

The following photos show a sample of a variety of embellishments needle felted onto a piece of commercial felt with a multineedle tool.

Embellishments used with needle-felted figures include beads, glass eyes, wool locks, prefelt, preyarn, and other props as needed. Beads or glass eyes

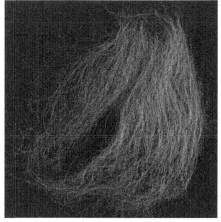

Silk top punches into the felt easily but doesn't hold very well. It would benefit from blending with other fibers that felt or being felted into wool.

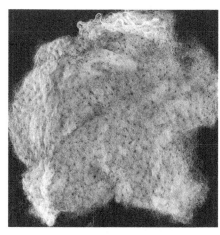

Silk caps felt into the surface well and adhere to the commercial felt satisfactorily. Visible needle holes are evident after needling.

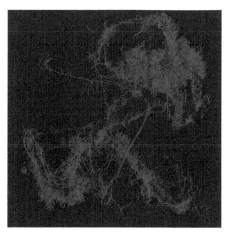

Silk throwsters waste punches in easily and remains well attached. Minimal needle holes are evident after needling.

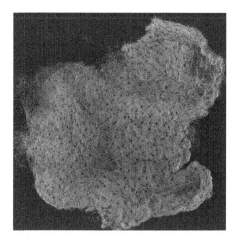

Silk hankies needle felt in a similar manner as silk cap—they felt easily and adhere well but show needle holes.

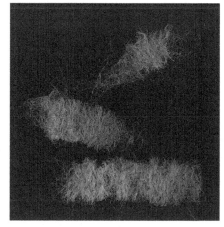

Silk carrier rods can be very thick and won't needle felt well. However, after soaking them in water and pulling apart the layers, the thinner layers will needle felt easily. They adhere well to the surface and due to the wispiness of the thin layers, don't show needle holes excessively.

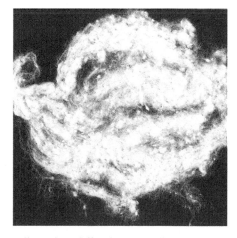

Silk noil is difficult to needle through thick layers but needle felts easily through thinner layers. It adheres well to the commercial felt and shows minimal needle holes.

(continued)

can be glued, sewn, or needle felted into eye sockets depending on the size of the eyes and whether or not they will be used as a toy. Long breed wools make excellent hair for figures or for needle-felted animals. Curly breed wool such as Wensleydale achieves a curly hairstyle while Merino top works well for straight hairstyles. Prefelt is an easy way to make clothing for figures. Clothing pattern shapes can be cut out of the prefelt and then needled together or to the figure. Preyarn works well for fine line accents. As it has very little twist, it is easier to needle down than yarn or roving. Preyarn makes an excellent fine line in detail areas such as eyes. Many needle felters use props such as glasses, hats, and other accessories to bring their needle-felted figures to life. These props can be hand crafted or purchased. These types of items can be found where doll and dollhouse accessories are sold.

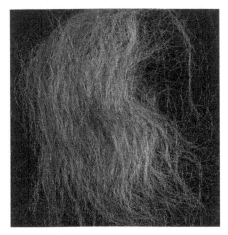

Nylon top punches into the commercial felt easily but has a tendency to pull right out. Other fibers such as wool would help it adhere better.

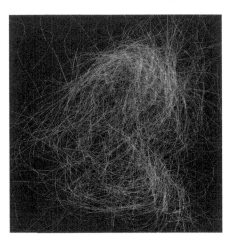

Angelina fibers punch in easily but pull right out and don't adhere well to the commercial felt. It would needle felt best blended with wool.

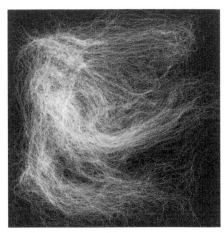

Fake cashmere needle felts easily but also pulls back out easily. It would adhere better blended with other fibers that felt.

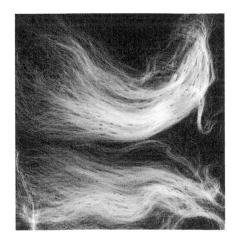

Tencel fiber punches into the commercial felt easily but doesn't adhere well. It would work better blended with other fibers or needled into wool.

Banana is another soft fiber that punches in easily but doesn't hold well. Blend with other fibers for better adherence.

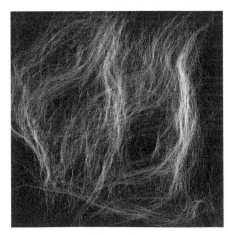

SeaCell fiber needle easily but doesn't adhere to the commercial felt well. Use other fibers that felt to help it stay better.

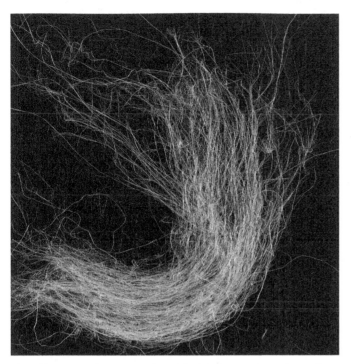

Flax fiber punches in well and holds better than the softer, silkier fibers. It would still benefit from the addition of wool or other fibers that felt.

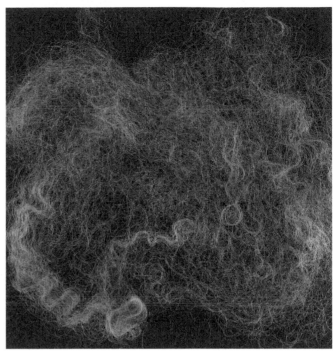

Wool locks felt in easily and hold well to the commercial felt. Lock structure can still be seen even after needling.

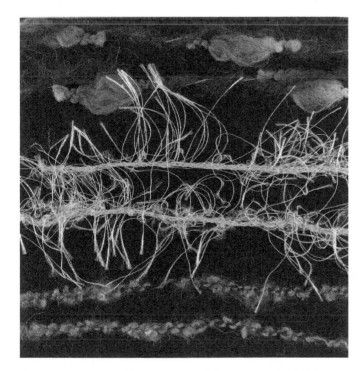

Specialty yarns needle in easily to the commercial felt. The yarns that are fuzzier hold better than the yarn tapes.

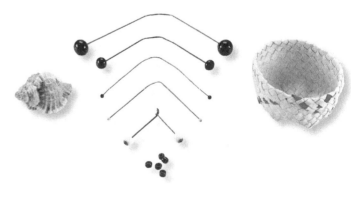

A variety of props and embellishments to use in needle felting with glass eyes ranging from 2 to 10 mm in size.

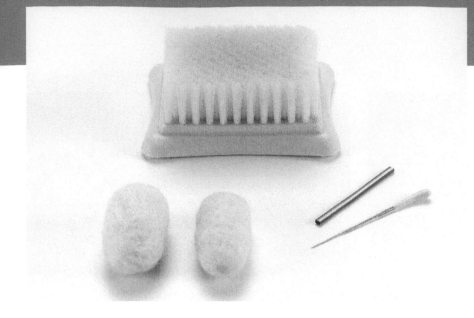

## YOU WILL NEED

- selection of felting needles from 36 to 42 gauges
- felting pad
- 1 oz. (28 g) medium coarse wool batt or roving such as Norwegian C1 (or use what you have)
- darning needle

## Needle Techniques

Every needle felter develops his or her own preferences of how the felting needle is handled. The following basic methods will get you started and can be used in different combinations to achieve varying effects. Try these ideas with a variety of needle gauges to see which is most effective for you. The photos and instructions use wool batting or batts, but roving can be substituted. If roving is used, it helps to pull apart pieces and blend them together by hand to form a mass of fibers that do not all run in the same direction.

## Standard Needle Stroke

The standard needle stroke is used in both two-dimensional and three-dimensional pieces. It is a simple in-and-out movement of the needle that will be used for the majority of the needle-felting action. The most important points to remember are to keep the needle at a consistent angle when moving in and out of the wool and to poke only to the depth of the working portion of the felting-needle blade. Wool batt is easier to use than roving or top, but either can be used.

**1** Pull off three pieces of wool batt approximately the size of your palm.

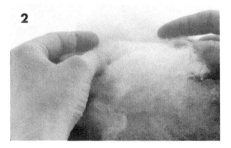

**2** Stack the pieces on top of each other and place them on the felting pad. Place a 36 to 38 star or triangle felting needle close to hand.

**3** Fold the two closest corners of the stack diagonally toward the back of the felting pad.

**4** Hold the folded corners and begin rolling the stack of wool into a roll. Press as much air out of the wool as possible as it is rolled.

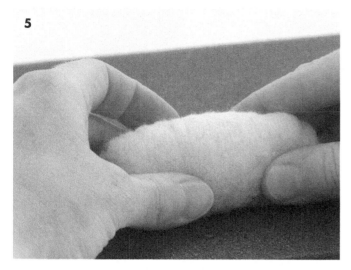

**5** Keep tucking in the sides of the wool stack and rolling until an ovoid shape of wool is formed.

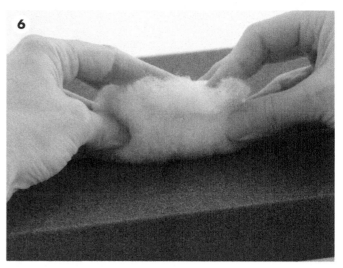

**6** Hold the wool shape with the loose edges of the wool at the top of the shape.

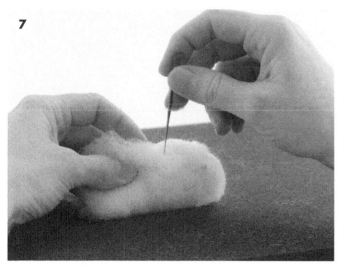

**7** Grasp the needle lightly and poke it into the wool at a 90-degree angle where the loose ends are located.

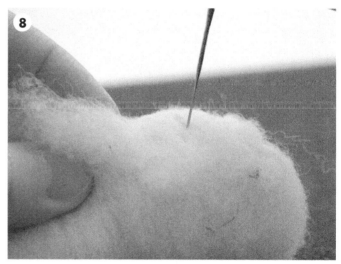

**8** Poke only to the depth of the working blade.

(continued)

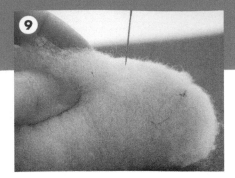

**9** Keep the needle at a 90-degree angle and pull the needle back out.

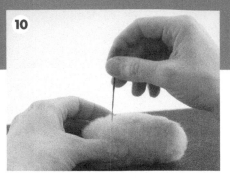

**10** Keep poking the needle gently in and out of the area with loose fibers.

**11** Once the fiber ends are poked in, let go of the wool, and the shape should hold together. If it doesn't hold together, repeat steps 3–12.

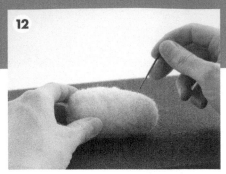

**12** Continue poking over the entire surface of the wool. Poke at different angles as you turn the shape on the felting pad. Just remember to keep the angle consistent when poking the needle in and out. Don't change the angle of the needle with the tip buried in the wool.

## Making a Line

A straight line or indentation with a felting needle is used mainly in three-dimensional needle felting. Poking the needle in and out over the same area of the wool in a line makes an indented valley. Indentations can be used to indicate a rib cage or define a muscle shape. A line can also be made with the felting needle to outline a shape on the felting pad to form an edge. Any kind of shape can be formed with this method. The first set of instructions shows how to make a three-dimensional indentation, and the second set is for outlining a flat shape.

## Three-dimensional Indentation

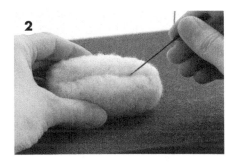

**1** Use an ovoid shape of wool (see instructions for the standard needling technique, page 150) and place the wool shape on the needle-felting pad.

**2** With a 36- or 38-gauge felting needle (star or triangle), poke the needle in and out, making a line down the length of the ovoid.

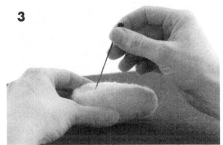

**3** Keep poking the needle in and out along this line, and an indentation will begin to form.

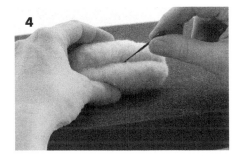

**4** For a deeper indentation, poke more deeply into the wool.

**5** Continue poking along the same line until you are satisfied with the depth of the indentation.

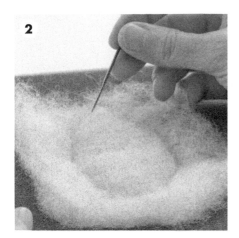

**1** Pull off one piece of wool batt approximately the size of your hand. Use a 36- to 38-gauge needle.

**2** Place the wool batt piece on the felting pad. Needle the outline of a shape on the wool batt, poking into the felting pad. This can be done freehand or around a pattern.

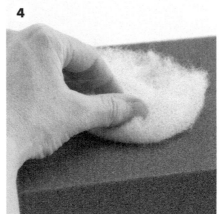

**3** Continue poking the needle to outline the entire shape.

**4** Fold the wool on the outside of the outlined shape in toward the center.

## Variations

Many different items can be used for a pattern. For a leaf shape, use a real leaf to needle around. Cut shapes out of coloring books and use these for a pattern. Cookie cutters can be placed on the wool, and the edge be used as a guide to form another shape.

**5** Use the standard needle stroke to poke the folded ends down into the body of the shape.

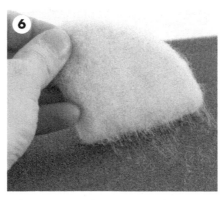

**6** Peel the shape off the felting pad, turn it over, and poke the loose wool down on the top side. Make shallow pokes to avoid pushing the wool into the felting pad.

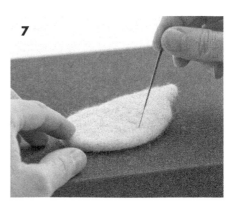

**7** Continue to use the standard needle stroke to firm the shape as needed.

## Blending Technique

The blending technique is used to blend fibers into a partially felted surface. Fiber needs to be blended in when wool is added to make a piece bigger, when parts with loose wool are added, and when outer wool is applied over core wool. All three of these techniques can be done in the same manner.

**1**

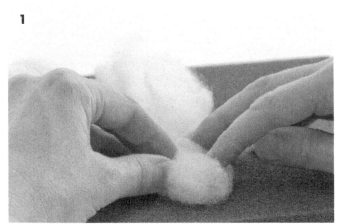

**1** Use an ovoid shape as the base. Place a small piece of wool batt approximately half the size of your hand on the felting pad and fold in the long edges of the batt.

**2**

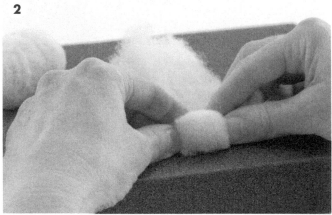

**2** Roll up one end leaving loose fibers on the opposite end.

**3**

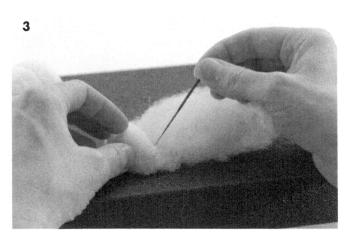

**3** Use the standard needle stroke to needle the rolled end to hold it together.

**4**

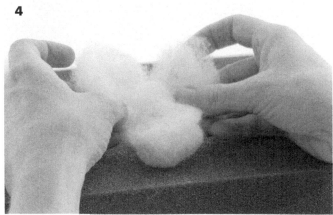

**4** Flare out the loose fibers so they aren't all clumped together.

**5**

**5** Place the smaller shape just made in the middle of the ovoid with the loose wool ends flaring upward. Pull off excess loose fiber.

**6**

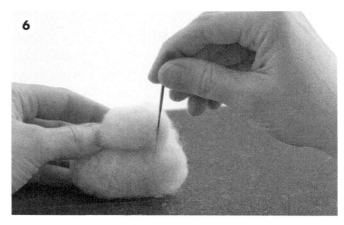

**6** Using the standard needle stroke, tack the rounded end of the smaller shape along the edges to the ovoid shape.

**7**

**7** To blend the loose fibers into the ovoid shape, hold the needle at an acute angle (almost parallel to the wool surface) with the point of the needle in the same direction as the ends of the loose fiber. Needle in and out gently along the surface of the loose fiber.

**8**

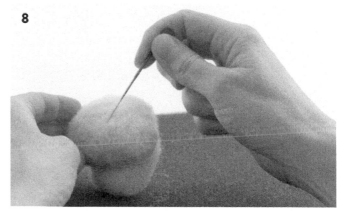

**8** Continue to needle in and out at an acute angle, pushing toward the ends of the loose fiber.

**9** Once all the ends have been needled in, use the standard needle stroke at a 90-degree angle and needle over the surface where the loose fibers were.

**9**

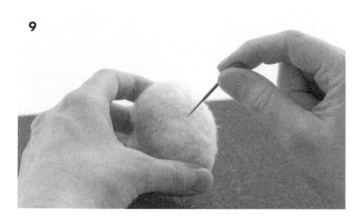

## Shaping Techniques

Three-dimensional needle felting is when you sculpt wool with a needle to make different shapes. Wool can be sculpted into any shape and the techniques are very versatile. Start the shaping process from the very beginning and continue to refine the shape as you work. Poking in one place repeatedly will create a hollow space or a crater, while poking in a line creates a groove. If one side of a shape is poked all over, that side will be flattened, but if the shape is rotated while poking, the needle will round the shape. Hollow places can also be erased if a mistake is made by using a darning needle to pull the wool back into a rounded shape again and then needling to hold. Shaping techniques define areas and enable you to make craters to form nostrils or shallow indentations above a collarbone on a figure.

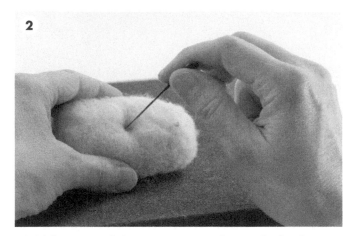

**1** Make an ovoid shape to start as in the standard technique instructions. Use a 36- to 38-gauge felting needle.

**2** Place the ovoid shape on the felting pad. Make a round indentation by poking the needle in and out in the same spot.

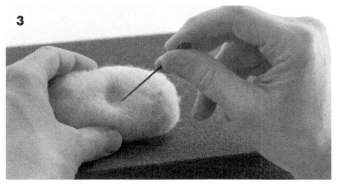

**3** To make the indentation or crater larger, work the needle in a circle around the center spot, widening the circle to enlarge the crater.

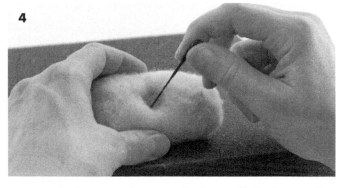

**4** To make the crater deeper, poke the needle farther into the wool in the center. Poke the needle deeper several times to force the fibers farther into the center. The surface of the wool can be formed into any shape by poking in and out in the areas that need to be concave and avoiding areas that will be convex.

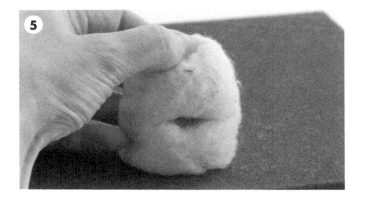

**5** Hold the ovoid shape with the crater facing forward. Squeeze the two ends together and place the squashed shape on the felting pad.

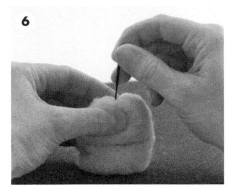

**6** With one hand pressing down from the top to hold the two ends together against the pad, needle deeply several times behind your fingers. Be aware of the location of the tip of the needle in the wool and avoid needling toward your fingers.

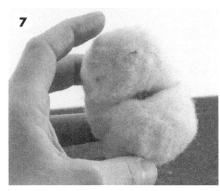

**7** Let go of the wool shape and see how this needle action changed the shape. By squeezing the wool together and then needling, the shape can be narrowed or changed in a variety of ways.

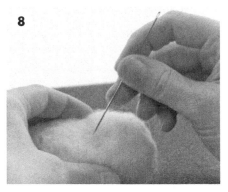

**8** To erase the previously made indentation, take a darning needle and scratch lightly across the surface of the crater.

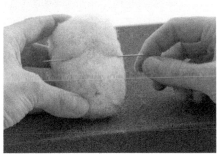

**9** Push the darning needle from one side of the crater and poke the end out on the opposite side.

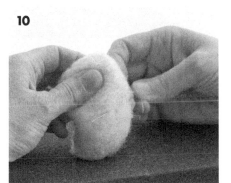

**10** Hold the wool shape in one hand and pull the wool held by the darning needle out and away from the shape to stretch it back out.

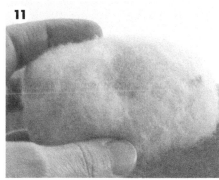

**11** Take the darning needle out to see the result.

**12** If the crater is still present, put the darning needle back in the wool again at a different angle and repeat step 10. Needle the shape to hold the wool in its new position.

## Technique

Erasing works best with wool that is not completely firm from needling.

## Attaching Techniques

There are a variety of ways to attach different needle-felted parts together, including leaving loose fibers on the part to be attached, deep needling, and wrapping core parts in a thin layer of wool to cover and attach the pieces at the same time. Attaching parts by leaving loose fibers was described in the blending section (page 154). The first method described here is deep needling followed by the wrapping method.

### Deep Needling

**1**

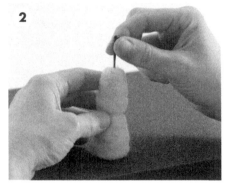

**1** Use two ovoid wool shapes and a 32- to 36-gauge felting needle. Place one ovoid shape on top of the other on the needle-felting pad.

**2**

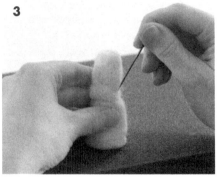

**2** Be aware of where your fingers are at all times to avoid poking yourself. Poke the needle down from the middle of the top ovoid shape into the lower shape. Jiggle the needle gently up and down while still in the wool. Do not change the angle of the needle.

**3**

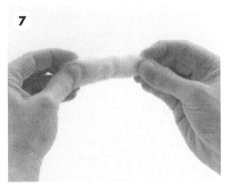

**3** Pull the needle all the way out and poke from the top shape down to the bottom one at a different angle. Jiggle the needle up and down in the wool.

**5**

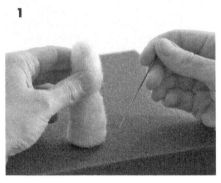

**4** Keep performing this deep needling technique from many different angles from the top down.

**5** Turn the two pieces upside down so the lower shape is now on the top.

**6**

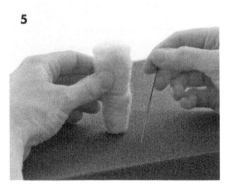

**6** Perform deep needling from many different angles from the new top shape to the bottom one.

**7**

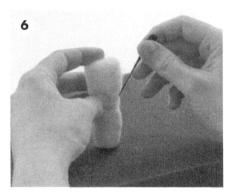

**7** Continue deep needling techniques until the two shapes hold together and will not pull apart.

## Wrapping

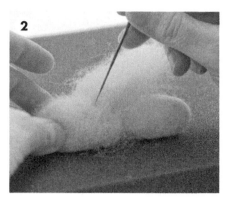

**1** Use two ovoid wool shapes and a 36- to 38-gauge felting needle. Use sheets of colored batting to wrap and cover the two shapes. Place both shapes on the felting pad.

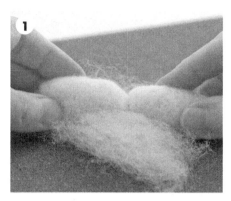

**2** Tack one end of a 2" to 3" x 6" (5 to 8 cm x 15 cm) wide strip of batting on the back side of one of the shapes by needling straight in and out through the batting into the ovoid shape.

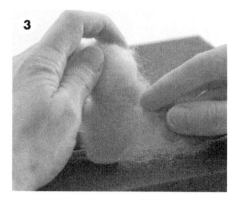

**3** With the end of the second ovoid shape pressed up against the end of the first one, wrap the batting around to the left and then to the front of both shapes.

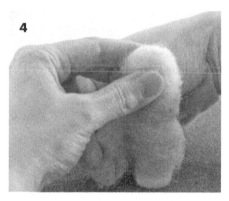

**4** Bring the end of the batting around toward the back of the second shape, making a figure-eight type of motion.

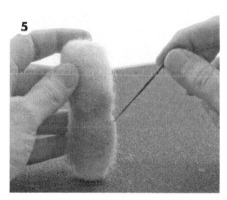

**5** Hold the batting in place as tightly as possible and needle in and out over both shapes, tacking the batting down.

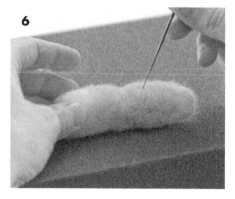

**6** Keep turning the two connected pieces on the felting pad, needling the batting completely onto the ovoid forms.

(continued)

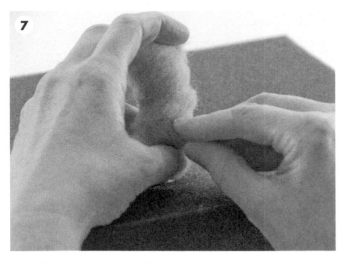

**7** Take a second piece of batting of similar size and repeat steps 3 and 4 but wrap from the back to the right side, then to the front and down around to the back of the lower ovoid.

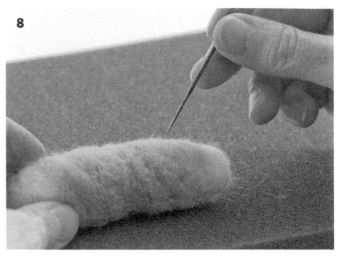

**8** Tack down the batting and then needle over the entire surface.

**9** The join between these two pieces will be bendable like a joint.

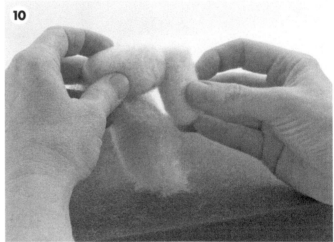

**10** If the joint needs to be in a bent position when the figure is complete, perform the entire process above with the two ovoid shapes at right angles to each other.

## Catching Stray Fibers

Needle-felted creations tend to be hairy with stray fiber ends sticking out. Several methods work to tame these stray fuzzies, but most creations will still have a few stray pieces present. The breed of wool used will also make a difference in the resultant surface after needle felting. Some needle felters finish their creations to a very firm surface, and others prefer a softer finish. A firmer surface tends to have fewer stray fibers. Some methods of taming fuzzies include felting with the needle nearly parallel to the wool surface, the use of wet-felting techniques, and using scissors or a razor to cut or shave stray fibers. For all these techniques, use a small ovoid or round shape that has been covered with colored wool and needled in. Use a 40- to 42-gauge felting needle and the felting pad. Each of the above methods is outlined below.

## Firm Surface

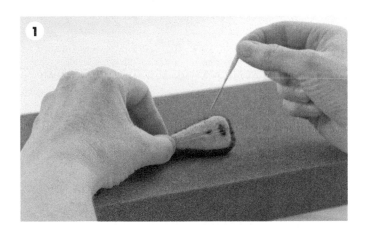

**1** To make a firm surface, needle over the entire surface, turning the shape on the felting pad as you needle.

**2** Continue to needle the shape until the surface becomes firm and the stray fibers have been poked into the surface.

**3** Be very careful, when making the surface firm, to keep the needle going in and out at the same angle. The more firm the wool, the more likely that the tip of the needle will snap off if lateral pressure is applied.

## Parallel Angle

1 Hold the felting needle almost parallel to the wool surface. Poke the needle in and out maintaining the acute angle. This is a surface motion and should penetrate only the very top layer of the wool.

2 Rotate the shape to needle over the entire surface in this manner.

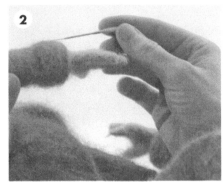

## Wet Felting

1 To tame fuzzies with wet felting, use your finger to wet felt the surface. The shape should be completely needled before beginning the wet-felting technique.

2 With a bowl of warm water close by, dip your fingers in the water and rub over the surface of the wool shape.

3 Keep dipping your fingers in the water and rubbing over the surface of the wool.

4 Continue this process until the loose ends have been felted into the surface.

5 Let the shape dry thoroughly.

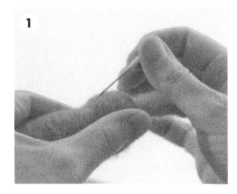

## Cutting

1 To cut the stray fibers, use a pair of manicure or embroidery scissors to trim the hairs from the shape.

2 Use a razor to shave over the surface of the shape and cut any stray fiber ends.

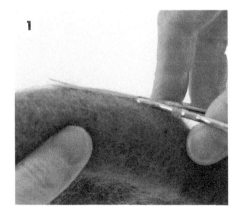
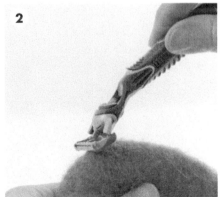

## Three-Dimensional Figures

An individual felting needle is an amazing piece of equipment when used to make three-dimensional figures. This small tool can sculpt wool into any shape with ease. By combining shaped wool pieces with the felting needle, an infinite number of possibilities can be the result. Take the information from the basic instructions found here, experiment, and make lots of figures, and you will find your own style.

Needle-felted fairies, Dandelion by Paula Rindal and Lichen by Cathy Martin, core wool, Norwegian C1, Merino, Angelina fibers, wool locks, and wired wings.

## Core Shapes

Core shapes are the building blocks of the figure being made. Core shapes are generally made from natural-colored wool that is less expensive than dyed batts or roving. Use down breeds, such as Dorset or Suffolk or other less expensive wool, as core wool. If a human figure is being made, the core shapes needed would be a body, head, upper arms, forearms, thighs, and calves. A simple shape to use for all of these is the ovoid, or egg shape, in a variety of sizes.

When making core shapes, it is important to squeeze as much air out of the wool as possible before needling. Roll the shape tightly and then needle in the ends so the wool won't spring back to its original shape. The more air removed at this stage, the less needling is needed later to form the figure. For better definition, start sculpting the core shapes early on in the process to form

(continued)

any craters, ridges, or indentations needed. Make the shapes as close to the finished shape. If you want a figure with a large belly and spindly legs, make the body shape rounder and the leg parts thin.

The surface of the core shapes will be covered completely with dyed wool, so the core should not be needled to a firm consistency. The shape needs to be soft so that more wool can easily be needled in. Don't worry about stray fibers on the core as these will all soon be covered. Several shapes are shown here to get you started. Try these and then branch out and try some shapes of your own.

## YOU WILL NEED

- 1 oz. (28 g) core wool batt
- needle-felting tools

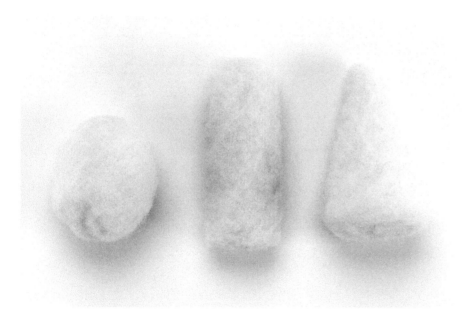

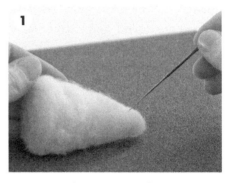

**1** An ovoid can be used for many core pieces such as a body, a head, and even arms and legs. Different sizes can be created by using smaller or larger amounts of wool. See the directions in the basic techniques section (page 150) to make an ovoid shape. An ovoid can also easily be reshaped into a cone by narrowing one end and flattening the other.

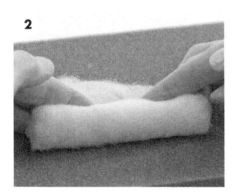

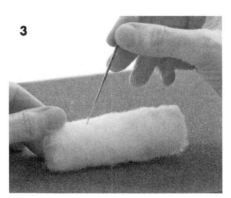

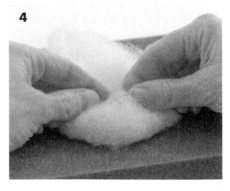

**2** To make a cylindrical shape, place 1 or 2 pieces of core wool batting on the felting pad. Fold in two edges and then roll into a cylinder.

**3** Needle the loose ends of the wool to hold the cylinder together. Keep turning the cylindrical shape on the felting pad as you needle.

**4** To make a sphere, place one sheet of core wool batting on the felting pad. Fold the front corners in diagonally.

**5**

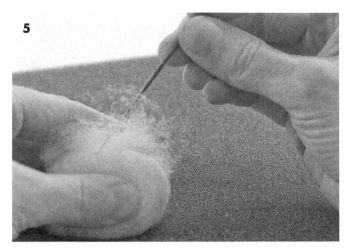

**5** Roll the folded wool up and keep folding the edges in to form a sphere of wool. Needle the ends to hold the shape together. Roll the ball in your hands as if making a ball of clay.

**6**

**6** Needle over the entire surface of the sphere to make it rounder.

## Using an Armature

An armature is a framework of wire that serves to support the wool in a needle-felted sculpture by providing sturdiness to the finished pieces and allowing for bendable appendages. An armature is not always necessary, and some needle felters use them while others don't. Try making a figure with an armature and one made with core shapes and determine which method works best for the specific project.

Armatures can be made into any shape by twisting wire pieces together. Use 20- to 22-gauge wire. Pipe cleaners will work but have a tendency to break if bent too often. Always bend the tips of the wire in a circle back on to itself. This will prevent the tips from poking through the wool. The wire can be covered with floral tape, which helps the first layer of wool to adhere to the wire.

Once the armature has been formed for the sculpture, it is wrapped with core wool. Wrap small amounts of wool around the wire, pull the wool tight, and carefully needle the wool together. Care must be taken to avoid hitting the wire underneath as it may cause needle breakage. Needle gently and avoid jabbing the needle in deeply.

Giraffe, needle felted over armature and core wool, mixed 56's wool, baby doll brown batting, Merino

## YOU WILL NEED

- four pieces 20- to 22-gauge wire 6" to 8" (15 to 20 cm) long

- wire cutters

- needle-nose pliers

- ½ oz. (14 g) of core wool

- needle-felting tools

- florist tape (optional)

Gradually build up layers of wool around the armature to make the core shape into the form required for the chosen figure. The core shape will then be covered with dyed wool for the skin and other details. Always avoid deep needling into the areas of the armature. The example shown here is making a basic animal body. The armature can be made in different sizes and shapes depending on what animal you choose to make.

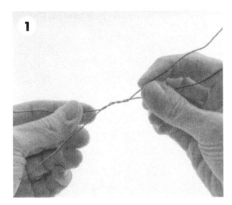

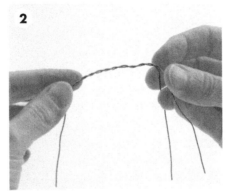

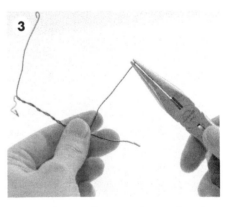

**1** Take two pieces of wire and twist together in the middle. The length of the twist will be the length of the body, and the remaining wire will form the legs.

**2** Bend all four ends of the wire down to form legs.

**3** Use the needle-nose pliers to bend the wire back on itself and make a small circle at the end of each leg.

**4**

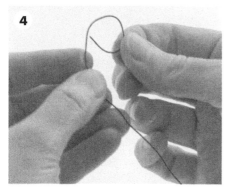

**4** Take another piece of wire and make a larger circle at one end for the head. This will not be the finished size of the head, as more wool will be added in later stages.

**5**

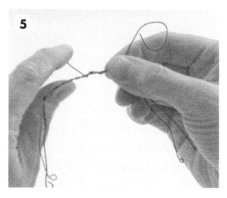

**5** Use the tail end of the wire from step 4 and wrap it onto the body framework previously made. The length of wire left between the head and the body will be the neck. Estimate the length of the neck by the physique of the animal chosen. A giraffe will have a much longer neck than a pig.

**6**

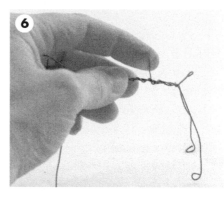

**6** Use the last piece of wire to make a tail. Again, the length will be determined by the animal chosen. Twist the wire around the body wire to attach the tail. Use the needle-nose pliers to bend the end of the tail back onto itself to make a small circle.

**7**

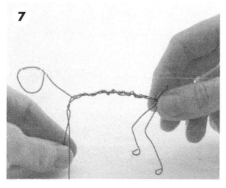

**7** Shape the armature as needed with your hands to resemble the form of the animal chosen. Wrap the armature in florist tape if desired.

**8**

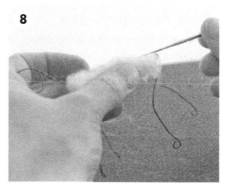

**8** Take a small piece of wool and wrap it around the body wire. Gently needle the ends of the wool to the wool wrapped beneath it. Needle the wool at an angle to avoid hitting the wire.

**9**

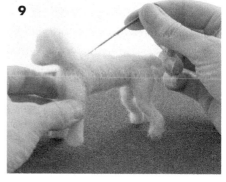

**9** Keep wrapping the wool around the entire armature until it is the appropriate size for the animal chosen. Remember that more outer wool will be added for the skin and details.

**10**

**10** Shape the wool as you proceed. If thin legs are needed, wrap with only small amounts of wool. For thicker sections, use more wool. It helps to have photos for reference.

**11** Once the armature is covered, needle gently over the entire surface to make sure all the wool is well attached.

### Covering the Core

Once the basic shape or shapes have been made, dyed wool needs to be added over the surface to cover the core wool. The colors chosen will depend on what is being made, but the process of covering the wool is the same. Batting works best to cover the wool since the fibers don't all run in the same direction. Therefore, a smoother surface is the result. Roving wrapped all in the same direction will show the lines of the fiber in the finished surface. If roving is all that is available, pull small pieces off the roving and mix them together in your hands to get the fibers running in different directions. Then apply this handmade batt over the surface and needle down.

When covering a figure made with an armature, remember not to needle deeply to avoid hitting the wire underneath. Use small pieces of batt and cover areas of the core wool. Needle in the center of the covering batt, working outward and blending in the edges as described in the needle-felting basics section (page 150). If a straight line of color butts up against another color, needle along the meeting line and fold any excess fibers back over into the same color and needle down.

As the outer wool is applied and needled in, the wool will continue to shrink and become denser. The shape of the figure should be continually sculpted as it is needled. Use the techniques from the basics section (page 150) to shape as desired. Avoid needling the figure firmly at this point, or it will be difficult to add further details. To cover core shapes made without an armature, it is generally better to cover and connect the parts at the same time. This method is described and shown in the basics section (page 150) and the connecting parts sections (pages 158 and 176).

### Adding Small Shapes

Once the core wool is covered, further small shapes made out of outer wool can be added to make ears, facial features, and hands and feet with fingers and toes, etc. The easiest method to apply small shapes is the blending method. Remember to leave loose fibers on a portion of the small wool shape so that it can easily be attached to the figure. A variety of shapes are shown here. One shape, such as a folded flap, could be used for a variety of parts such as eyelids or upper and lower lips depending on how the piece is applied and sculpted. Many other shapes are possible so keep experimenting and developing other shapes as you need them.

## YOU WILL NEED

- outer wool
- needle-felting tools

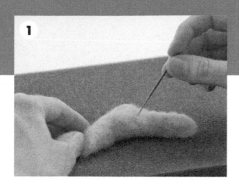

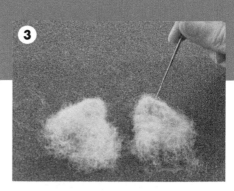

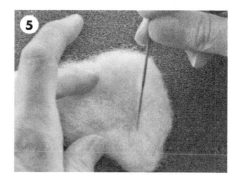

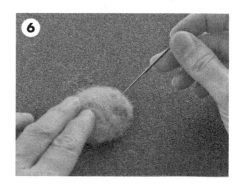

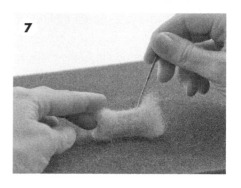

**1** To make a crescent roll shape that could be used to make a chin or an ear that lies low to an animal's head, use a triangle of outer wool batting. The size will be determined by the size of the figure. Roll up the triangle from the long end and then needle the point down. Turn the crescent roll shape on the pad to needle all over the center. Leave the ends loose for applying to the core figure.

**2** To make a smaller crescent shape to use as a lip, roll a small triangle of wool around a stick or skewer. Roll the wool-covered stick between your hands and then needle gently all over the surface of the rolled wool. Pull the wool off the stick and then attach the crescent shape as needed.

**3** To make a triangle that could be used for an animal's ear or for a dragon's scales, place a piece of outer wool batting on the felting pad. Outline the top portion of a triangle shape and make a flat shape as explained in the basic technique section (page 156). Leave the bottom ends loose for attachment.

**4** Make a folded flap for features such as eyelids, lips, or a kangaroo pouch. Place a rectangle of wool on the felting pad and fold it over a popsicle stick or skewer and needle the two sides of wool together. Needle the wool carefully along the edge of the stick but leave the fibers at the far edge from the stick loose for attachment. Remove the stick; needle and shape in the same manner as making a flat shape.

**5** To make a rolled-edge shape that could be used for a human ear or a brow or to emphasize an animal's eye socket, place a piece of outer wool on the felting pad. Roll up one edge of the rectangle and leave an edge of loose fibers. Needle the edge of the roll to hold it in place. Shape the rolled edge as needed but leave the loose fibers for attachment.

**6** Round pad shapes can be used for cheeks, bellies, or buttocks. Roll up a piece of outer wool into a ball and needle to hold together. Then flatten the shape against the felting pad and needle down to a disk shape. To attach these shapes, cover with outer wool and blend the edges in.

**7** A cylindrical shape with loose fibers on each end can be attached and shaped into a neck. A cylinder with one end of loose fibers could form a trunk. Roll up a sheet of outer wool and needle the edge down to the cylinder. Leave either both or one end of the fibers loose for attachment. Turn the cylinder on the felting pad and needle evenly to form a smooth surface.

A horizontal line is drawn halfway between the top of the head and the chin; this is the eye line. A vertical line splits the ovoid shape into two equal right and left halves. This line is the center of the nose. A line is drawn halfway between the eye line and the bottom of the chin. This line marks the bottom of the nose. Another line halfway between the bottom of the nose and the bottom of the chin is to assist in locating the mouth. The mouth sits slightly above this line. The mouth is closer to the bottom of the nose than it is to the bottom of the chin.

## Making a Face

To make a needle-felted face, small pieces of outer wool are added to the head and blended in with blending techniques. It helps to look carefully at the structure and proportions of the human face before beginning. This will provide you with guidelines of where each feature should be positioned and will result in a more realistic-looking face.

Many needle felters find that making faces is the most enjoyable part of making a figure, as different expressions can be developed with each new face. Faces can be needle felted to look like a certain person, but it is easier to make a face without preconceived ideas of how it should turn out. Start with a basic ovoid shape for the head and add each feature with blending and sculpting techniques. Let the face develop as you work and a little wool person with his or her own personality will grow before your eyes.

Human adult faces have certain proportions and features that are all alike. There are differences between males and females as well as changes that come with aging. The most important features to place correctly on the head are the eyes, nose, and mouth. Once those features are positioned appropriately, other features such as ears, cheeks, chins, brow bones, and eyebrows will follow easily.

The head is generally ovoid or egg shaped. The top of the head is normally bigger and narrows as it moves toward the chin. Look at the illustration of face proportions.

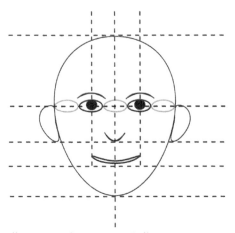

Illustration by Nanci Williams

To determine eye width, the width of the head is split into five equal sections. There is one eye width between the eyes and one eye width on either side of each eye to the side of the head. Therefore, the head should be approximately five eye-widths across. The width of the mouth is determined by a line drawn vertically down from the center of the eyes. Once the eyes, nose, and mouth have been placed, it is easier to place the ears, which start just above the eye line and end just at the bottom of the nose. The brow bone, cheekbones, and eyebrows can be placed depending on the sex and the age of the figure.

There are certain characteristic differences between the male and female facial features. Not everyone has all of these characteristics, but a predominance of male or female characteristics will determine whether a face looks male or female. When sculpting these facial features in wool remember these contrasting features to develop a male or female character.

Female faces tend to be rounder with fuller cheeks, have a more rounded forehead, a rounded or more pointed chin, with a tendency towards a heart-shaped face. The noses of females tend to be smaller with a thinner bridge. A female's eyes appear larger and the cheekbones are higher with the eyebrows sitting higher above the eyes. The jawbone of the female slopes gradually up from the chin to her ear.

Male faces tend to be a more square shape with flatter cheekbones and more pronounced brow bone over the eyes. Males usually have a squarer chin and jaw line. The jaw tends to drop straight down from the ear and then turns at an angle toward the chin. Males tend to have larger, more prominent noses, and there is a greater distance from the tip of the nose to the top of the upper lip. Males are also more likely to have a prominent Adam's apple.

The other differences noted in the facial features occur with aging. Due to the effects of gravity and the aging process, many features begin to sag, including the cheeks, which can form jowls; the corners of the mouth, which may turn down; the ears, which may elongate; and the area surrounding the eyes including the eyelids, which may sag. The skin of the face and forehead sag and develop wrinkles, causing the eyebrows to drop and flatten. Aging can cause the tip of the nose to enlarge, becoming bulbous as well as the entire nose becoming longer. Often the nose may develop a bump along the bridge as well. Consider these changes and perhaps exaggerate them to make a needle-felted character look older.

To sculpt the face of a baby or a young child, several features have different appearances than an adult face and must be considered. Babies' heads are large in proportion to their facial features. The forehead is larger, making the features lower on the head and closer together. A baby's eyes are bigger with short, flat eyebrows. The face tends to be rounder with plumper cheeks than an adult's face. A baby's nose tends to be small and short and have a turned-up end.

Study the features of different faces to find inspiration for the next wool face to sculpt. Exaggerate certain features as is done when drawing caricatures. Experiment sculpting different facial expressions and try to show different emotions in wool.

(continued)

The nose is the first feature to put on the sculpted wool face. It starts just below the eye line and ends halfway between the eye line and the chin. Noses come in all shapes and sizes, and the amount of wool used will determine the size of the nose. If the nose is too small or too large, don't worry; the size can be changed. Remember that the wool will shrink when needled down so start with a shape that is 40%–50% bigger than the final size.

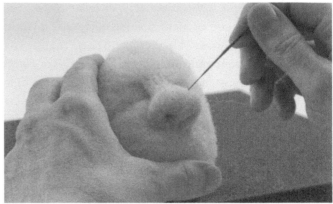

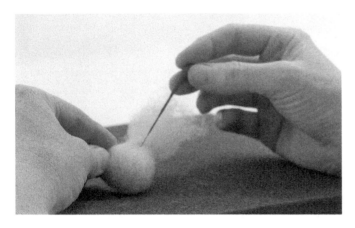

To make a nose, use a sheet of batting and roll up one end to make the larger tip of the nose. Leave the upper fibers loose at the top of the nose. Needle and shape the nose as desired. Before attaching the nose to the face, needle an eye line horizontally halfway between the top of the head and the chin. Attach the nose so the bridge begins on the eye line and the end of the nose is halfway between the eye line and the chin. Sculpt the nose to develop its shape and create craters for nostrils.

Our eyes are one of our most expressive features. Eyes will add life to the face being needle felted. Take a close look at your own eyes. Notice that the upper and lower eyelids are shaped differently. The upper eyelid covers the top of the iris and slightly overlaps the lower eyelid. The iris is not one solid color but tends to be lighter toward the center and darkens around the edges. The pupil is dark, and there is a reflection or glint in the eye. The upper eyelid casts a thin shadow along the top of the eyeball. Remember the facial proportions discussed earlier. The width of the face is equal to five evenly spaced eye-widths, with one eye-width between the eyes and one on each side of the eyes to the side of the head. To sculpt a more realistic eye, all of these factors should be taken into consideration.

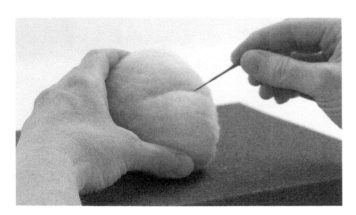

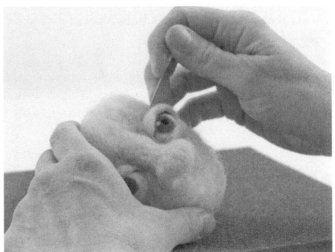

Needle the eye sockets on either side of the bridge of the nose. Use a sphere of white wool for the eyeball. Place the eyeballs in the middle of the eye sockets and needle carefully around the edge of the eyeballs to attach. Avoid needling in the center of the eyeballs. Make two small disks for the iris of the eye and needle carefully around the edge of the iris to attach to the eyeball. Roll up two tiny bits of dark brown or black wool into balls for the pupils. Place the pupils in the center of the iris and gently needle in place. Avoid deep needling as the pupil could be pushed too deeply into the wool. Add the glint in the eye with white wool in the same manner.

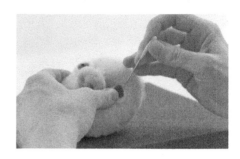

For the lower eyelids, use two small folded flaps. Place the lower eyelids to slightly overlap the bottom of the eyeball. The upper eyelids are made in the same manner as the lower eyelids, but the upper eyelids should be slightly thicker and wider than the lower eyelids. The upper eyelids overlap the eyeball and the top of the iris. The ends of the upper eyelid should overlap the ends of the bottom eyelid.

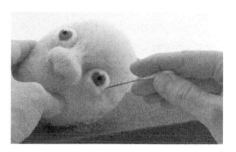

To add depth to the eye, use black or dark brown preyarn just under the edge of the upper eyelid to form a shadow on the eyeball. A very thin piece of roving can be substituted for the preyarn. Place the thin strip of wool just under the edge of the upper eyelid and needle into place.

The mouth is sculpted in two main pieces, the upper lip and the lower lip. The chin may need to be built up underneath the lower lip as the mouth is put together. The mouth should be placed slightly above the halfway mark between the bottom of the nose and the bottom of the chin. On the human face, the bottom lip is usually bigger than the top; it has more flesh and pouts outward. The upper lip tends to be thinner; it slopes inward and has the characteristic shape of a bow.

To form the upper lip, make a folded flap with loose fibers at the top edge to connect to the face.

Place the upper lip on the face below the nose, with the loose fibers flared out on both sides of the nose. Attach the lip in place over the upper edge just below the nose. Leave the outer and bottom edges of the upper lip free to allow the lower lip to be attached.

(continued)

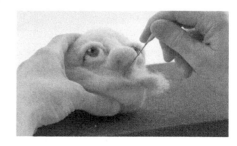

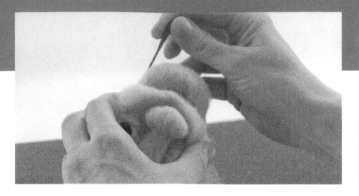 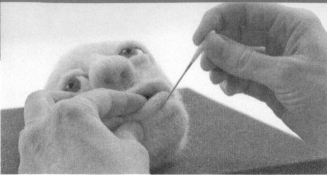

To form the chin, use a crescent roll shape. Fold the upper lip up out of the way and make a U shape with the rolled crescent shape. Place the U shape on the bottom end of the head below the lip area to form a chin and attach it by blending and shaping.

Form the lower lip with another folded flap shape. Place it on the face with the side edges underneath the upper lip and the loose ends running down over the chin. Attach by blending and shaping with the felting needle. Sculpt the expression of the mouth as it is attached. Needle the edges of the lower lip upward for a smile or more downward for a frown. The mouth can be shaped so it is more open or closed.

Once the lower lip is attached, pull the upper lip back down and needle the edges of the upper lip over the top of the lower lip edges. Add a small amount of dark brown wool into the mouth to give depth. Use a small crescent shape to enhance the lower and upper lip shapes. Needle it carefully along the edges to attach it to the base lip. The crescent shapes should be a slightly darker skin tone.

Adding the rest of the facial features will complete the face and give it an age and/or a gender. Not all of these features need to be added, use your discretion as to what the face needs. Consider whether the figure needs ears or whether it will be completely covered with hair, whether the cheeks and cheekbones need to be enhanced, if the addition of a stronger brow bone is needed, whether any wrinkles are needed, and what sculpting needs to be done to reinforce the facial expression.

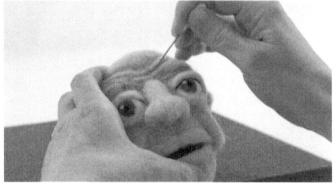

To form cheeks, use two small pad shapes. Place the cheeks where desired. Remember that higher, plumper cheek bones are a female trait; lower, sagging cheeks denote the jowls of an older face. Use outer wool over the cheek pads to blend them to the face

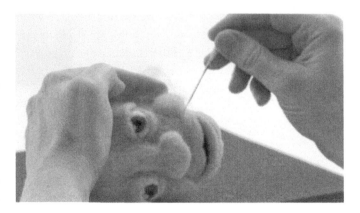

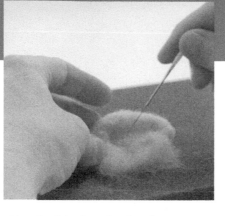

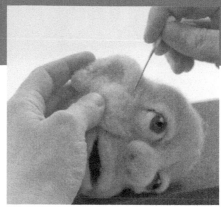

To make ears, use a small rolled edge shape. Sculpt the ears by needling the places that need to be smaller such as the earlobe. The top of the ear should begin at or just above the eye line and end just below the end of the nose. Place the ear on the side of the head about midway between the front and back of the head. After the ears are attached, needle deeply to form a crater in the area of the ear canal. Add a small amount of dark brown wool in the ear canal and needle into place.

For a heavier brow bone, which is a masculine trait, use a loose roll of wool and blend it in with small pieces of outer wool. To add eyebrows, use very small bits of hair-colored wool. Women's eyebrows tend to be higher than men's. Sagging and flattened eyebrows are a sign of age. To indicate wrinkles, use a very thin, long snake of outer wool covered and blended in with more outer wool. Needle into the indentations between the wrinkles and sculpt as needed.

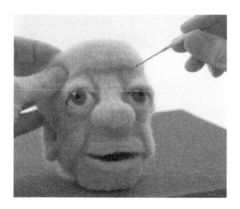

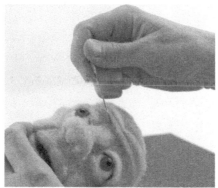

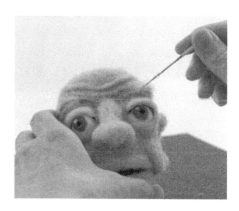

Sit back and take a good look at the face you have sculpted. What else does it need? Add wool to areas that appear too concave. Needle more deeply in areas that need to be more concave.

Do you want to make the entire face thinner? Place the head on the felting pad and push down to narrow the head. Poke the felting needle deeply up and down the side of the head. Does the head seem too long? Place the head chin down on the felting pad and push down on the top of the head. Perform deep needling techniques from the top of the head down. Does the nose stick out far enough from the face? Use the darning needle and push it through the lower end horizontally where the nose attaches to the face. Holding both ends of the darning needle, pull it away from the head, stretching the nose out more. The face can be shaped in this manner into almost any expression. Keep shaping until you are pleased with the face.

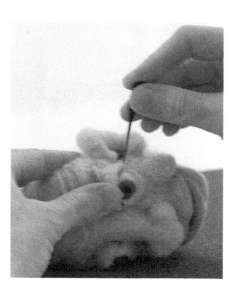

## Connecting Parts

As discussed in the basics section, there are several different ways to connect parts together on a needle-felted figure with a felting needle. Three methods will be shown here, including the wrapping method where the outer wool is used to connect the parts, the blending technique where loose fibers are left for attachment, and string jointing. String jointing is a doll-making technique usually used when making cloth dolls or teddy bears.

## Wrapping

The wrapping technique will show a hip joint of a human figure. Determine the position the figure needs to be in when completed. The parts need to be connected differently if the figure is to sit or stand when finished. An entire figure can be put together with this method. Work consistently by attaching the legs and then the arms and follow with the neck and head. The neck shape can be made as a small cylinder with fibers left free at both ends. Hands and feet should be added after the rest of the body has been connected. Add additional small parts such as small pads for buttocks or breasts as you work to sculpt the shape of the figure.

## Blending

## Technique

Decide whether the character is to be sitting or standing when completed, and attach the two parts in a bent position if it will be sitting and a straight position if it will be standing.

**1** Connect one set of the upper and lower leg core parts with wrapping techniques as described in Connecting Parts.

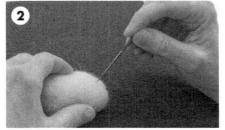

**2** Place the body shape on the felting pad. Needle one end of the ovoid shape to make it narrower than the other end.

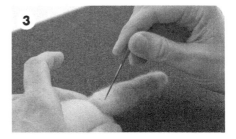

**3** With the skinny end of the body downward, place one of the legs on either side of the lower body. Perform deep needling techniques to tack the leg onto the body.

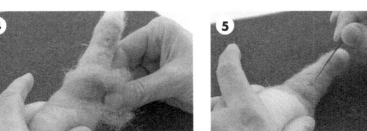

**4** Tack a strip of wool to the back of the body and wrap around the hip area covering the top of the leg.

**5** Needle the outer wool in completely.

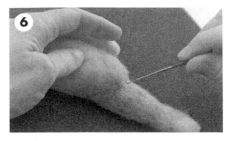

**6** Continue wrapping the hip area with wool and needling it in until the leg is completely joined with the body.

The blending technique works well for adding small parts such as ears, tails, horns, or antlers. For this technique to work, loose fibers need to be left on the smaller parts so that they can be attached to the main body. If the small part, such as an ear, is the same color as the body, the blending technique works well. If a small part is a different color use the deep needling method to attach the part.

## YOU WILL NEED

- small piece of outer wool
- needle-felting tools

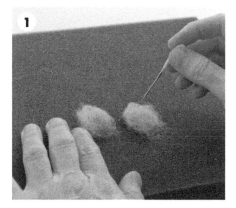

**1** Make two triangular small shapes for ears for the animal figure with loose fibers at the bottom.

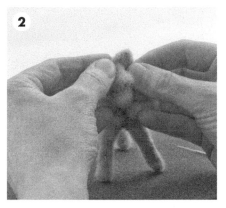

**2** Position the ear on the head with the loose fibers flaring out onto the head. Bend the ear into position to form the desired shape.

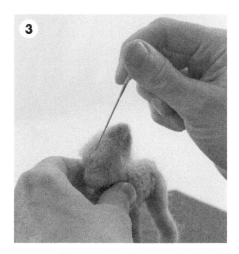

**3** Needle the loose fibers into the head, blending them into the surface.

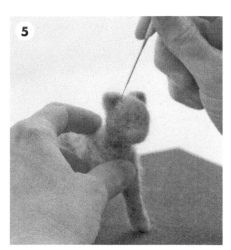

**4** Needle from the ear down into the head with deeper needle pokes.

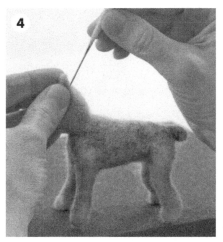

**5** Repeat with the other ear and continue needling over the head and ears until the ears are well connected.

## YOU WILL NEED

- needle-felted parts including a head, body, two arms, and two legs
- large darning needle
- heavy thread or unwaxed dental floss
- scissors

**1** Place the bear parts in easy reach. Thread the needle with the thread or dental floss. The thread should be a little more than double the width plus the length of the bear's body.

### String Jointing

String jointing is a method of connecting parts together with a needle and string. Use a heavy thread such as button thread or dental floss. The parts that are to be connected should be completely finished and covered with outer wool before connecting them together. The sample shown is a simple needle-felted bear.

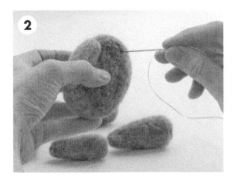

**2** Insert the needle into the right side of the body where the hip joint will be.

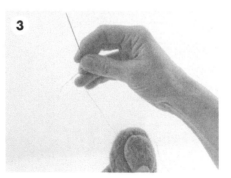

**3** Push the needle straight through the bear to the left hip joint area. Pull the thread through leaving at least a 6" to 8" (15 to 20 cm) tail emerging from the right hip joint.

**4** Take a deep stitch in the top inside of the left leg where the leg should attach at the hip joint.

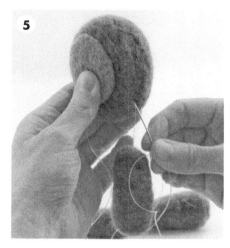

**5** Put the needle back into the same hole in the left hip joint on the body.

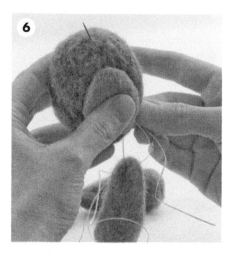

**6** Push the needle up through the bear's body exiting at the neck where the head will join.

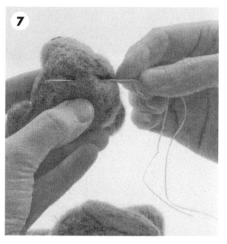

**7** Take a deep stitch in the bottom of the bear's head. This is where it will attach to the body.

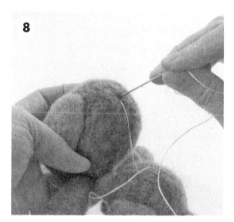

**8** Put the needle back into the same hole where it exited the body at the neck joint.

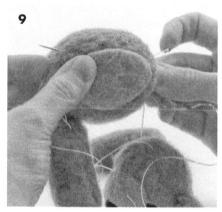

**9** Push the needle down through the bear's body to the right hip joint.

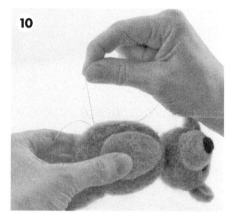

**10** Push the needle out where the thread first entered the hip joint.

(continued)

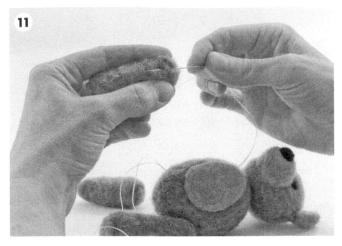

**11** Take a deep stitch in the top inside of the right leg where the leg will attach.

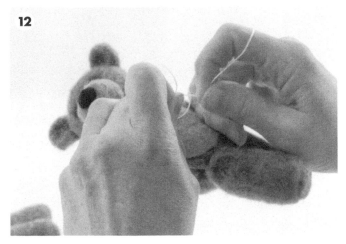

**12** Remove the needle and pull the two ends of thread very tightly.

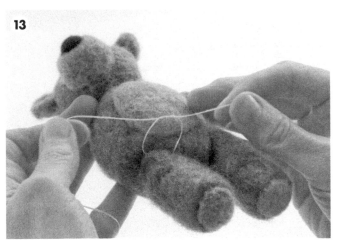

**13** Tie a square knot keeping the threads pulled very tightly. Tie a second square knot.

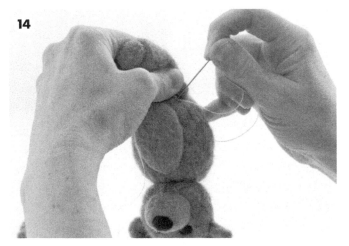

**14** Rethread one loose end of the thread; push the needle back into the bear's body at the hip joint.

**15** Push the needle out the other side of the body.

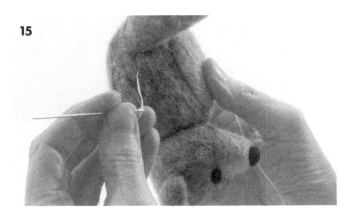

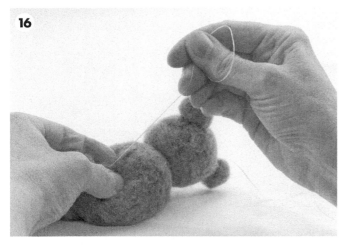

**16** Pull the thread tightly, pushing in the bear's body with your fingers as the thread is pulled with the other hand.

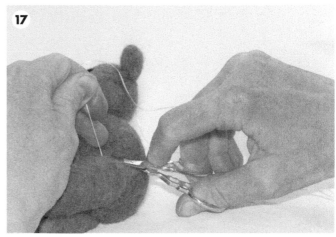

**17** Cut off the end of the thread as close to the bear's body as possible.

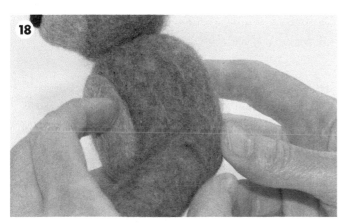

**18** The thread should be pulled back inside the bear's body to hide it.

**19** Repeat steps 14–18 for the other loose thread end.

**20** To attach the arms, rethread the needle with another piece of thread two times the width of the body plus 6" (15 cm).

**21** Insert the needle at the left shoulder joint.

**22** Push the needle through the body to exit at the right shoulder joint. Leave a 6" to 8" tail (15 to 20 cm) on the left side.

(continued)

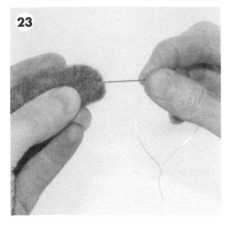

**23** Take a deep stitch on the inside of the right upper arm where the arm will attach at the shoulder.

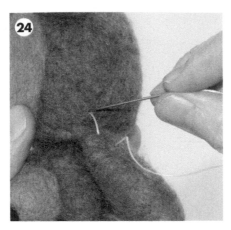

**24** Insert the needle back into the right side of the body in the same hole where it came out at the shoulder.

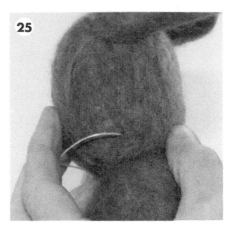

**25** Push the needle back through to the left side exiting the body where the thread first entered the left shoulder joint.

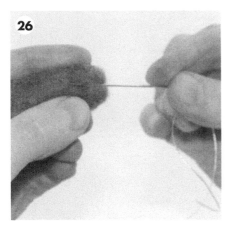

**26** Take a deep stitch in the inside top of the left arm to form the left shoulder joint.

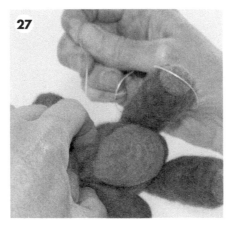

**27** Remove the needle and pull the threads tightly. Tie two square knots.

**28** Hide the thread ends in the body in the same manner as with the legs.

**29** Pose the bear as desired.

## Adding Details

To finish a needle-felted figure, hands, feet, hooves or claws, fur or hair, and any other details need to be added at this point. These details can be as simple or as elaborate as you want to make them. Other items can be added such as wings made from Angelina fiber, glasses, a walking stick, or even a musical instrument. For your first figure it might be best to keep it simple. As your skills improve, your needle-felted figures can become as elaborate as

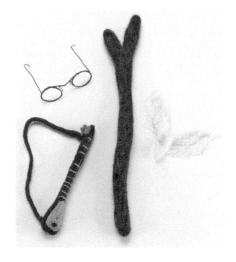

you wish. The materials needed are listed below for making hands and feet, applying hair or fur, and shading.

Making hands and feet for a needle-felted figure are similar processes. The shapes are a bit different for a hand as compared to a foot, but toes and fingers are made and attached by the same method. Put your hand up to your face to gauge its size as compared to your head. Exaggerating the size of the hands and feet often gives the character a cartoon quality.

## YOU WILL NEED

- needle-felted figure
- outer wool
- embellishing fibers such as curly locks for hair or animal fur
- small pieces of colored wool for shading
- needle-felting tools including popsicle stick or skewer

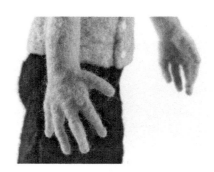

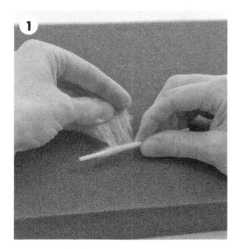

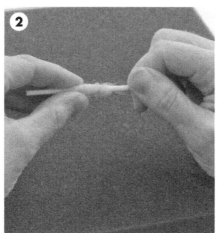

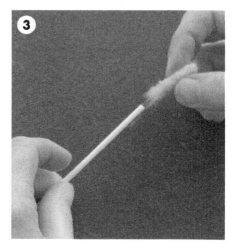

**1** To make fingers and toes, take a very small piece of outer wool. Wrap the wool around a stick or skewer. The amount of wool used will determine the length and thickness of the digit made.

**2** Roll the stick and wool between your fingers and hands to begin felting the wool together and needle along the wool lightly.

**3** Once the wool holds together on the stick, pull it off gently.

(continued)

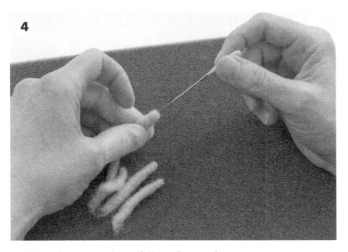

**4** Needle one end carefully to form a finger or toe. Leave loose fibers on the other end. Needle the finger until it is firm. Make as many fingers and toes as needed.

## Technique

It helps to make both hands simultaneously so they end up the same size and shape.

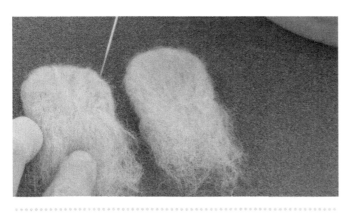

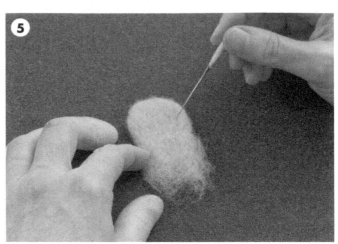

**5** Make a small paddle shape for the hand with loose fibers at the wrist area.

**6** To attach the fingers, use the blending technique to attach the loose fibers to the hand shape. Perform deep needling between the finger and the hand to strengthen the joint.

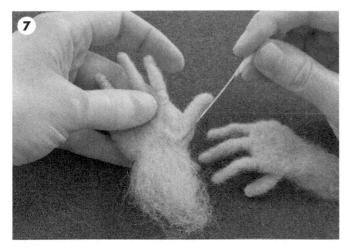

**7** Complete both hands with the blending technique, making sure that the thumb is in the correct position for each hand. Add small pieces of wool to form the pads on the hands and to fill out any fingers that are too thin.

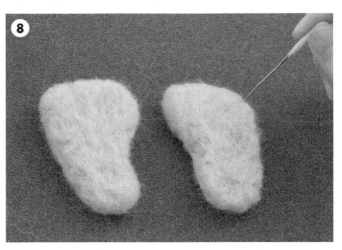

**8** To make a foot shape (think of the mark a wet foot makes on a bath towel), use the outlining method to make two flat foot shapes.

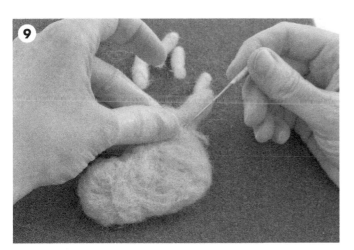

**9** Add toes with the same procedure used for attaching the fingers.

**10** Attach the hands and feet to the rest of the body using blending and wrapping techniques.

## Variation

If shoes will be added to the figure, toes are unnecessary, as they would be covered.

## Attaching Hair

Attaching hair to a figure's head and attaching longer fur for an animal use the same basic method. One end of the lock of wool is needled into the head or the body, and the other end is left free. The amount of hair added is up to you, and the hair can be cut and styled in different manners once it is attached. Hair can also be added as a mustache or a beard in the same way. When covering an animal figure, refer to a photo of the animal to see how the hair or fur grows naturally. Generally, it works best to start from a lower level on the animal's body and work up to the top layer of fur. The examples show the completion of the head made in earlier examples and the process of adding hair to the body of the dog from the Using an Armature section (page 165).

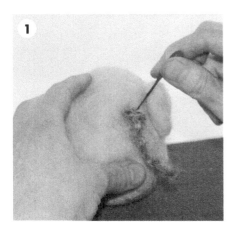

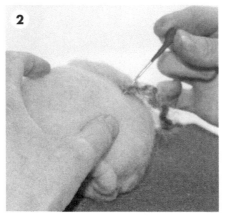

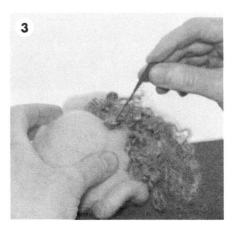

**1** Place the needle felted head on the felting pad. Take one lock of wool for hair and place it on the back of the head near the bottom hairline. Needle the end of the lock in to the head fairly deeply.

**2** Without pulling the needle out, gently twist the needle in the hole just made. Do not apply any lateral pressure to the end of the needle. This twisting motion helps to lock the hair in place.

**3** Continue needling in individual locks of hair over the entire head, working from the neck upward.

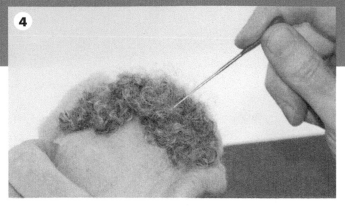

**4** Long curly locks will give a more feminine hairstyle. A curly lock with a shorter staple length works well needled in closely together without leaving loose ends for a shorter, curly style. Merino roving can be used for straighter hair. Any of the wool locks can be trimmed to change the hairstyle as desired.

**5** To cover an animal body with longer fur, use the same method as used with locks of hair. The body should already be covered with a base color of wool.

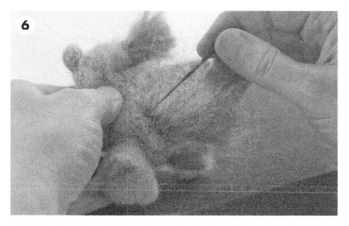

**6** Needle a line of hair along the body of the animal just above the tops of the legs. Trim each row of hair after it is needled in place.

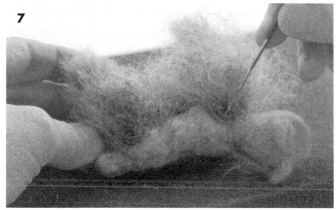

**7** Needle another line of hair along the body of the animal just above the last line.

## Technique

For longer staple wool, fold the wool pieces in half and needle the folded end into the animal's body.

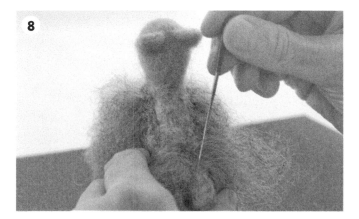

**8** Keep working all the way around both sides of the animal until there is just a small strip uncovered in the spine area. Lay the last locks of wool crosswise over the spine and needle down the center spine line to attach the wool.

## Shading

Shading is similar to painting with wool. Very thin layers of wool can be added and needled in to make cheeks rosy, add makeup to a female face, or add markings on an animal coat. The key to shading is to use very thin layers of wool and build the layers up gradually. The wool colors will blend, and only small amounts of extra color are needed to achieve a slightly shaded effect.

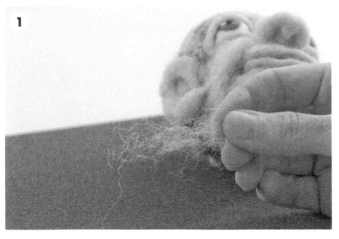

**1** To add color to cheeks, pull off a wisp of wool in the appropriate color.

**2** Pull off an even smaller piece from the wisp and spread it between your fingers to make a small cheek-sized piece of wool.

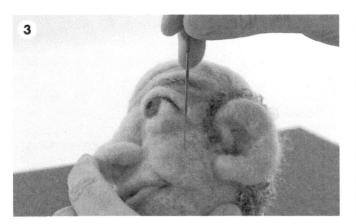

**3** Place it on the face and pat it down. If the shading is satisfactory, needle and blend the fibers into the cheek. If it is too much, pull it back off and try again with less wool.

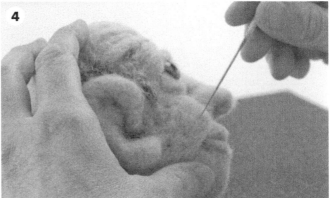

**4** Add the same amount of wool to the other cheek in the same manner.

**5** Add more color to both cheeks if they need to be darker.

**6** Shade any other areas of the face and body as desired.

## Clothing

There are many ways to make clothing for a needle-felted figure. Clothes can be sewn out of fabric just as you would for any type of doll clothing. But don't worry if you can't sew, because clothing can also be wet felted, nuno felted, or needle felted without any sewing required. Wet felting and nuno felting have already been covered and doll clothing can be made as you would in making clothing for yourself, only smaller. The simplest method for clothing needle-felted figures is to use prefelt, both handmade or commercial, and needling it directly to the figure. With this type of method, clothing will not be interchangeable.

When using prefelt for clothing, several layers of commercial prefelt need to be used, as one layer may be too thin for larger figures. If making your own prefelt, use at least two layers of wool to end up with a medium thickness of prefelt. The prefelt can be cut in a variety of shapes or pattern pieces to make the clothing. The shapes do not need to be elaborate as the details of the clothing can be sculpted with the felting needle. Rectangles in different sizes work well for shirts, vests, shorts, or pants. The example here is for a vest, but the same methods can be used for other items of clothing.

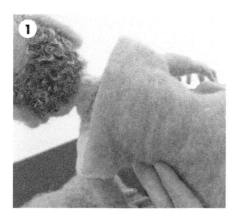

**1** To make a vest, cut one rectangle of prefelt large enough to cover the figure's back plus about 30% extra.

**2** Cut two more rectangles for the front of the vest giving enough room to overlap the edges.

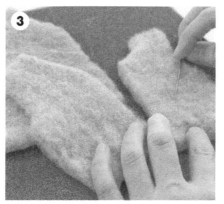

**3** Place all three pieces of prefelt on the felting pad and begin needling gently with a 40- to 42-gauge needle. Begin shaping the arm and neck holes as you needle.

**4** Avoid poking through to the felting pad. Flip the pieces over frequently to needle both sides evenly.

(continued)

## Technique

Use a felted edge or a folded edge of prefelt for any edges of the clothing that will be left free and not needled into the figure. Avoid leaving cut edges free as they are more difficult to needle completely.

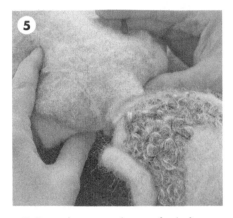

**5** Once the rectangles are fairly firm and shrunk down to the correct size, place the largest rectangle on the back of the figure with the top edge folded over onto the shoulders.

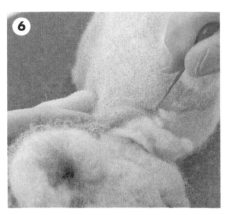

**6** Needle along the top edge of the prefelt into the shoulders to make seams at the top of the vest.

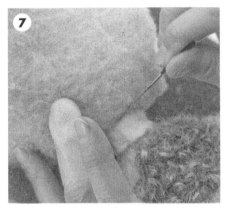

**7** Needle around the neckline, poking the prefelt edge to shrink it away from the neck.

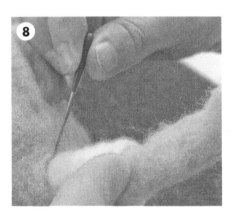

**8** Pull the sides of the rectangle down to the sides of the figure under the arms. Tack it in place along the side seams with the felting needle.

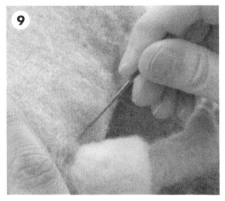

**9** Needle around the edges of the armholes to shrink the prefelt away from the arms. Keep needling the edges until they are the correct sizes around the arms.

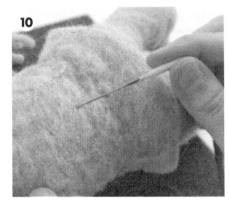

**10** Continue needling and shaping the back of the vest until it is well attached. Leave the bottom edge free.

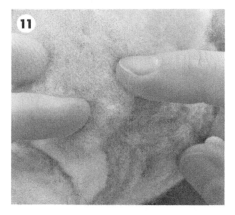

**11** Place one of the smaller rectangles on the right front with the top at the shoulder seam.

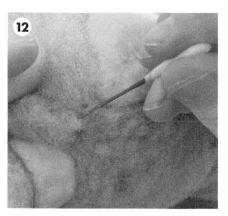

**12** Needle the top edge down into the shoulder seam.

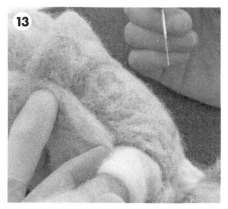

**13** Put the right edge of the rectangle along the side seam and around under the arm.

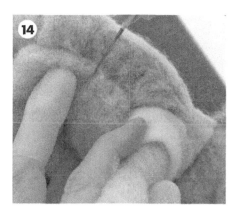

**14** Needle along the side seam to tack it in place.

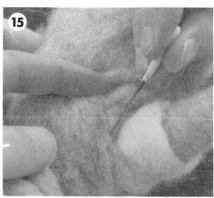

**15** Needle around the edge of the armhole to shrink the prefelt in this area.

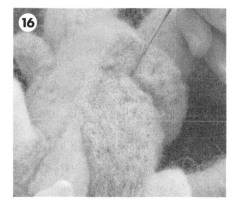

**16** Keep needling over the entire vest front until it is well attached.

**17** Repeat in the same manner for the left vest front.

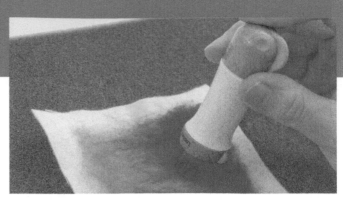

Bottle Study, 24" x 36" (61 cm x 91.5 cm), wool roving, Peace Fleece, wool batting; machine needle felted, machine trapunto using monofilament thread, by Linda Hall

## Two-Dimensional Needle Felting

Two-dimensional needle felting is often referred to as painting with wool. A variety of colors of wool can be used as paint, and the wool is needled on to a base fabric that is the canvas. Any subject can be painted with wool. Portraits, landscapes, still life, and representational or abstract paintings are just a few types of styles or subject matter to consider. Much can be learned from the painting world such as color theory, design basics, and even anatomical drawing. Use your local library to learn more about painting techniques to use in the making of wool paintings.

Multineedle tools are often used when making wool paintings to speed up the process and to cover more surface area than can be accomplished with a single needle. The fabric used for a base for wool paintings is the foundation of a piece, and various fabric options and their pros and cons will be discussed. Step-by-step instructions are given to make a wool painting from start to finish demonstrating the basic methods of two-dimensional felting. Choose a simple design to start and work up to more complex designs.

## Using Multineedle Tools

There are numerous devices or handles that allow the use of more than one needle to be used at one time. The main reason to use multiple needles is to cover more surface area with one needle action, which lessens the time needed to completely needle the fiber to a surface. Multineedle tools also work well to tack down a design before wet felting a piece.

When considering which device to purchase, it helps if you are able to hold different handles to see how they fit your hand. Make sure that the needles are interchangeable so that when a needle breaks, you can replace it. Some of the mechanisms available have a safety guard and a springlike action that assists in moving the needles in and out of the wool. With these devices, the needles are pushed down and then pressure is released and the needles spring back out of the wool automatically.

To make a multineedle tool, the simplest method is to use a rubber band to bind two to three needles together at the shanks. These needles can then be used like an individual needle. This use of multiple needles can be used with two-dimensional or three-dimensional works.

The multineedle tools that hold five or more needles generally work best with two-dimensional works. They can be used for large figures but tend to overwhelm smaller pieces. Use 36- to 42-gauge needles in a multineedle tool, depending on the breed of wool being used. Multineedle tools are also helpful when making flat pieces in three-dimensional works such as leaves.

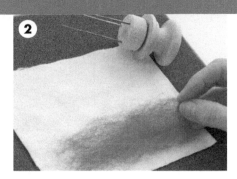

**2**

**3**

**1** Place the background fabric on the felting pad.

**2** Place thin wisps of wool on the fabric.

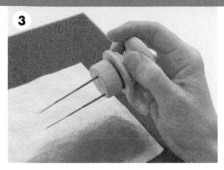

**3** Grip the multineedle tool lightly in your hand. Avoid a tight grasp as this will tire your hand and forearm muscles quickly.

## YOU WILL NEED

- multineedle tool with needles
- felting pad
- small pieces of different colored wool, other fibers, and embellishment fibers
- 5" x 7" (12.5 x 17.5 cm) background fabric such as flannel, a flat wet-felted piece, or other soft fabric

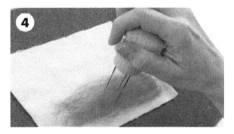

**4**

**4** Push the needles in and out over the wisp of wool. Do not push past the working portion of the blade. Make sure to push in and pull out at the same angle.

**5**

**5** Keep needling over the wisp of wool until it is completely adhered to the fabric.

**6**

**6** Pull the fabric up off the felting pad occasionally. Any pieces of wool that have been forced down into the pad will be pulled loose.

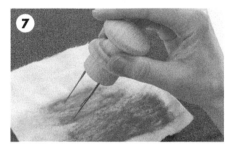

**7**

**7** Apply a different-colored piece of wool to the fabric and needle it in with the multineedle tool.

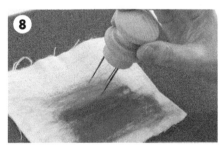

**8**

**8** Practice applying a variety of colors of fiber to the fabric. Experiment with color mixing and using different types of fiber. Put one color on top of another and then vice versa. See how the colors look different with one color on the top or underneath. Try a variety of colors to develop a palette for future wool paintings. Use the samples to make a 4" x 6" (10 cm x 15 cm) postcard.

## Technique

It works best to apply thin layers of wool building up the surface gradually. Thin layers allow the colors to blend more easily producing a more natural "painting" appearance.

## Backgrounds and Substrates

Almost any soft fabric can be used as a base for needle felting. However, some will give more support and cause less distortion than others. Try a variety of fabrics as one may work better for a certain project or technique than others. Some of the fabrics most often used for wool paintings are flannel, handmade wet felt, commercial felt, several layers of prefelt, or even a piece of fulled recycled sweater. Other soft fabrics can also be used depending on the effect desired.

Be aware that needle felting can cause distortion of the substrate, especially when using heavier fibers and large amounts of surface fiber. Experiment with a small sample before beginning a larger piece. Wet felting a piece after needle felting and then blocking it can decrease distortion.

The following examples show squares of a variety of background fabrics with thin layers of wool needled in with a multineedle tool. A description is given regarding ease of use, the gauge of needle best suited to the fabric, the distortion noted, and the resultant felted surface.

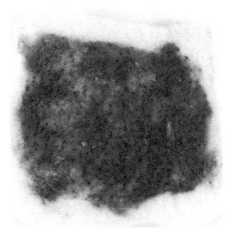

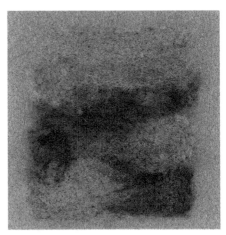

Flannel is an excellent fabric to use as a substrate as it has minimal distortion with needling, even with thicker layers of wool. Any gauge of needle can be used, but a 40- to 42-gauge needle leaves less noticeable needle holes. When needling from the back side, or reverse needling, the flannel doesn't show through to the front of the design.

Handmade wet felt is another excellent substrate as the design can be easily needle felted with any gauge needle. Slight distortion of the background is evident with heavier layers of wool needled to the surface. The background felt color will show through with reverse felting. If wet felting is performed after needle felting the surface, it is difficult to determine that the details were needle felted as they blend in with the original surface.

Commercial wool felt holds up well to any gauge of needle used to add surface wool or fiber. It does tend to distort slightly with heavy needling or heavy layers of surface wool. The color of the wool felt will come through to the front with reverse needling.

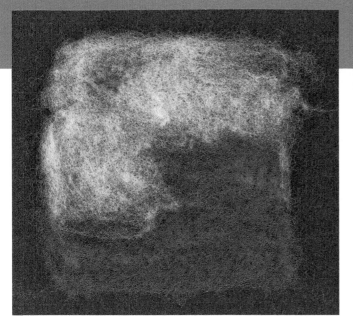

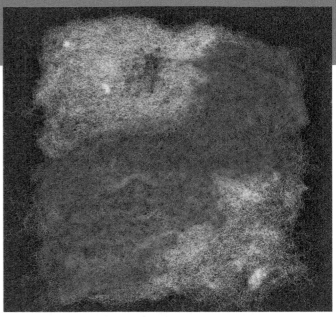

Commercial rayon felt is tough to penetrate with heavier gauge needles. Finer needles, such as 38 to 42 gauge, work better. Slight distortion is noted with heavier layers of wool and heavier needling. The rayon felt is very similar to the commercial wool felt and is a less expensive option.

Layers of commercial prefelt hold up well to lower-gauge needling but the finer gauges work better. The prefelt distorts easily due to the thinness of the material. Reverse felting will cause the color of the prefelt to come to the front. Wet felting would be beneficial after needle felting to form a thicker and more stable result.

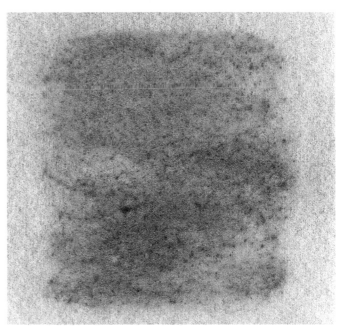

Handmade prefelt is another excellent choice for a background. It holds up well to any gauge of felting needle with minimal distortion. Reverse felting will cause the background color to show through. Further wet felting would be beneficial following needle felting.

The fulled recycled sweater was slightly tougher to penetrate with heavier gauge needles and the finer gauges work best. Slight to moderate distortion is noted and with heavy layers of surface wool added, there is quite a lot of distortion. Color will show through to the front with reverse needling.

(continued)

Fulled recycled wool blanket is very difficult to needle with lower-gauge needles. Use 40- to 42-gauge needles for the best result. The wool applied doesn't penetrate well and tends to sit on the surface of the blanket. The blanket does provide a stiff base with only slight distortion. Minimal color shows through with reverse felting.

Velvet holds up fairly well to higher needle gauges. There is some tearing of the fabric fibers with the lower gauges of needles. The velvet distorts easily, especially with heavy needling. With reverse felting, the color of the velvet will come through to the front design.

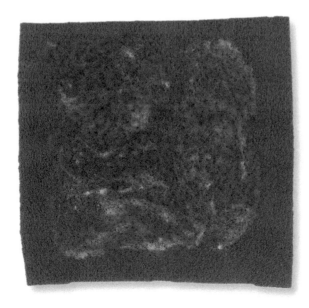

Velour tends to tear with lower-gauge needles but holds up well to finer-gauge needling such as 40 to 42. The layered wool felts in easily with slight to moderate distortion. No color shows through with reverse needling.

8-mm habotai silk is fragile and tears easily with lower-gauge needles. Use 40- to 42-gauge needles to avoid as much tearing of the silk fibers. Distortion is a major factor when using silk as a base and ruching of the fabric occurs even with minimal needling. Reverse felting reveals minimal transfer of color from the silk fabric.

Polyester fleece is difficult to penetrate with lower-gauge needles but felts easily with higher-gauge needles. Slight distortion occurs with heavy application of fiber and heavy needling. Minimal color is noted on the front design after reverse felting.

Denim is a very sturdy base and is difficult to penetrate with lower-gauge needles. Use higher-gauge needles such as 40 to 42 and be careful to avoid needle breakage. Wool and other fiber will sit on the surface instead of felting into the fabric. It is easier to needle felt if the denim is stretched taut when needling. Minimal color is noted from the denim with reverse felting.

## Wool Paintings

Painting with wool and other fibers is an exciting and versatile way to express your creativity. This fairly simple process can produce sophisticated pieces of artwork with practice. When beginning, choose a simple subject to portray; once you have some experience, try a more complex composition. There are a variety of styles that can be developed with wool paintings. Some are very flat and look more like a traditional painting, while others have more texture to their surface.

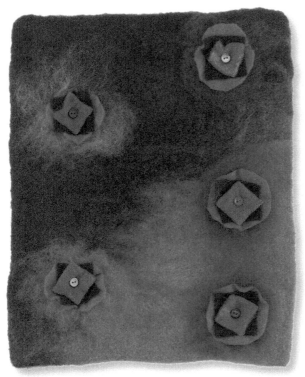

**Night Sea, machine** needle felted, Falkland wool, commercial and handmade prefelt, buttons, thread

Underpainting is an important first step to achieve a more realistic look in wool paintings. First developed by oil painters to provide a base layer of paint in a monochromatic (one hue) color scheme to act as a guide in the composition, underpainting with wool allows the colors to blend with the subsequent layers and imparts more depth to the finished piece.

As subsequent layers are added to the wool painting, more details will be applied. These overpainted layers will blend together giving form to the composition. Many different types of fibers can be used for the detail work in wool paintings. Unlike oil or acrylic paint, each fiber has its own texture and sheen, thus more distinctive effects can be achieved.

Planning and design should be considered when painting with wool. Determining the subject matter, developing a pattern to follow, and picking a color scheme before you start will provide a foundation from which to work. A rough value sketch that shows the areas of dark and light in the composition will help to determine where darker and lighter fiber should be placed in the underpainting.

### Underpainting

There are several reasons why underpainting should be the first step of a wool painting. The first is that it will act as a guide to follow in laying out the composition. Since there are many things such as value, center of interest, color choices, and other design principles to consider when developing a painting, an underpainting helps to break these down into steps.

Another reason to underpaint is because the value patterns can be established early in the process. The

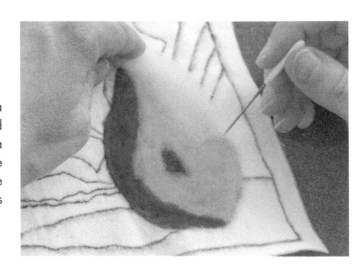

dark and light areas can be distributed appropriately, and changes can be made more easily if an area's value is incorrect. Underpainting also allows you to envision the final outcome and see if there are certain details that could be eliminated, thereby strengthening the overall design. Areas that appear too dark can be lightened, and errors can be corrected before the composition has progressed too far.

The depth of color achieved by underpainting is hard to attain by any other method. Volume and substance are portrayed more realistically due to the subtle shadows and highlights from the underpainting. Underpainting allows you to think about big blocks of color and value that can serve as the foundation for the details to follow.

There are different kinds of underpainting. Monochromatic underpainting is made with only one hue, usually earth tones or grays. It establishes the values of the composition. Use a white background or substrate and cover the lightest values with white or light wool to provide the brightest contrasts and highlights. Monochromatic underpainting resembles a black-and-white photograph.

Color-block underpainting uses a variety of colors to block out the basic color of each object in the design. These base colors will blend with the subsequent layers and details added. Value patterns should be created with color-block underpainting just as in the mono-chromatic method.

To determine the colors to use when underpainting, think about the emotions or mood that you are trying to express; the hues of the underpainting will be the basis for establishing that mood. Also consider the colors in the shadows from your source of inspiration. Cool colors in an underpainting will make shadows that contrast nicely with warm overpainted hues. Yellow tones in an underpainting will tend to make a composition feel warm while blue will feel cool. Contrasting underpainted hues will give a more dramatic look to a piece while analogous colors will be more subdued.

## Transferring Designs

There are many methods for transferring designs to a base fabric. The design can be drawn free hand; a light box (or sunny window) can be used to trace the design; or the design can be projected on to the fabric hung on the wall from an overhead projector. An overhead projector allows for easier enlargement of the design. Use a washable marker or a water-erasable fabric-marking pen (found where quilting supplies are sold) to mark the design on the base fabric. The fine details do not need to be included when the design is transferred, just the main outlines.

**1** Tape the black-and-white photo to a light box or a sunny window.

**2** Place the piece of white flannel over the photo, centering the photo in the fabric. Hold the fabric in place while tracing the outlines. The fabric can be taped down, but the edges tend to fray when the tape is removed.

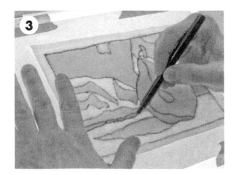

**3** Draw a 5" x 7" (13 cm x 18 cm) rectangle tracing the outside of the photo with the water-erasable marker. Trace the outlines of the main shapes in the photo.

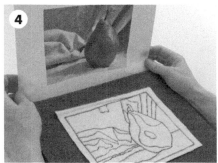

**4** Once the design is completed, place the flannel on the felting pad with the color photo nearby for guidance.

**5** Place a thin layer of wool over one of the main shapes in the design.

## Technique

Work systematically and apply the darkest values first, followed by midrange values up to the lightest values.

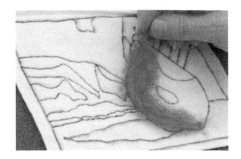

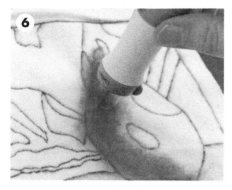

**6** Start in the middle of the covered shape and use the multineedle tool to needle the wool into the flannel. For smaller areas, use the single needle.

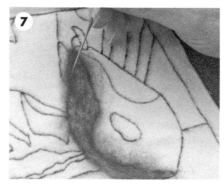

**7** Use the single felting needle to needle along the outline of the shape.

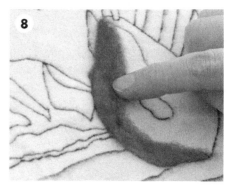

**8** Fold any stray fibers in toward the middle of the shape.

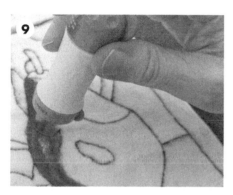

**9** Needle stray fibers down with the multineedle tool.

**10** Continue needling using a combination of the single needle and the multineedle tool until the wool adheres to the fabric.

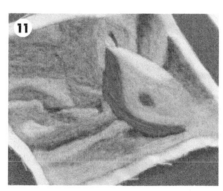

**11** Fill in each shape with the appropriate colors and follow steps 5–10 until the entire rectangle is filled.

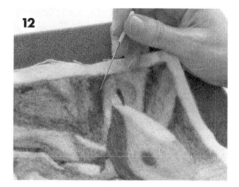

**12** Pin the piece to a bulletin board or design board; step back and view the underpainting. Look for any areas that need to be darker or lighter. Add different values of wool as needed.

**13** Use this piece for the following instructions on painting and adding details.

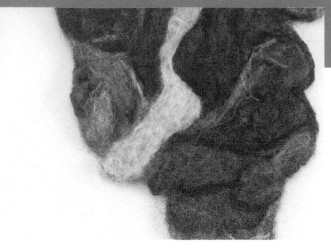

## Painting

Adding thin layers of colored wool or other fiber over the underpainting brings the composition to life. The use of very thin layers of fiber allows for further color mixing as the painting develops. Think of the layers as you would a wash of watercolor. Many thin layers of color can be added to achieve the final effect desired. When color is added over the underpainting, it should be the same value as the corresponding value underneath. Since the value patterns have already been determined in the underpainting, this is one less decision to make at this point. Think of each color on a value scale from one to ten where one is the lightest color value and ten is the darkest. Then determine what value a particular shape has in the underpainting and use the same number value to overpaint with the correct color of wool.

Detail, Avalanche Creek

mottled effect of a tree's foliage in the distance, use a batt of mixed green wools and other green fibers instead of only one shade of green. Different colors of fiber can be previewed by placing very thin layers over the prior layer of wool and then patting it down on the surface. Pin the piece to a design board or bulletin board, step back and look at the result. If the color is suitable, go ahead and needle it in. If it doesn't seem appropriate, just pull the fiber layer away and try another color.

Keep building the layers of fiber and needling them in as you work until you are satisfied with the result. For lines or outlines, use preyarn or thin pieces of roving. Use an individual felting needle to add the finest details. Save the details for the last step so that they won't be covered by subsequent layers of fiber. The most detailed areas should be in or near the center of interest in the composition. Background areas should have less detail.

Look closely at the source of inspiration to determine color placement and details that need to be added. There are many color variations in most objects even if the object overall is one color. Light, shadows, and nearby objects affect the colors seen. Many times, especially with a small composition, fiber may need to be shorter than the available staple length. In that case, tear the fibers to fit in small spaces before needling them in. Cut fibers are harder to needle felt down than torn fibers.

Use a variety of different types of fiber for overpainting to take advantage of the textures and sheens available. For example, if shiny glints are needed, such as in water, use a fiber with a higher sheen like silk. To show the

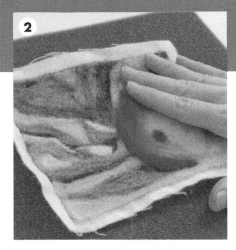

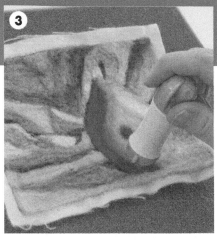

**1** Place the flannel with the underpainting on the felting pad. Keep the inspirational photo nearby. Have a multineedle tool and individual needle at hand.

**2** Look at the inspirational photo closely and choose one shape in the design to begin. Pick out a color of wool to cover the shape on the underpainting. Use the same value as used in the underpainting. Place a thin layer of wool over the shape and pat it down.

**3** If the color is satisfactory, use the multineedle tool to needle the wool in place.

## YOU WILL NEED

- underpainting from previous section
- inspirational photo
- felting pad
- ¼ to ½ oz. (7 to 14 g) wool in a variety of colors
- variety of embellishing fibers
- multineedle tool with 38- to 42-gauge needles
- individual 38- to 42-gauge felting needle

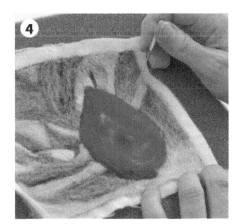

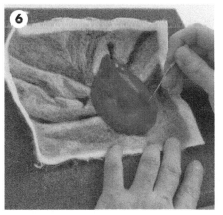

**4** Continue to choose and place colors of wool in thin layers over the shapes in the composition, needling each layer of wool in place.

**5** Work from the background to the foreground. Leave the background less detailed. Remember that objects in the distance will appear less bright and grayer in color.

**6** Add multiple thin layers of wool as above to achieve a blended effect. Refer back to the inspirational photo often for a guide in color placement.

**7** Once the basic composition is satisfactory, use the multineedle tool to needle over the entire surface.

**8** Peel the piece off the felting pad intermittently to pull loose any fiber needled into the pad.

(continued)

## Technique

Use a photo-editing program to help determine actual colors seen in a photo. Crop out a small section of the photo, enlarge that section, and use the eyedropper tool to see what the true color is. Many times you will be surprised to see that the actual color is different than you think it is.

**9** Flip the piece over and needle all over the back surface.

**10** Flip the wool painting back over and needle again over the entire front surface. Avoid deep needling into the pad.

**11** Use a 40- to 42-gauge individual needle to add details. Tear any fibers that are too long. Use very small wisps of wool, embellishing fiber or preyarn for detailed areas. The center of interest should be the most detailed area. Use high value contrasts to emphasize the areas of interest.

**12** Continue to add details with the single needle until you are pleased with the design. Use the single needle to adhere the detailed areas thoroughly to the painting.

**13** Use this piece for the finishing instructions that follow.

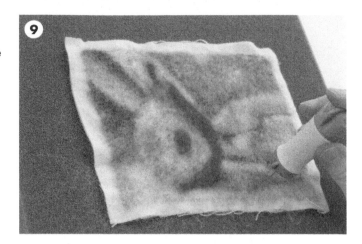

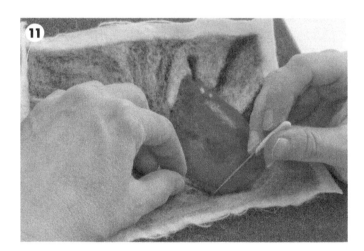

## Design Hints

One of the most important aspects of drawing and painting is to train your eyes to really see an object. Because our brains must process so much information, we learn to recognize objects without really seeing all the details. However, if you are going to portray an object by painting it, whether with wool or paint, you need to see the details. Look at the object closely and see the areas of darkness and light. Try to see the different shapes that are part of the object. Don't let your brain override what your eyes are seeing. For example, if you are planning a still life with a pear, your brain will say, "That's a pear, draw a pear shape." But every pear is different, and you need to depict the shape of the pear in front of you, not a generic pear shape.

If you haven't already, read the section on design (page 48). The wool paintings you create will be enhanced by planning and design. When planning the center of interest, remember the rule of thirds. Avoid placing the center of interest in the exact center of the composition. Use elements such as line and value change to draw the eye around the piece. Contrasting elements will draw the eye, so make shapes and lines that are not exactly alike. Use warm and cool colors to portray depth. Warm colors appear to advance, and cool colors recede, which gives a landscape a more realistic feel.

Spend time looking at artists' work that you admire. Try to see what it is that you like about their work. Is it the color scheme that draws your eye or the good use of contrasting values? Ask yourself questions about how the artist used design elements and principles in completing an artwork. Could you use the same methods in a wool painting? Write down the ideas generated from viewing other artwork into a journal to use the ideas for future projects.

## Finishing

Many needle felters use only needle-felting techniques to finish a two-dimensional piece. However, there are many benefits to wet felting a wool painting after it has been needled. The wet felting locks all the layers together, adhering most stray fibers left by needle felting. The colors in the wool painting will mix more thoroughly allowing more of the underpainting to show through. Therefore, the colors will have smoother transitions and look more natural. Another benefit to wet felting a needle-felted wool painting is to erase any needle holes. The resultant piece will be smoother, stronger, and more durable. Because the fiber has been needle felted already, there will be minimal shifting of the fibers, and the design will not be moved or changed.

Refer back to the wet felting section (page 52) for instructions on how to wet felt a piece if needed. The needle-felted wool painting can be treated like any other piece of flat felt to wet felt. Rolling to full will provide the most even shrinkage and the smoothest surface. The wool tends to felt together from each side of the background fabric first. Avoid fulling to the point where the background fabric begins to ruche. Fifty to one hundred rolls from each direction are usually enough rolling to flatten the wool painting without excessive shrinkage. The painting can then be blocked to dry so that its edges remain square.

## Machine Needle Felting

In the last decade, home needle-felting machines have become popular with fiber artists, felters, and even quilters. The machine speeds up two-dimensional felting considerably. It works just like a multineedle tool but allows the work to be completed in less than half the time. Needle-felting machines can be found where sewing machines are sold. Most sewing machines companies make a needle-felting machine, and there are numerous brands from which to choose.

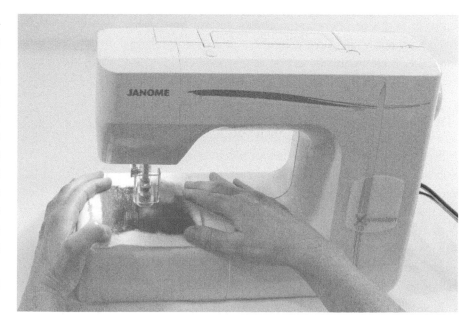

(continued)

The needle-felting machine looks like a sewing machine, but it has no thread or bobbin mechanism. The machine can apply design onto fabric with no sewing or thread necessary. Machines can hold from one to fifteen needles depending on the brand. Interchangeable heads, where individual needles can be replaced, are the most economical because needles break occasionally, especially with beginners. Some machines also come with yarn guides to allow for more ease when couching or punching yarn down to a base fabric.

The mechanical action of the needle-felting machine is called a variety of things including needling, felting, embellishing, or punching. These terms are used interchangeably in literature about the needle-felting machine. It all means the action of the needles going in and out of fiber or fabric.

The needle-felting machine is very versatile, and due to its speed and force, can achieve effects that would be more difficult by hand. The needle-felting machine can needle two pieces of soft fabric together, enhance surface texture on a fabric, trap fibers or embellishments between two pieces of sheer fabric, needle yarns and ribbons to the surface of a base fabric, and needle loose wool or other fiber together to form prefelt. Other techniques can be performed on the machine such as making folds or tucks in felt or soft fabric, appliquéing pieces of fabric or felt to a

base fabric, making a cord from a combination of yarns, and even reverse punching where a patterned fabric is needled onto the back side of the base fabric making a misty pattern appear on the front of the base fabric.

The basic parts of a needle-felting machine are shown here, but each brand will be slightly different. Follow the manufacturer's instructions for the type of machine used. Most needle heads use screws to hold the needles in place; again follow the instructions for your specific machine.

A variety of fabrics can be used in the needle-felting machine. Experiment with different soft fabrics but avoid heavy or stiff fabrics as they will tend to cause needle breakage. Try the basic techniques shown here and then continue to develop the methods on your own. The needle-felting machine can really speed the wool painting process and allow work on a larger scale than can be attempted by hand.

### Machine Anatomy

The basic parts of the needle-felting machine that differ from a standard sewing machine are the needle plate, the needle unit or head, the finger/eye guard, and the bed area under the needles where lint or dust accumulates. Just like a sewing machine, the needle-felting machine also has a presser foot, a hand wheel, a presser foot lifter, and a foot control pedal that varies the needling speed. Extension tables are available for most needle-felting machines as an additional accessory. The table provides more surface area for large pieces of work.

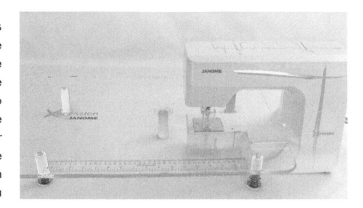

The following photos review the basic parts of the machine and how they work. Turn the power off and unplug the machine whenever the parts are removed or changed.

The needle plate is located on the base of the machine. Many machines have more than one needle plate with either one hole or multiple holes. Plates can be exchanged by loosening the screws with a screwdriver and switching plates. Always raise the presser foot before changing the plates.

Needle heads can hold one needle or more depending on your brand. To replace or change the needle head or unit, raise the finger guard and use the screwdriver tool supplied with the machine to loosen the needle clamp screw. Pull the needle unit/head out of the clamp. Most needle heads fit only one way into the clamp. Make sure that the replacement needle head is lined up correctly to fit back into the clamp. Tighten the screw on the needle clamp. Make sure to check that the needles will go down in the needle plate holes easily. Use the hand wheel to lower the needles slowly into the needle plate.

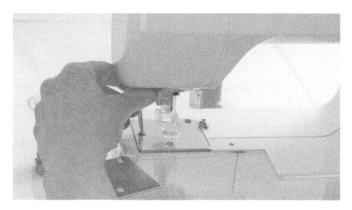

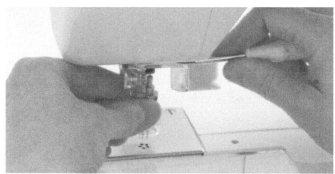

The needle unit or head fits up into a needle clamp mechanism and is held by a screw. Most machines come with one or more heads. Some heads have interchangeable needles, while other companies consider this an optional accessory. The finger guard is to protect fingers from the sharp needles. It should always be lowered whenever the machine is running. Raise the finger guard to make any adjustments to the presser foot or to change the needle unit.

The presser foot holds the fabric against the needle plate and can be adjusted depending on the thickness of the material being needled. To adjust the presser foot height, loosen the screw that holds it in place. Move the presser foot up or down to match the height of the fabric or fiber being needled. Tighten the screw to hold the presser foot at the appropriate height. Use the presser foot lifter to lower the presser foot and check for the correct height.

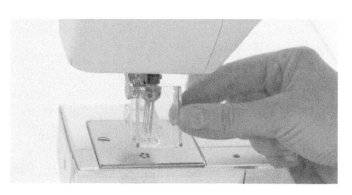

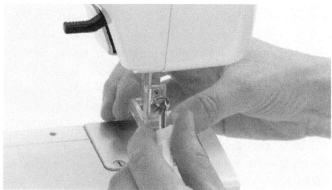

## Needles

Most manufacturers supply only one size needle with their machines and often don't even indicate what gauge needle it is. These needles work fine for most projects but a finer or coarser gauge needle might work better for certain projects. Any of the gauges of felting needles 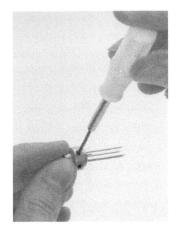 previously discussed will work in a needle-felting machine. The problem is the crank on the end of the needle. It needs to be removed before the needle will fit up into the needle head or unit. Since the needles are made from carbon steel, they are difficult to cut at home. Suppliers for machine needles of a variety of sizes are available.

Selecting the correct gauge of needle for each different project is similar to selecting an individual needle for a hand-needle project. The coarser needles will work best for coarser fibers and to produce more texture on fabrics. Use a finer-gauge needle for fine fiber and for application of fiber to fabrics. The finer needle will leave smaller holes and cause less damage and buckling of the base fabric. For wool painting, use a 40- to 42-gauge needle if available.

Investing in a needle head with interchangeable needles is recommended. Needle breakage is fairly common, and needle heads with fixed needles can be expensive to replace. It can be discouraging for a beginner to break needles when starting out and be unable to replace them easily. The interchangeable needle head uses screws to hold the needles in place and replacing the needles is a simple process. Remove the interchangeable head from the needle-felting machine as shown in the machine anatomy section (page 205). Loosen the screw by the broken needle by turning counter clockwise. Pull the broken needle out of the head and throw it away. Often the broken end will be stuck in the fibers of the project, and it will need to be taken out and thrown away as well. Place a new needle into the open hole and push it all the way in. Tighten the screw to clamp the needle in place. Reinsert the needle head into the machine and retighten. Check with the hand wheel to make sure all the needles move freely into the needle plate.

## Maintenance and Cleaning

Needle-felting machines require little maintenance if used properly. Follow the manufacturers' instructions for appropriate care. One of the most important tasks to remember is to clean out the bed area to prevent excessive lint buildup. Each machine will 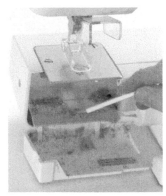 have a cover or a door that opens to allow access to the bed area. The top mechanism, which moves the needle of most machines, can also be cleaned by removing the faceplate and using a lint brush. Always turn off and unplug the machine before cleaning. Move the needles to the highest position to avoid accidentally brushing against the needles. Frequent cleaning is recommended.

To clean under the needle plate, remove the extension table if present. Open the bed cover and remove lint or dust that has accumulated. Brush away remaining particles with the lint brush. Close the bed cover. To clean inside the faceplate, remove the faceplate cap and screw with a screwdriver. Pull off the faceplate and brush away lint and dust with the lint brush. Replace the faceplate and screw back into place. Replace the cap over the screw.

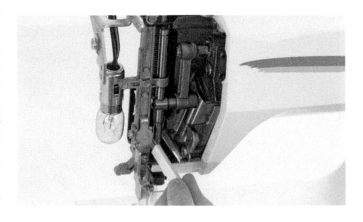

## Machine Needle Felting on Fabric

Almost any soft fabric can be used when machine needle felting. Sheer fabrics, silk, velvet, flannel, and commercial felt all work well. A fabric with pile such as velvet or velour can be cut up into pieces and needled to a base fabric either on the wrong or right side of the fabric. Sheer or thin fabrics can be textured by needling, or yarns and fibers can be trapped between two pieces of sheer fabric. The options are endless and again, experimentation is the key. Try a variety of soft fabrics. See how needling the fabric affects the texture. Try adding a variety of fibers and needling them down. Cut up small pieces of fabric and needle them to a base of commercial felt.

The following samples show various types of fabric after being machine needle felted with a layer of Merino wool. An explanation is included to describe how the fabrics react to needling with 36-gauge triangular needles.

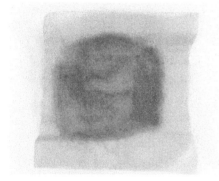

Organza sheer fabric worked well for machine needle felting with minimal tearing of the fabric noted. The wool needles in easily with minimal distortion of the fabric. The wool tends to sit on the surface of the sheer fabric.

Silk fabric distorts easily with machine needle felting and slight tears in the fabric occur, especially if the fabric is needled excessively in one area. The wool sits on the surface of the fabric after needling.

A recycled fulled sweater provides a good support for machine needle felting. There is no fabric tearing and minimal distortion. The wool felts into the base instead of sitting on the surface of the fabric.

Velour fabric held up well to machine needle felting with only slight distortion noted. There is minimal fabric tearing, and the wool felts into the fabric fairly well.

Commercial felt provides a good base for machine needle felting with slight distortion of the fabric noted with heavier wool layers. The wool felts into the surface, and the commercial felt holds up to heavy needling.

Flannel is a good fabric to use as a base when machine needle felting as it holds up well with minimal distortion. The wool sits more on the surface of the fabric, but there is no fabric tearing with needling unless heavier gauge needles are used.

## Basic Techniques

The needle-felting machine is similar to using a multineedle tool by hand but saves the repetitive motions that have to be done by hand. Try out each of the basic methods and make a few samples. Any of the fabrics that have been needled by machine could be used in a variety of projects. After trying out the basics, you will gain enough confidence to progress to more challenging techniques such as wool painting by machine.

The basics of raising and lowering the presser foot, using the needle guard, and raising the needles out of the fabric will be shown in the first technique of applying wool to fabric. These instructions are not repeated in subsequent techniques, but remember to follow them for all techniques.

## Avoiding Needle Breakage

Everyone will break a needle eventually, but there are a few things you can do to make it less likely to happen. To avoid needle breakage as much as possible, keep the following precautions in mind:

- When the needles are in the fabric or fiber, don't pull on the fabric.

- When needling is stopped, use the hand wheel to raise the needles to their highest position.

- When needling a large area, push all the way down on the foot pedal to move the needles quickly, while moving the fabric slowly and gently.

- Avoid harder and thicker fabrics. Test fabrics with the hand wheel. If it is difficult to get the needles to pass through the fabric by hand, the needle will be more likely to break when machine needling.

- Avoid using harder and thicker embellishments like nepps, slubs, thick silk cocoons, or carrier rods.

- Make sure to adjust the presser foot to match the height of the piece that is being needled.

- Always lift the presser foot up and put the needles at the highest position when removing the fabric from the machine.

## Safety

The needle-felting machine is very safe if used appropriately. Make sure to place the machine on a sturdy table as excess motion can develop if the surface is not firm. Always use the finger/eye guard and do not place your fingers near the needles. Hold the fabric at the edges to move it around under the needles. Always turn off and unplug the machine when removing or inserting any of the parts. The needles are very sharp and should be handled with care. Store any extra needles in a safe place. Follow all manufacturers' instructions.

## Filling Shapes

Whether making a wool painting or a small wool embellishment on a piece of clothing, filling in a shape and applying wool to a piece of fabric is a simple process. Start with a small sample to see how the wool reacts and shrinks as it is needled to the fabric.

**YOU WILL NEED**

- needle-felting machine
- variety of fabrics in 10" (25 cm) squares including flannel, commercial felt, silk, velvet, velour, sheers, and quilt batting
- yarns and soft ribbons
- variety of colors of medium to fine wool
- netting or tulle
- water-soluble marker
- scissors

**1** Draw a flower shape in the center of a square of flannel with a water-soluble marker.

**2** Place a thin layer of wool over one of the petal shapes.

**3** Set the presser foot to the correct height to hold the flannel and wool against the needle plate. Put the presser foot in the up position after it has been adjusted.

**4** With the hand wheel, turn the needles to the highest point.

(continued)

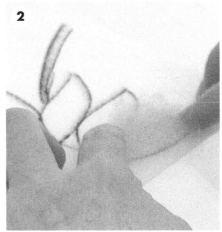

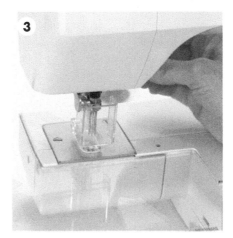

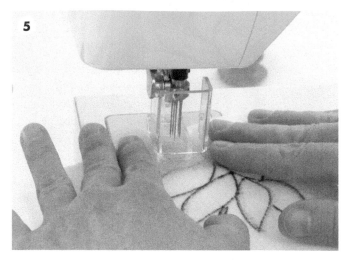

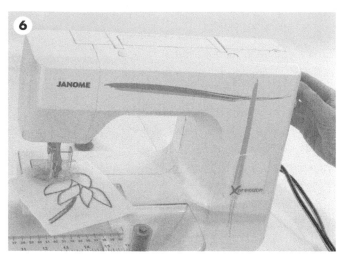

**5** Slide the flannel and wool under the needles. Put the needle guard down. Position the fabric to start in the center of the flower petal. Put the presser foot down.

**6** Use the hand wheel to move the needle in and out of the fabric and wool several times to test the thickness.

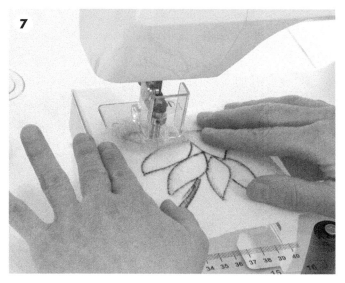

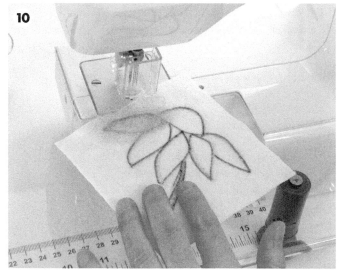

**7** Gently push down on the foot pedal to begin needling.

**8** Work from the center outward moving the fabric slowly as the needles move.

**9** Avoid needling repetitively in the same place.

**10** Raise the needles up to the highest position, raise the presser foot, and pull out the fabric.

**11** Examine the wool and see how it shrunk with needling.

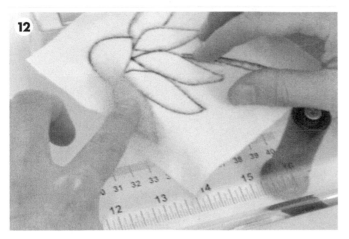

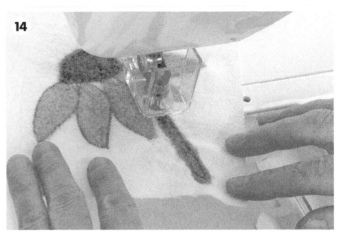

**12** Fold over the loose wool on the edges and needle in place. Add more fiber in the petal shape if needed and continue needling in the same manner.

**13** Continue filling in the marked flower shapes with wool, needling down the fiber each time on the machine.

**14** After all the shapes are filled; needle over the entire flower to make sure all the fiber is well attached.

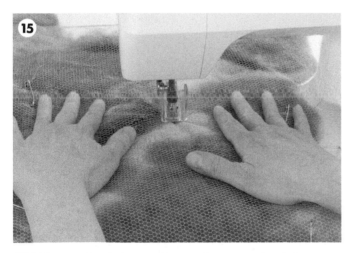

**15** When making a larger piece such as a wool painting, attach fiber in place by hand first. Then cover the painting with a piece of tulle or netting before machine needling. Use safety pins to baste the layers together. Avoid the safety pins when machine needling. Remove the safety pins as you work and needle in the area where the safety pins were. The netting will help to keep the fiber in place when moving the painting around while needling. The netting won't felt into the surface and can be pulled off and reused for the next painting.

## Technique

Use a single felting needle to tack fibers down in small spaces or tight corners.

## Outlining

Outlining a shape with yarn is quick and easy with the needle-felting machine. A variety of yarn can also be attached or couched to the fabric without having to sew it on. It may be easier to needle the yarn down with the use of the single needle head. Try both the multineedle head and the single needle head to see which method works best for the yarn used.

**1** Use the flower piece made in the last section.

**2** Place a piece of yarn to form the stem of the flower. The yarn should be longer than the drawn stem as it will shrink.

**3** Needle the top end of the yarn to the fabric by using the hand wheel to attach.

**4** Needle the yarn along the drawn line holding the far end in your hand. If your machine has a yarn guide, use that for couching and outlining.

**5** Once the yarn is needled in place, snip the top end with scissors to the correct length.

**6** Needle over the yarn again to make sure it is well adhered.

**7** Outline the petals or center of the flower as desired in the same manner. To remove ink lines, soak the piece in cool water for a few minutes. Let dry thoroughly.

**8** Use a 10" (25 cm) square piece of commercial felt and try needling down a variety of yarns or ribbons in the same manner.

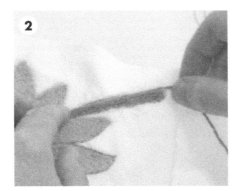

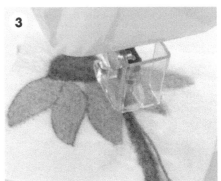

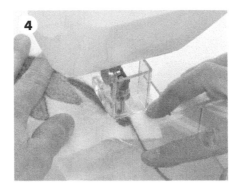

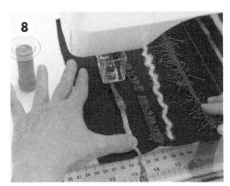

## Technique

Use a longer piece of yarn that extends past the end of the design. Needle the yarn down along the drawn line and then snip the yarn at both ends to the appropriate length. For narrow yarns, use a single needle instead of the multineedle head.

### Making Prefelt

Needle-felted prefelt can be used in wet-felting, needle-felting, or nuno-felting projects. The simplest method is to use one or two layers of wool batting and needling them with the machine. If batting is unavailable, lay out two layers of fiber at right angles to each other as previously shown in the wet-felting section (page 52).

**1** Put the laid out wool, either batting or two layers of wool at right angles, on the machine with the needles in the center of the wool.

**2** Start needling slowly, moving the wool gently in a circular motion. Avoid sudden jerks or sharp pulls.

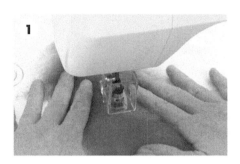

**3** Continue increasing the speed of the needles and make sure to needle over the entire surface.

**4** Turn the needled wool upside down and needle over the opposite side thoroughly.

**5** Continue machine needling until the wool has become firm.

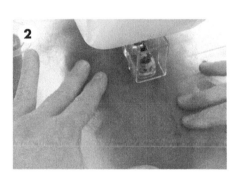

## Technique

Fold the edges under to make a straighter edge on the prefelt.

### Appliqué

A variety of soft fabrics can be felted to the surface of wool or commercial felt. Softer fabrics with pile will felt the easiest, but most soft fabrics will work. Try scraps of different fabrics to see the different effects that can be achieved. Fabrics can also be needled to the back of the base and will give a soft patterning result on the front side.

(continued)

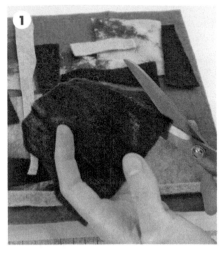

1 To appliqué one soft fabric to another, use a 10" (25 cm) square of commercial felt. Cut up small pieces of soft fabrics like silk, velvet, velour, sheers, or flannel.

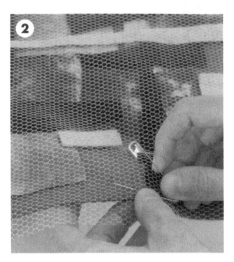

2 Place the pieces of fabric over the felt and cover with a piece of netting or tulle. Secure with safety pins to baste the fabrics together.

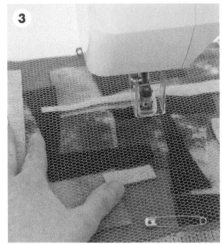

3 Slide this sandwich of fabrics under the felting needles and begin needling. Avoid the safety pins.

4 Keep needling and remove the safety pins as you work.

5 Make sure all the safety pins are removed and needle over the entire surface.

## Reverse Pattern Felting

A soft, diffused pattern can be replicated from a fabric design by needling the patterned fabric to the reverse side of the base fabric. If the patterned fabric is cut into a shape, that shape will appear on the front of the fabric. This technique works best with lower gauge needles such as 36 to 38.

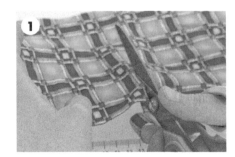

1 Use a soft patterned fabric. Cut the fabric into the desired shape.

2 Place the fabric on the back side of a square of commercial felt.

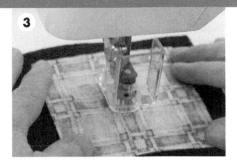

**3** With the back side facing up, place the two fabric layers under the needles on the needle-felting machine.

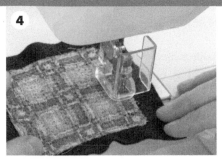

**4** Needle over the entire fabric shape several times. Avoid needling continuously in one area. Make several passes over the fabric shape to achieve an even pattern on the reverse side.

**5** Pull the fabric out and turn it over to see the pattern on the front side.

**6** Put the fabric back under the needles with the back side up and needle to increase the patterning seen on the front of the felt.

## Texturing Fabric

Needling over different types of fabric will give different textures. Interesting patterns and textures can be developed. Lower gauges of needles tend to cause greater fabric distortion. These fabrics could then be used in a variety of ways to enhance sewing projects such as clothing or bags.

**1** Place a 10" (25 cm) square of thin fabric such as silk over a square of quilt batting.

**2** Place the fabric and batting under the needles at the center bottom edge.

**3** Begin needling and gently pull the fabric forward, making a straight line of needle texture in the center of the fabric.

**4** Continue to needle in the same manner making stripes of texture across the fabric.

**5** Try different types of fabric on top to see the variety of textures that can be achieved.

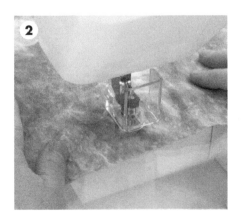

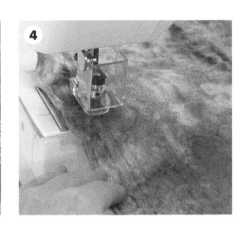

## Making Tucks and Folds

Once a piece of felt has been needle felted with a design, the needle-felting machine can be used to further enhance the texture. Tucks and folds can be made by needling the folded felt. A piece of felt could be cut into strips, the strips woven together, and then machine needle felted at the joins.

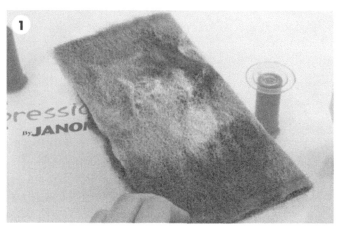

**1** Machine needle felt a variety of wool and other fiber to the surface of a 10" (25 cm) square of commercial felt. Fold the felt in half with the right side of the fabric on the outside.

**2** Place the folded felt under the needles of the machine after adjusting the presser foot. Needle felt along the folded edge of the felt carefully to form the tuck.

**3** Take the felt out of the machine and open it back out flat. A ridge will form where the felt has been needled together.

**4** Fold the felt again in another place to make another tuck, and needle along the folded edge.

**5** Experiment folding the felt in different ways to achieve different effects.

## Making Cords

The needle-felting machine is an excellent tool for making cords. These cords can be used for ties on clothing, for straps on bags, or for wrapping around a book cover to keep it closed. At least one of the yarns used needs to be fairly thick and wooly. It doesn't necessarily have to be wool yarn but should have enough fiber to felt well to the other yarns used.

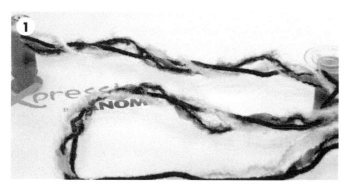

**1** Use 3 to 4 different coordinating yarns, one of which is fairly thick with lots of fiber. Twist the ends of the yarns together and pull about a yard (meter) of yarn off the ball or skein. Do not cut the ends yet as the yarns will shrink and it is hard to determine how much shrinkage will occur.

**2** Hold the twisted yarn ends in one hand and place the twisted rope of yarn under the needles on the machine. Give yourself plenty of room to hold the yarn without being close to the needles.

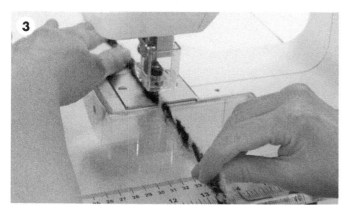

**3** Hold the other end of the yarn in your other hand. Begin needling the yarn together, holding them taut under the needles and flat against the needle plate.

**4** Twist and pull the yarn under the needles as the needles move up and down. Avoid pulling quickly or sharply.

**5** Needle up and down the yarn cord several times until the cord is felted together.

**6** Move on to the next section of yarn, needling them together in the same manner.

**7** Continue needling until the cord is long enough for the intended purpose.

**8** Cut off any loose ends that were not completely felted.

# Gallery

Feast your eyes on these wonderful felted pieces by a myriad of felt makers from all over the world. You can see the versatility of felt and the variety of options that are open to you as a felt maker in the examples shown here. Visit these felt maker's websites to gain further inspiration. You can find me online at www.feltingandfiberstudio.com.

**Horst Couture**
http://horstcouture.com/
*Tribal*

Tribal, made from Falkland wool and wet-felting techniques, was created in separate pieces. The skirt was made first, with yellow, textural organic shapes felted to its surface. The top was created second, with black roving creating the detailing, and hand-felted dreads attached to its hemline. They were then attached together by burring up the edges with a cat comb, and felted together, forming one piece. Each of Horst's gowns is a one of a kind creation transforming the body of its wearer into art itself.

## Ann McElroy
http://www.shepherdsspringfarm.ca/
*Viking Hats*

The gray hat is made from Corriedale wool and the colored hats from Merino. Each hat is wet felted around a resist, and the final shaping is done around a hat block. The strap is placed over the top and needle felted into place using loose fiber to create the rivets. The rivets are then needled in around the base of the hat. The horns are first shaped into cones and curled using the felting needle. Then they are needle felted onto the hat.

## Ruth Lane
http://ruthsfiberphotos.blogspot.com/
*The Rhythm of Autumn*

Inspired by one of my favorite times of the year, The Rhythm of Autumn represents Montana's rich fall season. It is a mixed-media piece with a wet-felted base from Merino wool fibers and various bits of yarn and silk that was rust dyed. It also includes appliquéd leaves from commercial fabric, hand stitching, and free motion machine embroidery over Jacob's lamb fleece.

## Patti McAleenan
http://www.dreamfelt.com/
*Gretchen*

Gretchen was my first needle-felted creation, made while taking an online needle-felting class. She was created on a piece of foam covered with wool felt. Her body was created using core wool and covered with C1 Norwegian wool. Her hair is wool dreadlocks. All the glass beads were created by me and assembled in pieces that complement her outfit. When my grandchildren saw it, they immediately said it was "Grandma." It is often said that your first piece of needle felting a doll is usually a self-portrait.

### Zed

http://www.flickr.com/photos/
zedster01/
*Felt Lampshade*

The lampshade cover was wet felted with four fine layers of wool. The inner layer consists of Mohair, Wensleydale, and Blue-faced Leicester locks and curls that were sandwiched between two fine layers of Merino. The top layer includes wool locks, Merino, silk top, and silk lap. A template was made from a commercial lampshade and the felt was cut out in the shape of the template. The felt shade was sewn together with a running stitch and edged with blanket stitch and then slipped over the commercial shade.

### Linda Hall

www.fabricartbylinda.com
*Provincetown*

31" x 45" (79 cm x 114 cm)
The style of the Impressionistic painters of the nineteenth century, such as Claude Monet, Auguste Renoir, and Vincent Van Gogh has always looked more like fabric than paint to me, and I've wanted to try to duplicate their painting style using the medium of wool fibers. Using flannel as a base fabric, I used many different types of fibers from my stash and machine needle felted them in place. To create the look of Impressionistic painting, I found that gradually building up the layers of wool was better than just felting one layer of color in place. I used Merino wool and the shorter Waldorf wool I dyed myself as the working wool for underpainting and fill holes and wherever else I needed more wool, with a fluffy nonlinear color. Peace Fleece creates the foliage instantly and easily and brings everything to life. I used upholstery fabric for the borders because the texture seems to better suit the felted painting.

Elis Vermeulen
www.elisv.nl
*Installation, Do Not Watch the Waves*

This installation was exhibited at the Abbey of Middelburg in 2010. The boat is nearly 8.7 yd. (8 m) long, made with two pieces of handmade felt, wood, and lots of rope filled with raw wool blankets and pillows.

**Elis Vermeulen**
www.elisv.nl
*Raw Wool Bag*

The bag was made from raw wool, roving, and leather. It was wet felted using the roving to assist in catching the ends of the raw wool and felting the piece together.

**Christie Wareham-Norfolk**
www.panachelace.com.au
*Purple Parade*

A nuno-felted circular sleeveless jacket was made with the base fabric of silk paj hand dyed in graduated shades of purple from the dark base to the light upper section. A circular shape was cut out and edged with hand-dyed Merino wool. Swirls and spirals of Merino wool were laid over the silk and extra wool positioned where the armholes would be. After felting, armhole slots were cut through the felt.

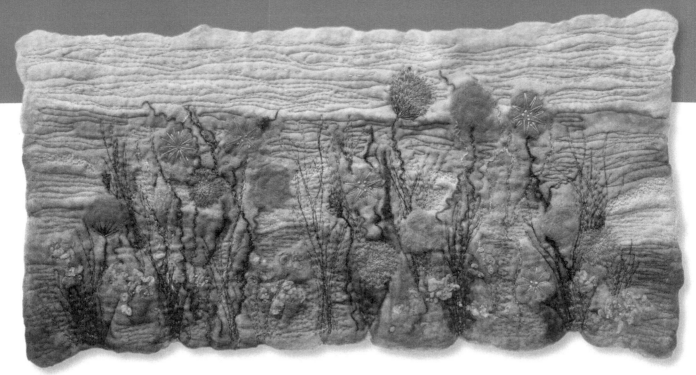

**Annie Watkins and Lyn Clinton**
www.rosiepink.typepad.co.uk
*Flowers on Coverack Beach*, 33" x 17" (83.8 cm x 43 cm)

Flowers on Coverack Beach was wet felted from four layers of Merino wool top; fluffy yarn was used for stems; and puffs of pink Merino wool were used for flower heads. After felting, the picture was backed with stabilizer; then free-motion machining was used to make grasses, flower detail, and texture in the sand, sea, and sky. A few hand running stitches and French knots completed the embroidery. The picture was backed with calico and hand-stitched in place, and a hanging rod was secured just below the top edge of the picture so that it would seem to float against the wall.

**Christie Wareham-Norfolk**
www.panachelac.com.au
*Sunset at Sea*, 15.7" x 11.8" (40 cm x 30 cm)

This wall hanging was wet felted from Merino wool with silk hankies and mixed threads blended in to add sheen and texture. After being partially fulled, uneven squares and rectangles were cut out and then further fulled to soften the edges. The pieces were assembled and embellished with beading, hand-stitching, sari thread–wrapped washers, and kumihimo braiding.

**Paula Rindal**
*Santa*

Santa was sculpted with a single felting needle out of core wool and Norwegian C1 wool. Wool locks were used for the hair and beard. Small details were added with a variety of colors of Merino wool.

**Paula Rindal**
*Man with Binoculars*

This figure was needle felted using a single needle. He was constructed of core wool and Norwegian C1 wool. His combover is Merino wool as are other details.

**Pam DeGroot**
www.pamdegroot.com.
*Nuno-Felted Silk Dress*

This nuno-felted dress was made with eucalyptus-printed pongee silk and 19-micron organic Merino wool. The bodice was felted, and then the rest of the gown was sewn together.

**Pam DeGroot**
www.pamdegroot.com
*Nuno-Felted Silk Dress*

The short dress was made using chiffon prefelt, which was cut and sewn before felting together and dyeing. Eucalyptus-printed silk has been added to the front and bottom. The wool used was 19-micron, organic Merino wool.

**Judith Colvin**
www.bitterrootranch.net
*Cloche Hat and Nuno-Felted Wrap*

The cloche hat was made with wet-felting techniques using Blue-faced Leicester wool from my own sheep. The hat was embellished with silk and bamboo fibers. The coordinated wrap was made by felting superfine Merino through silk fabric. The surface of the wrap was embellished with silk and bamboo fibers.

**Birgitte Krag Hansen**
www.feltmaking.dk
*Soft Granite Woman*

This woman figure was needle felted entirely from Gotland wool. The natural colors of the wool give the look of granite.

**Birgitte Krag Hansen**
www.feltmaking.dk
*Raw Fleece Lion Head*

The lion head was needle felted from Spelsau wool. Raw fleece was used to give a more natural look and feel to the mane.

**Birgitte Krag Hansen**
www.feltmaking.dk
*Eagle Head*

The eagle head was needle felted from Spelsau wool.

**Michelle Dibdin**
http://www.michelledibdin.com/
*Shibori Wall Hanging*

The shibori wall hanging was created by making six pieces of wet felt, which were dyed. Marbles were stitched into the dyed felt to create the sweeping pattern. It was steamed, dried, the marbles removed, and then stitched together along the sides.

**Michelle Dibdin**
http://www.michelledibdin.com/
*Ruffled Scarf*

The ruffled scarf was made with wet-felting techniques using Merino fibers in the center and a Merino and mulberry silk blend around the edges.

**Michelle Dibdin**
http://www.michelledibdin.com/
*Cobweb Scarf*

The cobweb scarf was made with wet-felting techniques using a blend of Merino and mulberry silk. It was dyed with acid dyes.

**Karen Erickson**
www.karensfeltworks.blogspot.com
*Mixed Media Wall Hanging,*
15½" x 9½" (39 cm x 24 cm)

The background was wet felted using a mix of Merino, silks, and Gotland fiber. The main flower heads were also wet felted using a blend of Merino and Blue-faced Leicester. The piece was then embellished with hand-spun yarns, embroidery threads, and beads throughout.

**Carol Cypher**
www.carolcypher.com
*In Honor of Hemlock Necklace*

This necklace was made with wet-felted Merino medallions strung with carved gemstone pinecones by Gary Wilson, swirling borosilicate beads by Nancy Tobey, seed beads, dagger beads, and a magnetic closure.

**Carol Cypher**
www.carolcypher.com
*Felted Complex Cane Bead Necklace*

The beads were Merino wet felted into a complex cane, which was then cut into beads. The beads are strung into a necklace with a magnetic closure.

**Kasey Sorsby**
www.tanglewoodthicket.com
*"Rainbow Sprite" Woolie Wog Goblin*

Needle felted entirely with one 38-gauge needle using British Columbia–grown wool that was dyed 100% with Kool-Aid and Wilton's Icing Dye. Goblin's hair was hand-dyed silk.

**Karen Erickson**
www.karensfeltworks.blogspot.com
*Happy Troll*

The troll was made using a single barbed needle-felting needle. His core is a Merino cross fleece and the outer layer is Norwegian C1 fiber. His jacket was also needle felted using a blend of Blue-Faced Leicester and Merino. He stands 16" (41 cm) tall and has a button for an earring.

**Teri Canepa**
www.tericanepa.com
*Squirrel, Bear, Mushroom, and Sunflower*

These figures were all needle-felted wool without armatures. The gray on the squirrel is the natural wool color. For the yellow colors, I used pickling alum as a premordant. The pinks and browns were dyed without any mordant. The mushroom was dyed with goldenrod flowers and the snail with onionskins and copper blue. All of the other yellow colors were dyed with brown onionskins. The green leaves were yellow dyed with onionskins with a copper blue modifier. The pink on the feet and belly of the bear were dyed with birch twigs and bark. His nose was dyed with sweet woodruff roots and his muzzle with chokecherry bark. The bear's eyes were dyed with black walnut hulls.

# Glossary of Terms

**Bamboo Shade/Window Blind:** A roller blind made of small sticks or bamboo used for rolling felt more aggressively.

**Barb:** A notch on the edge of a felting needle. The barb catches the wool during the felting process.

**Batt, Batting:** A sheet of wool as it comes off the drum carder.

**Blending:** Combining different fibers together, whether different colors or different types of fibers.

**Breed:** A kind or type of sheep with common ancestry and common characteristics; different breeds produce wool with different characteristics.

**Brush Matt:** A small brush similar to an upside-down nail or scrub brush. Used as a surface to needle felt on, it protects the needle's tip and the table's surface from the felting needle.

**Bubble Wrap:** Plastic packaging with enclosed pockets of air that is used to roll a felt project to felt or full.

**C1 Wool:** A crossbreed of sheep with medium coarse wool that is often used in needle felting.

**Carding:** A method of processing wool using either hand carders or a mechanical carder in which steel teeth separate and align the fibers, remove vegetable matter, and blend different fibers together.

**Carding Cloth:** Heavy fabric or leather with embedded teeth that covers the drums in a drum carder.

**Color Fast:** A dye that is stable and resists fading in the sun and through washing.

**Combed Top:** A long continuous length of wool that has the short and broken fibers removed, while the long fibers are aligned in the same direction. The preparation was originally for spinning worsted yarn.

**Combing:** The process following carding where the long fibers are separated from shorter fibers to make tops.

**Core Wool:** The wool used as the base or in the middle of a 3D wool sculpture in needle felting.

**Crimp:** The natural waviness of wool fibers, which varies with fiber diameter and breed of sheep.

**Crossbreed:** A sheep bred from one or more breeds.

**Diz:** A thin disk with a small hole that is used to make roving from a drum carder or to make tops from combed fiber.

**Drum Carder:** A mechanical device that uses a system of drums covered in carding cloth that straighten and separate fibers. This can be hand or motor powered.

**Dry Felting:** Another term for needle felting, a process using barbed needles to matt fibers together to form felt without the use of water.

**Dyeing:** The application of color to fiber or fabric.

**Embellishment:** Additional fibers, fabrics, or yarns incorporated into the felt project or other finishing details such as hand embroidery or beading.

**Feltability:** The property of wool and some other fibers to interlock with each other to create felt.

**Felt:** An ancient technique that produces a nonwoven sheet of matted wool created by the entanglement of a mass of fibers.

**Felting Machines:** Mechanical devices used to make felt that can either agitate or needle the wool.

**Felting Needles:** Barbed needles originally manufactured for the industrial machines that make nonwoven fabric or felt. The needles are used for felting without water and are now used for hand-needle felting with individual needles.

**Felting:** The matting of wool fibers by a process of heat, moisture, soap, and agitation. Felting causes the scales of the wool fiber to open, become locked together irreversibly, and shrink the resulting fabric. This is the traditional type of felting; see needle felting for further information.

**Fiber:** A continuous filament from the wool or hair from sheep or other animals as well as from plants, manmade fibers, or silk.

**Fleece:** The shorn wool from a single animal.

**Flick Carder:** Single hand carder used on locks to separate the fibers without disturbing the alignment of the lock. They are usually much smaller than hand cards.

**Felting Pad:** A dense piece of foam used in needle felting. It protects the needle and the table's surface from the felting needles.

**Fulled:** The result of fulling.

**Fulling:** Use of heat, moisture, and agitation to shrink and strengthen wool fabrics.

**Guard Hair:** Long, stiff, usually coarse fiber that projects from the wooly undercoat of a mammal's pelt.

**Hand Carders:** Wood and wire brushes used to straighten or blend fibers for felting or spinning.

**Handle or Hand:** How the wool or felt feels as assessed by touch.

**Lambswool:** Wool shorn from a lamb up to 8 months old, the softest wool of each breed usually shorter then regular wool.

**Laminate Felt:** Another term for nuno felt, sometimes used in the context of both sides of the fabric being covered with wool or wool sandwiched between two pieces of fabric.

**Lanolin:** A yellow, waxy substance secreted by the sebaceous glands of wool-bearing animals. It makes the raw wool feel greasy.

**Locks:** Small, finger-sized bits of wool that tend to stay together when shorn from the sheep.

**Loft:** The amount of air in the wool relating to the thickness of wool batting.

**Luster:** The light reflective quality of fiber exhibited in shine and gloss.

**Machine Felting:** Any process that employs a mechanical device to make either needle felt or wet felt.

**Micron:** Unit of measurement equaling a micrometer, which is one-millionth of a meter, that is used to measure the diameter of a wool fiber for grading purposes. The smaller the micron count, the finer and softer the wool.

**Multineedle Tool:** A tool that holds two or more needles for hand-needle felting.

**Needle Felting:** The matting or entanglement of wool or other fibers using barbed needles.

**Needle Gauge:** The thickness of the needle; the higher the number, the finer the needle.

**Nep:** A small knot of short, tangled fibers.

**Noils:** Short, sometimes defective, fibers combed from the long fibers in the process of making yarn.

**Nuno Felting:** Combining loose wool and woven fabric through felting to make a new fabric that is formed by migration of the wool fibers through the weave of the fabric.

**Palming:** Rubbing soft felt between the palms of the hands to make sure fibers are tangling together tightly.

**Picking:** A process of opening and teasing apart locks of fiber and removing foreign matter.

**Pinch Test:** Grabbing a small bit of felt between the thumb and forefinger and lifting the felt to see if the fibers are holding together.

**Prefelt:** Partially felted material that has not been fulled. It can be cut and added to another felting project.

**Preyarn:** Very thin roving or top, made for spinning into yarn, works well for embellishment in felting.

**Raw Fleece:** Freshly sheared fiber off an animal such as alpaca or llama that has not been washed.

**Raw Wool:** Freshly sheared fiber off the sheep that has not been washed.

**Resist:** A piece of plastic or other material used to prevent two sections of wool felt from sticking to each other while being made. For example, a resist is placed between the two sides of a purse before felting.

**Rolag:** Fluffy roll of wool pulled off a hand carder, fibers are in a nonparallel formation.

**Rolling:** A method of agitating the wool to turn it into felt.

**Roving:** A continuous length of wool that is made by a carding machine. It has not had the short fibers removed and is not as aligned as combed top. This preparation was originally for spinning woolen yarn.

**Scale, or cuticle:** The outer layer of cells on the wool fibers, which are hard and flattened. Scales do not fit together evenly, their surfaces overlap and open with heat and water.

**Scouring:** Washing fiber.

**Shaping:** Stretching and manipulating wet felt to get the form wanted. In needle felting, using the barbed needle to sculpt a form.

**Shearing:** Process of cutting or shaving wool off a sheep.

**Shrinkage:** The difference between the size of the dry wool laid out and the finished piece after felting.

**Skirting:** Removing stained unusable or undesirable portions of a fleece.

**Sliver:** Carded fiber in a continuous strand.

**Staple:** The length of a lock of shorn wool, which is measured without stretching or distorting the crimp.

**Superwash:** A mild chemical treatment applied to the wool fibers. It forms a permanent microscopic film of resin coating the fiber surface and scales of the fiber. Prevents felting by reducing friction and fiber entanglement allowing wool garments to be washed and dried by machine without shrinkage. Trademark owned by The Wool Bureau Inc.

**Throwing:** Part of the fulling process in wet felting.

**Tops:** Roving that has been combed to align fibers and remove any short fibers and lumps.

**Vegetable Matter:** The plant matter and debris that ends up in the fleece of the sheep, goats, alpacas, etc., from being out on pasture or being hay-fed during winter.

**Virgin Fiber:** Wool that has not previously been used for anything in any way; i.e., not recycled.

**Wet Felting:** The process of making nonwoven fabric using animal fiber, water, and agitation.

# Resources

Contact these wonderful suppliers for wool, fiber and equipment suitable for felting projects.

**Canada**

**Dream Spin Fibres**
Dreamspin Fibres
271 Percy Boom Road
Campbellford, Ontario
Canada, K0L 1L
www.dreamspinfibres.ca
*felting wools, silk fibers, silk fabrics*

**United Kingdom**

**World of Wool**
Unit 8, The Old Railway Goods Yard
Scar Lane
Milnsbridge
Huddersfield
West Yorkshire
HD3 4PE
www.worldofwool.co.uk
*dyed, blended and natural wool tops; effect, specialty, and synthetic fibres; felt and prefelt; silk and yarns; books, magazines, and DVDs*

**United States**

**Carol Cypher**
PO Box 916
Port Ewen NY 12466
www.carolcypher.com
*turbo felting boards, felting needles, felting kits*

**Dharma Trading Company**
1604 Fourth St.
San Rafael, CA 94901
www.dharmatrading.com
*dye supplies, silk and cotton fabrics, silk and cotton dyeables, wools, other fibers, felting equipment and tools, felting kits, books, DVDs*

**Dream Felt**
PO Box 420613
Kissimmee, FL
www.dreamfelt.com
*Dream Felt needle felting wool, prefelt, wool locks, needle felting equipment.*

**Finger Gloves** ™
PO Box 832
Colorado Springs, CO 80901
www.fingergloves.com
*finger gloves - enter special online coupon code "RuthLane" for 10% off all products*

**Frank's Cane and Rush Supply**
7252 Heil Avenue
Huntington Beach, CA 92647
www.franksupply.com
*poly hat blocks*

**New England Felting Supply**
84 Cottage Street
Easthampton, MA 01027
www.feltingsupply.com
*wools, fibers, embellishing fibers, prefelt, wet felting and needle felting equipment, books, DVDs*

**Outback Fibers**
PO Box 55
13756 CR 45
Coaldale, CO 81222
www.outbackfibers.com
*wools, silk fibers, prefelt, nuno felting kits, felting needles, needle felt adaptor, wet felting kits, books, DVDs*

# Acknowledgments

Many people assisted in the creation of this book and I want to thank everyone that offered tips, suggestions, and support. The book wouldn't have been the same without this remarkable community of felters, and I appreciate you all. I'm sorry if I have forgotten to mention you by name.

Thanks to Kay for sending Linda in my direction. Thank you to Linda and the rest of the staff at Creative Publishing international for all your hard work, professional expertise, finding of photos, answering of questions, and for taking my ideas and developing such a wonderful end product.

I really appreciated the generous donation of a variety of fibers from Amanda, Zed, Jo, Karen, Bunny, Barb, and Sherry. Sherry also took the time to send a photo of one of her Wensleydale sheep, the only breeder who responded to my inquiries. Thanks to Una for the shoe lasts, to Carole for the light box, and to Bunny for the use of her hand carders and drum carder.

I am grateful for the photos that were generously shared by Diane of her fiber mill; Patti of the Maryland Sheep and Wool Festival; Kate from Ashford of their hand and drum carders; Horst and Jessica for the dyeing photo; and Judith for the use of her picker, combs, and flick carder. Thanks to Ethan for the time and knowledge spent in setting up the online work site. Thanks also to the generous felting suppliers listed in the resource section. Go check out their websites for wonderful fiber goodies!

I can't forget all the support and tips kindly shared by the members of the Felting Forum; you guys are the best. Thanks to all of the artists whose inspiring work is shown in the gallery. It made a wonderful ending for the book and illustrates the amazing versatility of felting.

Thanks to Nanci for drawing and digitizing the illustrations. You made my explanations much more clear. Thanks to Ann and Karen for reviewing the manuscript and providing your felting knowledge. I am grateful to Cindy for reminding me that a giraffe has a mane and to Rhonda for noticing the "missing spot."

To Zed, you are amazing, and your feedback, felting knowledge, and critique was invaluable. Thanks for finding all the missing commas, adding those pesky the's, and for correcting my Americanisms. It wouldn't have been the same book without you.

To my loving husband Dennis, I am so grateful that you were willing to assist me in this journey. Thanks for those many hours of taking and retaking the photographs and your tolerance for all things felting taking over our house and our lives. I love you. We make a great team, don't we?

Last of all, I thank you for reading this book. I hope you will take as much pleasure in your felting experience as I have and that this book will encourage you in exploring further. Enjoy!

# Contributors

## About the Author

Ruth Lane is a self-taught fiber artist who enjoys the ancient technique of felt making combined with a variety of mixed media. As the co-owner of a fine craft gallery she has long had a love for handcrafted work and supports the resurgence of American craft. Through the store, Ruth has exhibited her own fiber art and the work of other felt makers to educate the general public about felt making in all its forms.

Teaching, learning, and playing with fiber are some of Ruth's favorite activities. She resides in Kalispell, Montana, with her husband Dennis and two Yorkies, Symphony and Hardy.

## Illustrations
Nanci Williams drew and digitized all of the illustrations for the book. Nanci has no idea what she is going to be when she grows up. In the meantime, she is living in Kalispell, Montana, disguised as a graphic designer, swim instructor, and door opening person for her dogs. She also lives with her partner of 26 years who also might be a graphic designer when he grows up.

## Needle Felting
Patti McAleenan was a great resource for the needle felting section. Patti was raised right outside New York City. As a young child Patti was always encouraged to pursue her creativity. People all over the world own Patti's creations. Patti is a proud recipient of a "TELLY AWARD" for a how-to-video, along with being a guest on several TV Shows: Home Shopping Network and QVC as well as appearing on such TV shows as NBC's Today Show - Weekend in New York, and Oprah's Oxygen Network She Commerce. Today Patti has a very successful business Dream Felt that sells needle-felting supplies to people all over the world.

## Felting and Fiber Preparation
Ann McElroy contributed many ideas for all of the felting chapters and about fiber preparation. She also helped with the glossary of felting terms. Ann lives on a working sheep farm in Eastern Ontario with her extended family. She has been felting for more than 10 years and takes pleasure in teaching and sharing her work through the Ottawa Valley Weavers and Spinners Guild, as well as at her farm. Ann enjoys exploring the many felting possibilities offered by different wools and fibers, with the combination of fine wool and woven fibers into nuno felt as a particular favourite. Ann has great enthusiasm for expanding her knowledge and skills by taking classes from other felters whenever possible.

## Photography
Dennis Green, the author's husband, took all the step-by-step photographs throughout the book. Dennis is an amateur photographer and very understanding of his wife's enthusiasm for all things woolly. He has been educating everyone he knows, and even complete strangers, about felting and this book.

# Index

**DON'T MISS THE OTHER BOOKS IN THE SERIES!**

**The Complete Photo Guide to Textile Art**
Susan Stein

ISBN: 978-1-58923-505-2

**The Complete Photo Guide to Art Quilting**
Susan Stein

ISBN: 978-1-58923-689-9

**The Complete Photo Guide to Sewing**

ISBN: 978-1-58923-434-5

**The Quilting Bible**

ISBN: 978-1-58923-512-0

**The Complete Photo Guide to Ribbon Crafts**
Elaine Schmidt

ISBN: 978-1-58923-469-7

**The Complete Photo Guide to Cake Decorating**
Autumn Carpenter

ISBN: 978-1-58923-669-1

**The Complete Photo Guide to Perfect Fitting**
Sarah Veblen

ISBN: 978-1-58923-608-0

**The Complete Photo Guide to Needlework**
Linda Wyszynski

ISBN: 978-1-58923-641-7

**The Complete Photo Guide to Knitting**
Margaret Hubert

ISBN: 978-1-58923-524-3

**The Complete Photo Guide to Crochet**
Margaret Hubert

ISBN: 978-1-58923-472-7

**The Complete Photo Guide to Window Treatments, Second Edition**
Linda Neubauer

ISBN: 978-1-58923-607-3

**The Complete Photo Guide to Jewelry Making**
Tammy Powley

ISBN: 978-1-58923-549-6

**The Complete Photo Guide to Creative Painting**
Paula Guhin and Geri Greenman

ISBN: 978-1-58923-540-3

**The Complete Photo Guide to Doll Making**
Nancy Hoerner, Barbara Matthiessen and Rick Petersen

ISBN: 978-1-58923-504-5

**The Complete Photo Guide to Paper Crafts**
Trice Boerens

ISBN: 978-1-58923-468-0

**ONLINE OR AT YOUR LOCAL CRAFT OR BOOK STORE.**

Creative Publishing
international

www.CreativePub.com

**OUR BOOKS ARE AVAILABLE AS E-BOOKS, TOO!**

Many of our bestselling titles are now available as E-Books.
Visit www.Qbookshop.com to find links to e-vendors!

CPSIA information can be obtained at www.ICGtesting.com
Printed in the USA
LVOW05s1615110915

453819LV00004B/4/P